# DISCRETE WAVELET TRANSFORMS - A COMPENDIUM OF NEW APPROACHES AND RECENT APPLICATIONS

Edited by **Awad Kh. Al - Asmari**

**Discrete Wavelet Transforms - A Compendium of New Approaches and Recent Applications**
http://dx.doi.org/10.5772/3424
Edited by Awad Kh. Al - Asmari

**Contributors**

Masahiro Iwahashi, Hitoshi Kiya, Chih-Hsien Hsia, Jen-Shiun Chiang, Nader Namazi, Tilendra Shishir Shishir Sinha, Rajkumar Patra, Rohit Raja, Devanshu Chakravarty, Irene Lena Hudson, In Kang, Andrew Rudge, J. Geoffrey Chase, Gholamreza Anbarjafari, Hasan Demirel, Sara Izadpenahi, Cagri Ozcinar, Dr. Awad Kh. Al-Asmari, Farhaan Al-Enizi, Fayez El-Sousy

**Published by InTech**
Janeza Trdine 9, 51000 Rijeka, Croatia



**Publishing Process Manager** Iva Lipovic
**Technical Editor** InTech DTP team
**Cover** InTech Design team

Additional hard copies can be obtained from orders@intechopen.com

Discrete Wavelet Transforms - A Compendium of New Approaches and Recent Applications, Edited by Awad Kh. Al - Asmari
p. cm.
ISBN 978-953-51-0940-2

For EU product safety concerns:
IN TECH d.o.o., Prolaz Marije Krucifikse Kozulić 3, 51000 Rijeka, Croatia,
info@intechopen.com or visit our website at intechopen.com.

# Meet the editor

Awad Kh. Al-Asmari was born in Balasmer, Saudi Arabia in 1959. He received his B.Sc and M.Eng from King Saud University, Riyadh, Kingdom of Saudi Arabia and Ohio State University, Columbus, Ohio, U.S.A, respectively. He then proceeded to the University of Toledo, Toledo, Ohio, U.S.A. where he obtained his PhD in 1991 specialising in communication and signal processing. Since 1991 he has been a faculty member at the College of Engineering, King Saud University, Saudi Arabia, where he rose through the ranks to become a full professor in 2003. In addition to this, he was appointed Vice Rector for Graduate Studies and Research at the Salman Bin Abdulaziz University, Kharj in 2009. Prof. Awad Alasmari is deeply involved in numerous services to his immediate constituencies, both geographical and professional. He has been a senior member of the IEEE since 1996 and has co-authored numerous publications in the areas of image processing, information security, telecommunications, nanotechnology and quantum computing. He can be reached at www.alasmari.com.

# Contents

# Preface

Discrete Wavelet Transform (DWT) is a wavelet transform that is widely used in numerical and functional analysis. Its key advantage over more traditional transforms, such as the Fourier transform, lies in its ability to offer temporal resolution, i.e. it captures both frequency and location (or time) information. DWTs enable a multi-resolution and analysis of a signal in frequency and time domains at different resolutions making it an effective tool for digital signal processing. Its utility in a wide array of areas such as data compression, image processing and digital communication has been effectively demonstrated. Since the first DWT, the Haar wavelet, was invented by Alfred Haar, DWTs have gained widespread applications mainly in the areas of signal processing, watermarking, data compression and digital communication.

Recently, however, numerous variants of the DWT have been suggested, each with varying modifications suited for specific state-of-the-art applications. This book presents a succinct compendium of some of the more recent variants of DWTs and their use to come up with solutions to an array of problems transcending the traditional application areas of image/ video processing and security to the areas of medicine, artificial intelligence, power systems and telecommunications.

To effectively convey these recent advances in DWTs, the book is divided into two sections. Section 1 of the book, comprising of three chapters, focuses on applications of variants of the DWT in the traditional field of image and video processing, copyright protection and watermarking.

Chapter 1 presents a so-called non-separable 2D lifting variant of the DWT. With its reduced number of lifting steps for lower latency, the proposed technique offers faster processing of standard JPEG 2000 images.

In chapter 2, the focus turns to the use of DWTs for copyright protection of digital images. Therein, a pyramid-wavelet DWT is proposed in order to enhance the perceptual invisibility of copyright data and increase the robustness of the published (copyrighted) data.

The last chapter of this section, chapter 3, discusses a new video resolution enhancement technique. An illumination compensation procedure was applied to the video frames, whilst simultaneously decomposing each frame into its frequency domains using DWT and then interpolating the higher frequency sub-bands.

Section 2 of the book comprises of five chapters that are focused on applications of DWT outside the traditional image/video processing domains. Where required, variations of the standard DWT were proposed in order to solve specific problems that the application is targeted at. The first chapter in this section, Chapter 4, presents an adaptive resolution method using DWT for humanoid-robot vision systems. The functions of the humanoid vision system include image capturing and image analysis. A suggested application for proposed techniques is its use to describe and recognize image contents, which is necessary for a robot's visual system.

In Chapter 5, the DWT was used to solve some problems encountered in modelling and simulation for recognition of physiological and behavioral traits through human gait and facial image.

Chapter 6 focusses on a medical application for DWTs. Therein, a density estimation and wavelet thresholding method is proposed to assess agitation and sedation in Intensive Care Unit (ICU) patients. The chapter uses a so-called wavelet probability band (WPB) to model and evaluate the nonparametric agitation-sedation regression curve of patients requiring critical medical care.

In Chapter 7, an intelligent maximization control system with Improved Particle Swarm Optimization (IPSO) using the Wavelet Neural Network (WNN) is presented. The proposed system is used to control a self-Excited Induction generator (SEIG) driven by a variable speed wind turbine feeding a grid connected to double-sided current regulated pulse width modulated (CRPWM) AC/DC/AC power converters.

Finally, in Chapter 8, the application domain of the DWTs is shifted to the field of telecommunications. Therein, DWT was used to suggest a demodulation of FM data in free-space optical communication systems. Specifically, the DWTs were used to reduce the effect of noise in the signals.

Together the two sections and their respective chapters provide the reader with an elegant and thorough miscellany of literature that are all related by their use of DWTs.

The book is primarily targeted at postgraduate students, researchers and anyone interested in the rudimentary background about DWTs and their present state-of-the-art applications to solve numerous problems in varying fields of science and engineering.

The guest editor is grateful to the INTECH editorial team for extending the invitation and subsequent support towards editing this book. Special thanks also to Dr. Abdullah M. Iliyasu and Mr. Asif R. Khan for their contributions towards the success of the editorial work. A total of 17 chapters were submitted from which only the eight highlighted earlier were selected. This suggests the dedication and thoroughness invested by the distinguished reviewers that were involved in various stages of the editorial process to ensure that the best quality contributions are conveyed to the readers. Many thanks to all of them.

*Chapter 7* is written by Manal K. Zaki and deals with fibre method modelling (FMM) together with a displacement-based finite element analysis (FEA) used to analyse a three-dimensional reinforced concrete (RC) beam-column. The analyses include a second-order effect known as geometric nonlinearity in addition to the material nonlinearity. The finite element formulation is based on an updated Lagrangian description. The formulation is general and applies to any composite members with partial interaction or interlayer slip. An example is considered to clarify the behaviour of composite members of rectangular sections under biaxial bending. In this example, complete bond is considered. Different slenderness ratios of the mentioned member are studied. Another example is considered to test the importance of including the bond-slip phenomenon in the analysis and to verify the deduced stiffness matrices and the proposed procedure for the problem solution.

I hope this book benefits graduate students, researchers and engineers working in resistance design of engineering structures to earthquake loads, blast and fire. I thank the authors of the chapters of this book for their cooperation and effort during the review process. Thanks are also due to Ana Nikolic, Romana Vukelic, Ivona Lovric, Marina Jozipovic and Iva Lipovic for their help during the processing and publishing of the book. I thank also of all authors, for all I have learned from them on civil engineering, structural reliability analysis and health assessment of structures.

**Awad Kh. Al - Asmari**
College of Engineering, King Saud University, Riyadh, Saudi Arabia
Salman bin Abdulaziz University, Saudi Arabia

Section 1

# Traditional Applications of DWT

Chapter 1

# Non Separable Two Dimensional Discrete Wavelet Transform for Image Signals

Masahiro Iwahashi and Hitoshi Kiya

Additional information is available at the end of the chapter

http://dx.doi.org/10.5772/51199

## 1. Introduction

Over the past few decades, a considerable number of studies have been conducted on two dimensional (2D) discrete wavelet transforms (DWT) for image or video signals. Ever since the JPEG 2000 has been adopted as an international standard for digital cinema applications, there has been a renewal of interest in hardware and software implementation of a lifting DWT, especially in attaining high throughput and low latency processing for high resolution video signals [1, 2].

Intermediate memory utilization has been studied introducing a line memory based implementation [3]. A lifting factorization has been proposed to reduce auxiliary buffers to increase throughput for boundary processing in the block based DWT [4]. Parallel and pipeline techniques in the folded architecture have been studied to increase hardware utilization, and to reduce the critical path latency [5, 6]. However, in the lifting DWT architecture, overall delay of its output signal is curial to the number of lifting steps inside the DWT.

In this chapter, we discuss on constructing a 'non-separable' 2D lifting DWT with reduced number of lifting steps on the condition that the DWT has full compatibility with the 'separable' 2D DWT in JPEG 2000. One of straightforward approaches to reduce the latency of the DWT is utilization of 2D memory accessing (not a line memory). Its transfer function is factorized into non-separable (NS) 2D transfer functions. So far, quite a few NS factorization techniques have been proposed [7, 14]. The residual correlation of the Haar transform was utilized by a NS lifting structure [7]. The Walsh Hadamard transform was composed of a NS lossless transform [8], and applied to construct a lossless discrete cosine transform (DCT) [9]. Morphological operations were applied to construct an adaptive prediction [10]. Filter coefficients were optimized to reduce the aliasing effect [11]. However, these transforms are not compatible with the DWT defined by the JPEG 2000 international standard.

In this chapter, we describe a family of NS 2D lifting DWTs compatible with DWTs defined by JPEG 2000 [12, 14]. One of them is compatible with the 5/3 DWT developed for lossless coding [12]. The other is compatible with the 9/7 DWT developed for lossy coding [13]. It is composed of single NS function structurally equivalent to [12]. For further reduction of the lifting steps, we also describe another structure composed of double NS functions [14]. The NS 2D DWT family summarized in this chapter has less lifting steps than the standard separable 2D DWT set, and therefore it contributes to reduce latency of DWT for faster coding.

This chapter is organized as follows. Standard 'separable' 2D DWT and its latency due to the total number of lifting steps are discussed, and a low latency 'non-separable' 2D DWT is introduced for 5/3 DWT in section 2. The discussion is expanded to 9/7 DWT in section 3. In each section, it is confirmed that the total number of lifting steps is reduced by the 'non-separable' DWT without changing relation between input and output of the 'separable' DWT. Furthermore, structures to implement 'lossless' coding are described for not only 5/3 DWT but also for 9/7 DWT. Performance of the DWTs is investigated and compared in respect of lossless coding and lossy coding in section 4. Implementation issue under finite word length of signal values is also discussed. Conclusions are summarized in section 5. References are listed in section 6.

## 2. The 5/3 DWT and Reduction of its Latency

JPEG 2000 defines two types of one dimensional (1D) DWTs. One is 5/3 DWT and the other is 9/7 DWT. Each of them is applied to a 2D input image signal, vertically and horizontally. This processing is referred to 'separable' 2D structure. In this section, we point out the latency problem due to the total number of lifting steps of the DWT, and introduce a 'non separable' 2D structure with reduced number of lifting steps for 5/3 DWT.

### 2.1. One Dimensional 5/3 DWT defined by JPEG 2000

Fig.1 illustrates a pair of forward and backward (inverse) transform of the one dimensional (1D) 5/3 DWT. Its forward transform splits the input signal $X$ into two frequency band signals $L$ and $H$ with down samplers $\downarrow 2$, a shifter $z^{+1}$ and FIR filters $H_1$ and $H_2$. The input signal $X$ is given as a sequence $x_n$, $n \in \{0,1,\cdots,N\text{-}1\}$ with length $N$. The band signals $L$ and $H$ are also given as sequences $l_m$ and $h_m$, $m \in \{0,1,\cdots,M\text{-}1\}$, respectively. Both of them have the length $M$=$N$/2. Using the z transform, these signals are expressed as

$$X(z)=\sum_{n=0}^{N-1} x_n z^{-n},\ L(z)=\sum_{m=0}^{M-1} l_m z^{-m},\ H(z)=\sum_{m=0}^{M-1} h_m z^{-m} \tag{1}$$

Relation between input and output of the forward transform is expressed as

http://dx.doi.org/10.5772/51199

$$\begin{bmatrix} L(z) \\ H(z) \end{bmatrix} = \begin{bmatrix} 1 & H_2(z) \\ 0 & 1 \end{bmatrix} \begin{bmatrix} 1 & 0 \\ H_1(z) & 1 \end{bmatrix} \begin{bmatrix} X_e(z) \\ X_o(z) \end{bmatrix} \tag{2}$$

where

$$\begin{bmatrix} X_e(z) \\ X_o(z) \end{bmatrix} = \begin{bmatrix} \downarrow 2[X(z)] \\ \downarrow 2[X(z)z] \end{bmatrix} = \downarrow 2\left[\begin{bmatrix} 1 \\ z \end{bmatrix} X(z)\right] \tag{3}$$

The backward (inverse) transform synthesizes the two band signals *L* and *H* into the signal *X'* by

$$X'(z) = [1 z^{-1}] \begin{bmatrix} \uparrow 2[X_e'(z)] \\ \uparrow 2[X_o'(z)] \end{bmatrix} = [1 z^{-1}] \uparrow 2 \begin{bmatrix} X_e'(z) \\ X_o'(z) \end{bmatrix} \tag{4}$$

where

$$\begin{bmatrix} X_e'(z) \\ X_o'(z) \end{bmatrix} = \begin{bmatrix} 1 & 0 \\ -H_1(z) & 1 \end{bmatrix} \begin{bmatrix} 1 & -H_2(z) \\ 0 & 1 \end{bmatrix} \begin{bmatrix} L(z) \\ H(z) \end{bmatrix} \tag{5}$$

In the equations (3) and (4), down sampling and up sampling are defined as

$$\begin{bmatrix} \downarrow 2[W(z)] \\ \uparrow 2[W(z)] \end{bmatrix} = \begin{bmatrix} 1/2 & 0 \\ 0 & 1 \end{bmatrix} \begin{bmatrix} W(z^{1/2}) + W(-z^{1/2}) \\ W(z^2) \end{bmatrix} \tag{6}$$

respectively for an arbitrary signal *W*(*z*). In Fig.1, the FIR filters $H_1$ and $H_2$ are given as

$$\begin{bmatrix} H_1 \\ H_2 \end{bmatrix} = \begin{bmatrix} H_1(z) \\ H_2(z) \end{bmatrix} = \begin{bmatrix} -1/2 & 0 \\ 0 & 1/4 \end{bmatrix} \begin{bmatrix} (1+z^{+1}) \\ (1+z^{-1}) \end{bmatrix} \tag{7}$$

for 5/3 DWT defined by the JPEG 2000 international standard.

### 2.2. Separable 2D 5/3 DWT of JPEG 2000 and its Latency

Fig.2 illustrates extension of the 1D DWT to 2D image signal. The 1D DWT is applied vertically and horizontally. In this case, an input signal is denoted as

$$X(z_1, z_2) = \sum_{n_1=0}^{N_1-1} \sum_{n_2=0}^{N_2-1} x_{n_1,n_2} z_1^{-n_1} z_2^{-n_2} \tag{8}$$

Down sampling and up sampling are defined as

$$\begin{bmatrix} \downarrow 2_{z1}[W(z_1, z_2)] \\ \downarrow 2_{z2}[W(z_1, z_2)] \end{bmatrix} = \begin{bmatrix} 1/2 & 0 \\ 0 & 1/2 \end{bmatrix} \begin{bmatrix} W(z_1^{1/2}, z_2) + W(-z_1^{1/2}, z_2) \\ W(z_1, z_2^{1/2}) + W(z_1, -z_2^{1/2}) \end{bmatrix} \tag{9}$$

and

$$\begin{bmatrix} \uparrow 2_{z1}[W(z_1, z_2)] \\ \uparrow 2_{z2}[W(z_1, z_2)] \end{bmatrix} = \begin{bmatrix} W(z_1^2, z_2) \\ W(z_1, z_2^2) \end{bmatrix} \tag{10}$$

respectively for an arbitrary 2D signal $W(z_1,z_2)$. The FIR filters $H_1$ and $H_2$ are given as

$$\begin{bmatrix} \mathrm{H}_1 \\ \mathrm{H}_2 \end{bmatrix} = \begin{bmatrix} H_1(z_1) \\ H_2(z_1) \end{bmatrix} = \begin{bmatrix} -1/2 & 0 \\ 0 & 1/4 \end{bmatrix} \begin{bmatrix} (1 + z_1^{+1}) \\ (1 + z_1^{-1}) \end{bmatrix} \tag{11}$$

$$\begin{bmatrix} \mathrm{H}_1^* \\ \mathrm{H}_2^* \end{bmatrix} = \begin{bmatrix} H_1(z_2) \\ H_2(z_2) \end{bmatrix} = \begin{bmatrix} -1/2 & 0 \\ 0 & 1/4 \end{bmatrix} \begin{bmatrix} (1 + z_2^{+1}) \\ (1 + z_2^{-1}) \end{bmatrix} \tag{12}$$

for Fig.2, instead of (7) for Fig.1.

The structure in Fig.2 has 4 lifting steps in total. It should be noted that a lifting step must wait for a calculation result from the previous lifting step. It causes delay and it is essentially inevitable. Therefore the total number of lifting steps (= latency) should be reduced for faster coding of JPEG 2000.

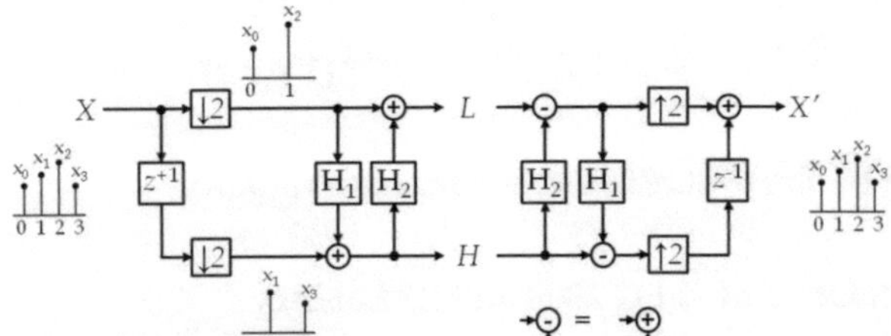


**Figure 1.** One dimensional 5/3 DWT defined by JPEG 2000.

The procedure described above can be expressed in matrix form. Since Fig.2 can be expressed as Fig.3, relation between input vector X and output vector Y is denoted as

$$Y = (L_{H_2^*, H_1^*} P_{23})(L_{H_2, H_1} P_{23}) X \tag{13}$$

for

$$X = [X_{11} \quad X_{12} \quad X_{21} \quad X_{22}]^T, \quad Y = [LL \quad LH \quad HL \quad HH]^T \tag{14}$$

and

$$P_{23} = \begin{bmatrix} 1 & 0 & 0 & 0 \\ 0 & 0 & 1 & 0 \\ 0 & 1 & 0 & 0 \\ 0 & 0 & 0 & 1 \end{bmatrix} L_{p,q} = \begin{bmatrix} \begin{bmatrix} 1 & p \\ 0 & 1 \end{bmatrix}\begin{bmatrix} 1 & 0 \\ q & 1 \end{bmatrix} & \begin{bmatrix} 0 & 0 \\ 0 & 0 \end{bmatrix} \\ \begin{bmatrix} 0 & 0 \\ 0 & 0 \end{bmatrix} & \begin{bmatrix} 1 & p \\ 0 & 1 \end{bmatrix}\begin{bmatrix} 1 & 0 \\ q & 1 \end{bmatrix} \end{bmatrix} \tag{15}$$
$$\text{for } p, q \in \{H_1, H_2, H_1^*, H_2^*\}$$

Fig.4 illustrates that each of the lifting step performs interpolation from neighboring pixels. Each step must wait for calculation result of the previous step. It causes delay. Our purpose in this chapter is to reduce the total number of lifting steps so that the latency is lowered.

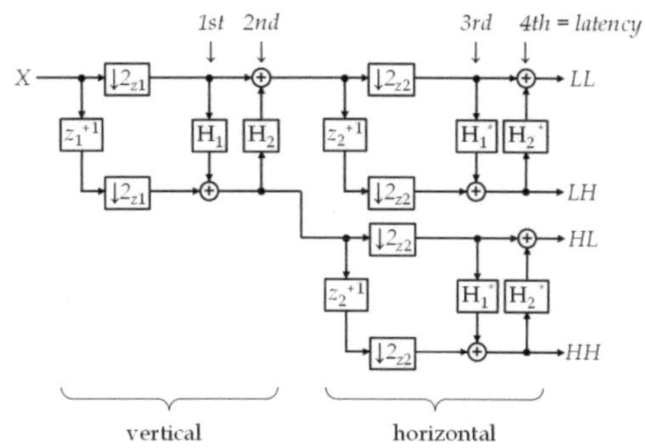


**Figure 2.** Separable 2D 5/3 DWT defined by JPEG 2000.

### 2.3. Non Separable 2D 5/3 DWT for Low latency JPEG 2000 Coding

In this subsection, we reduce the latency using 'non separable' structure without changing relation between X and Y in (13). Fig.5 illustrates a theorem we used in this chapter to construct a non-separable DWT. It is expressed as

*Theorem* 1;

$$Y = N_{d,c,b,a} X \tag{16}$$

for

$$\mathbf{X}=[x_1\ \ x_2\ \ x_3\ \ x_4]^T,\ \ \mathbf{Y}=[y_1\ \ y_2\ \ y_3\ \ y_4]^T \tag{17}$$

where

$$\mathbf{N}_{d,c,b,a}=\begin{bmatrix} 1 & d & b & -bd \\ c & 1 & 0 & b \\ a & 0 & 1 & d \\ ac & a & c & 1 \end{bmatrix} \tag{18}$$

for arbitrary value of $a$, $b$, $c$ and $d$. These values can be either scalars or transfer functions. Therefore, substituting

$$\mathbf{L}_{d,c}\mathbf{P}_{23}\mathbf{L}_{b,a}\mathbf{P}_{23}=\mathbf{N}_{d,c,b,a} \tag{19}$$

with

$$[a\ \ b\ \ c\ \ d]=[\mathrm{H}_1\ \ \mathrm{H}_2\ \ \mathrm{H}_1^*\ \ \mathrm{H}_2^*] \tag{20}$$

into (13), we have

$$\mathbf{Y}=\mathbf{N}_{\mathrm{H}_2^*,\mathrm{H}_1^*,\mathrm{H}_2,\mathrm{H}_1}\mathbf{X} \tag{21}$$

for X and Y in (14).

Finally, the non-separable 2D 5/3 DWT is constructed as illustrated in Fig.6. It has 3 lifting steps in total. The total number of lifting steps (= latency) is reduced from 4 (100%) to 3 (75%) as summarized in table 1 (separable lossy 5/3). Signal processing of each lifting step is equivalent to the interpolation illustrated in Fig.7. In the 2nd step, two interpolations can be simultaneously performed with parallel processing. Note that the non-separable 2D DWT requires 2D memory accessing.

### 2.4. Introduction of Rounding Operation for Lossless Coding

In Fig.1, the output signal *X'* is equal to the input signal *X* as far as all the sample values of the band signals *L* and *H* are stored with long enough word length. However, in data compression of JPEG 2000, all the sample values of the band signals are quantized into integers before they are encoded with an entropy coder EBCOT. Therefore the output signal *X'* has some loss, namely $X'-X \neq 0$. It is referred to 'lossy' coding.

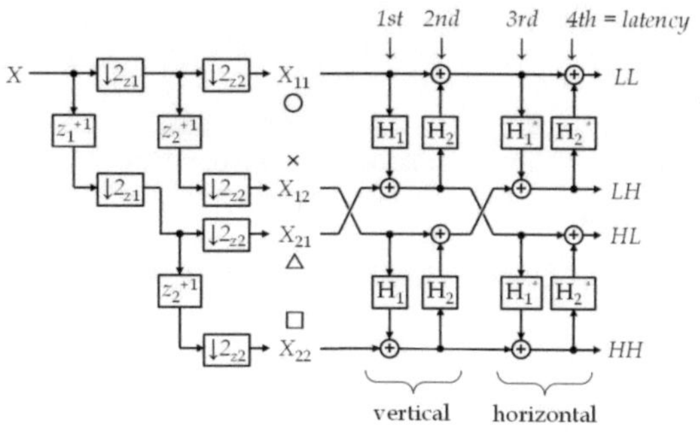


**Figure 3.** Separable 2D 5/3 DWT for matrix expression (5/3 Sep).

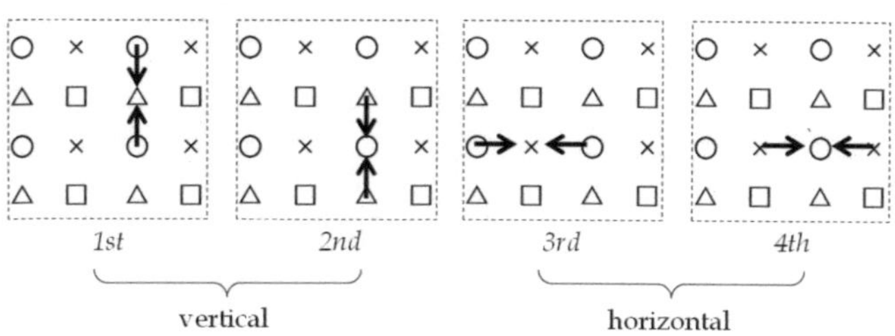


**Figure 4.** Interpretation of separable 2D 5/3 DWT as interpolation.

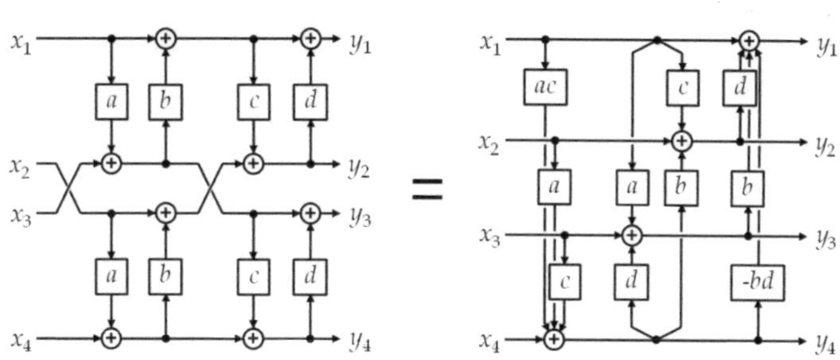


**Figure 5.** Theorem 1.

However, introducing rounding operations in each lifting step, all the DWTs mentioned above become 'lossless'. In this case, a rounding operation is inserted before addition and subtraction in Fig.1 as illustrated in Fig.8. It means

$$\begin{cases} y^{*}=x+Round[x_0+x_1+x_2] \\ x'=y^{*}-Round[x_0+x_1+x_2] \end{cases} \tag{22}$$

which guarantees 'lossless' reconstruction of the input value, namely $x'$-$x$=0. In this structure for lossless coding, comparing '5/3 Sep' in Fig.3 and '5/3 Ns1' in Fig.6, the total number of rounding operation is reduced from 8 (100%) to 4 (50%) as summarized in table 2. It contributes to increasing coding efficiency.

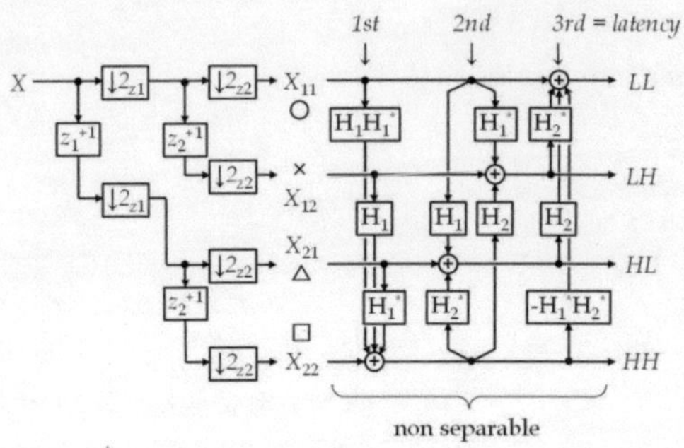


**Figure 6.** Non Separable 2D 5/3 DWT (5/3 Ns1).

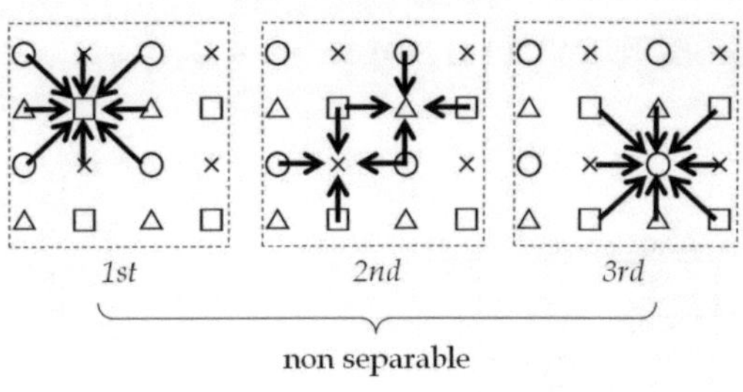


**Figure 7.** Interpretation of non-separable 2D 5/3 DWT as interpolation.

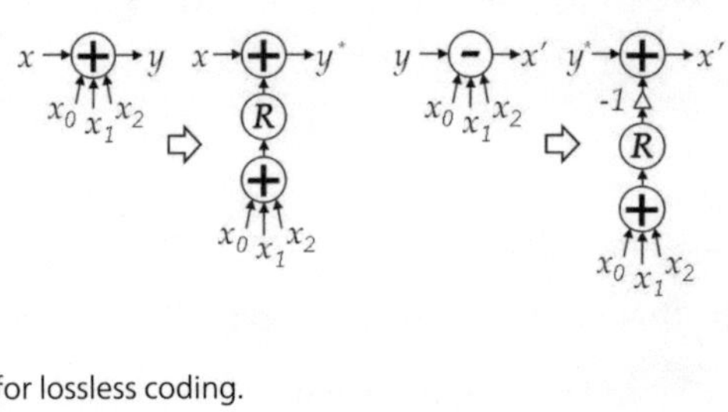

**Figure 8.** Rounding operations for lossless coding.

# 3. The 9/7 DWT and Reduction of its Latency

In the previous section, it was indicated that replacing the normal 'separable' structure by the 'non-separable' structure reduces the total number of lifting steps. It contributes to faster processing of DWT in JPEG 2000 for both of lossy coding and lossless coding. It was also indicated that it reduces total number of rounding operations in DWT for lossless coding. All the discussions above are limited to 5/3 DWT. In this section, we expand our discussion to 9/7 DWT for not only lossy coding, but also for lossless coding.

## 3.1. Separable 2D 9/7 DWT of JPEG 2000 and its Latency

JPEG 2000 defines another type of DWT referred to 9/7 DWT for lossy coding. It can be expanded to lossless coding as described in subsection 3.4. Comparing to 5/3 DWT in Fig.1, 9/7 DWT has two more lifting steps and a scaling pair. Filter coefficients are also different from (7). They are given as

$$\begin{bmatrix} H_1(z) \\ H_2(z) \end{bmatrix} = \begin{bmatrix} \alpha & 0 \\ 0 & \beta \end{bmatrix} \begin{bmatrix} (1+z^{+1}) \\ (1+z^{-1}) \end{bmatrix}, \begin{bmatrix} H_3(z) \\ H_4(z) \end{bmatrix} = \begin{bmatrix} \gamma & 0 \\ 0 & \delta \end{bmatrix} \begin{bmatrix} (1+z^{+1}) \\ (1+z^{-1}) \end{bmatrix} \tag{23}$$

and

$$\begin{cases} \alpha = -1.5861343420599 24\cdots, \ \beta = -0.052980118572961\cdots \\ \chi = +0.8829110755309 34\cdots, \ \delta = +0.443506852043971\cdots \\ k = +1.230174104914001\cdots \end{cases} \tag{24}$$

for 9/7 DWT of JPEG 2000. Fig.9 illustrates the separable 2D 9/7 DWT. In the figure, filters are denoted as

$$\begin{bmatrix} \mathrm{H_1H_3} \\ \mathrm{H_2H_4} \end{bmatrix} = \begin{bmatrix} H_1(z_1)H_3(z_1) \\ H_2(z_1)H_4(z_1) \end{bmatrix} \tag{25}$$

$$\begin{bmatrix} \mathrm{H_1^*H_3^*} \\ \mathrm{H_2^*H_4^*} \end{bmatrix} = \begin{bmatrix} H_1(z_2)H_3(z_2) \\ H_2(z_2)H_4(z_2) \end{bmatrix} \tag{26}$$

It should be noted that this structure has 8 lifting steps.

Fig.10 also illustrates the separable 2D 9/7 DWT for matrix representation. Similarly to (13), it is expressed as

$$\boldsymbol{Y} = (\boldsymbol{J}_k \boldsymbol{L}_{\mathrm{H_4^*,H_3^*}} \boldsymbol{L}_{\mathrm{H_2^*,H_1^*}} \boldsymbol{P}_{23}) \cdot (\boldsymbol{J}_k \boldsymbol{L}_{\mathrm{H_4,H_3}} \boldsymbol{L}_{\mathrm{H_2,H_1}} \boldsymbol{P}_{23}) \boldsymbol{X} \tag{27}$$

for

$$\boldsymbol{X}=[X_{11} \quad X_{12} \quad X_{21} \quad X_{22}]^T, \boldsymbol{Y}=[LL \quad LH \quad HL \quad HH]^T \tag{28}$$

and

$$\boldsymbol{P}_{23}=\begin{bmatrix} 1 & 0 & 0 & 0 \\ 0 & 0 & 1 & 0 \\ 0 & 1 & 0 & 0 \\ 0 & 0 & 0 & 1 \end{bmatrix}, \begin{bmatrix} \boldsymbol{L}_{p,q} \\ \boldsymbol{J}_k \end{bmatrix}=\begin{bmatrix} diag[\boldsymbol{M}_{p,q} \quad \boldsymbol{M}_{p,q}] \\ diag[\boldsymbol{K}_k \quad \boldsymbol{K}_k] \end{bmatrix} \tag{29}$$
$$for\, p,\, q \in \{\mathrm{H}_r,\, \mathrm{H}_r^*\},\; r \in \{1, 2, 3, 4\}$$

In (29), a scaling pair $K_k$ and filter a matrix $K_{p,q}$ are defined as

$$\boldsymbol{K}_k=\begin{bmatrix} k^{-1} & 0 \\ 0 & k \end{bmatrix}, \boldsymbol{M}_{p,q}=\begin{bmatrix} 1 & p \\ 0 & 1 \end{bmatrix}\begin{bmatrix} 1 & 0 \\ q & 1 \end{bmatrix} \tag{30}$$

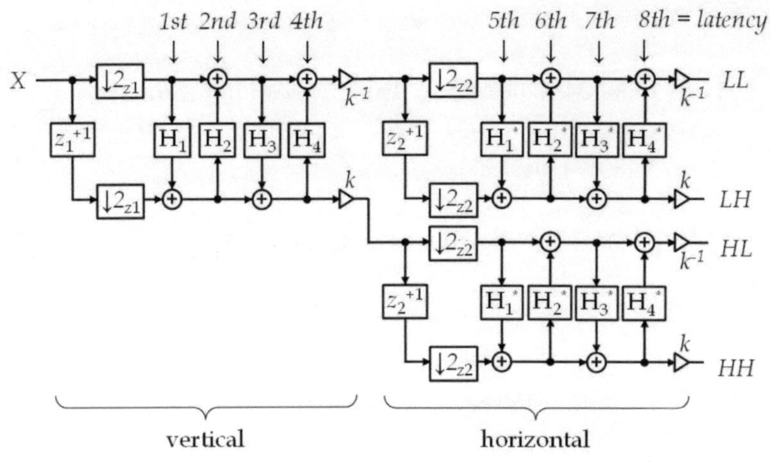


**Figure 9.** Separable 2D 9/7 DWT in JPEG 2000.

### 3.2. Single Non Separable 2D 9/7 DWT for Low latency JPEG 2000 coding

In this subsection, we reduce the latency using 'non separable' structure without changing relation between X and Y in (27), using the theorem 1 in (16)-(18) illustrated in Fig.5. Starting from Fig.10, unify the four scaling pairs $\{k^{-1}, k\}$ to only one pair $\{k^{-2}, k^2\}$ as illustrated in Fig. 11. It is denoted as

$$
\begin{aligned}
&(\boldsymbol{J}_k \boldsymbol{L}_{\mathrm{H}_4^*,\mathrm{H}_3^*} \boldsymbol{L}_{\mathrm{H}_2^*,\mathrm{H}_1^*} \boldsymbol{P}_{23})(\boldsymbol{J}_k \boldsymbol{L}_{\mathrm{H}_4,\mathrm{H}_3} \boldsymbol{L}_{\mathrm{H}_2,\mathrm{H}_1} \boldsymbol{P}_{23}) \\
&= \boldsymbol{J}_k^* \cdot \boldsymbol{L}_{\mathrm{H}_4^*,\mathrm{H}_3^*} \boldsymbol{L}_{\mathrm{H}_2^*,\mathrm{H}_1^*} \boldsymbol{P}_{23} \boldsymbol{L}_{\mathrm{H}_4,\mathrm{H}_3} \boldsymbol{L}_{\mathrm{H}_2,\mathrm{H}_1} \boldsymbol{P}_{23} \\
&= \boldsymbol{J}_k^* \cdot \boldsymbol{L}_{\mathrm{H}_4^*,\mathrm{H}_3^*} (\boldsymbol{L}_{\mathrm{H}_2^*,\mathrm{H}_1^*} \boldsymbol{P}_{23} \boldsymbol{L}_{\mathrm{H}_4,\mathrm{H}_3} \boldsymbol{P}_{23}) \boldsymbol{P}_{23} \boldsymbol{L}_{\mathrm{H}_2,\mathrm{H}_1} \boldsymbol{P}_{23}
\end{aligned}
\tag{31}
$$

where

$$
\boldsymbol{J}_k^* = diag[k^{-2} \quad 1 \quad 1 \quad k^2]
\tag{32}
$$

Next, applying the theorem 1, we have the single non-separable 2D DWT as illustrated in Fig.12. It is denoted as

$$
\begin{aligned}
&\boldsymbol{J}_k^* \cdot \boldsymbol{L}_{\mathrm{H}_4^*,\mathrm{H}_3^*} (\boldsymbol{L}_{\mathrm{H}_2^*,\mathrm{H}_1^*} \boldsymbol{P}_{23} \boldsymbol{L}_{\mathrm{H}_4,\mathrm{H}_3} \boldsymbol{P}_{23}) \boldsymbol{P}_{23} \boldsymbol{L}_{\mathrm{H}_2,\mathrm{H}_1} \boldsymbol{P}_{23} \\
&= \boldsymbol{J}_k^* \cdot \boldsymbol{L}_{\mathrm{H}_4^*,\mathrm{H}_3^*} (\boldsymbol{N}_{\mathrm{H}_2^*,\mathrm{H}_1^*,\mathrm{H}_4,\mathrm{H}_3}) \boldsymbol{P}_{23} \boldsymbol{L}_{\mathrm{H}_2,\mathrm{H}_1} \boldsymbol{P}_{23}
\end{aligned}
\tag{33}
$$

As a result, the total number of lifting steps (= latency) is reduced from 8 (100%) to 7 (88%) as summarized in table 1 (non-separable lossy 9/7).

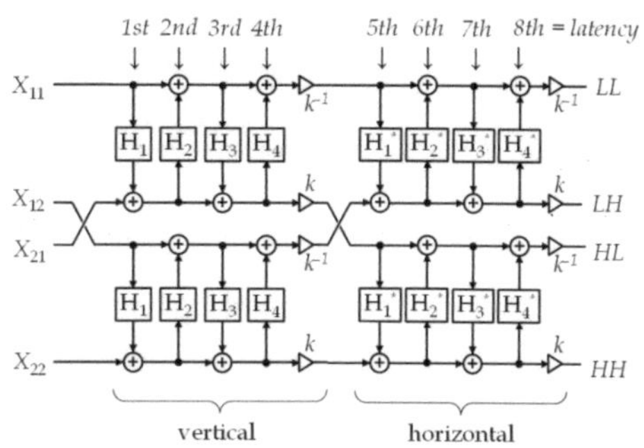


**Figure 10.** Separable 2D 9/7 DWT for matrix expression.

### 3.3. Double Non Separable 9/7 DWT for Low latency JPEG 2000 Coding

In the previous subsection, a part of the separable structure is replaced by a non-separable structure. In this subsection, we reduce one more lifting step using one more non-separable structure. Starting from equation (31) illustrated in Fig. 11, we apply

*Theorem* 2;

$$
\boldsymbol{L}_{\mathrm{H}_s^*,\mathrm{H}_r^*} \boldsymbol{P}_{23} \boldsymbol{L}_{\mathrm{H}_q,\mathrm{H}_p} \boldsymbol{P}_{23} = \boldsymbol{P}_{23} \boldsymbol{L}_{\mathrm{H}_q,\mathrm{H}_p} \boldsymbol{P}_{23} \boldsymbol{L}_{\mathrm{H}_s^*,\mathrm{H}_r^*}
\tag{34}
$$

Namely, (31) becomes

$$\begin{aligned} & J_k^* \cdot L_{H_4^*,H_3^*}(L_{H_2^*,H_1^*} P_{23} L_{H_4,H_3} P_{23}) P_{23} L_{H_2,H_1} P_{23} \\ &= J_k^* \cdot L_{H_4^*,H_3^*}(P_{23} L_{H_4,H_3} P_{23} L_{H_2^*,H_1^*}) P_{23} L_{H_2,H_1} P_{23} \end{aligned} \quad (35)$$

as illustrated in Fig.13. Then the theorem 1 can be applied twice as

$$\begin{aligned} & J_k^* \cdot (L_{H_4^*,H_3^*} P_{23} L_{H_4,H_3} P_{23})(L_{H_2^*,H_1^*} P_{23} L_{H_2,H_1} P_{23}) \\ &= J_k^* \cdot N_{H_4^*,H_3^*,H_4,H_3} N_{H_2^*,H_1^*,H_2,H_1} \end{aligned} \quad (36)$$

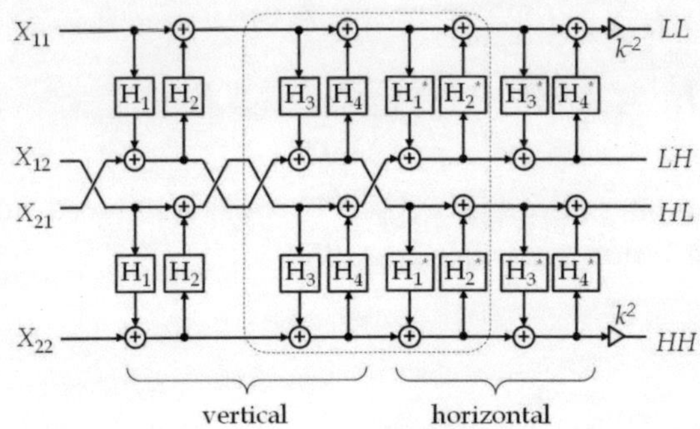


**Figure 11.** Derivation of single non separable 2D 9/7 DWT (step 1/2).

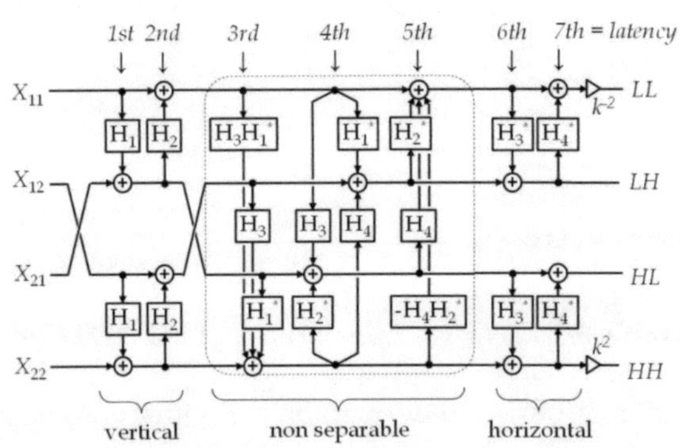


**Figure 12.** Derivation of single non separable 2D 9/7 DWT (step 2/2).

and finally, we have the double non-separable 2D DWT as illustrated in Fig.14. The total number of the lifting steps is reduced from 8 (100%) to 6 (75 %). This reduction rate is the same for the multi stage octave decomposition with DWTs.

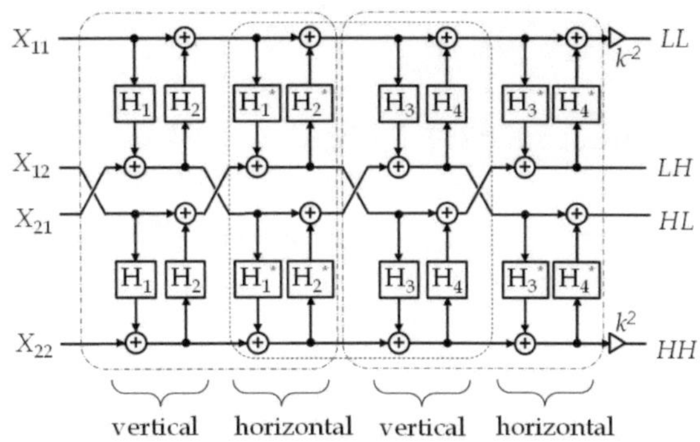


**Figure 13.** Derivation of double non separable 2D 9/7 DWT (step 1/2).

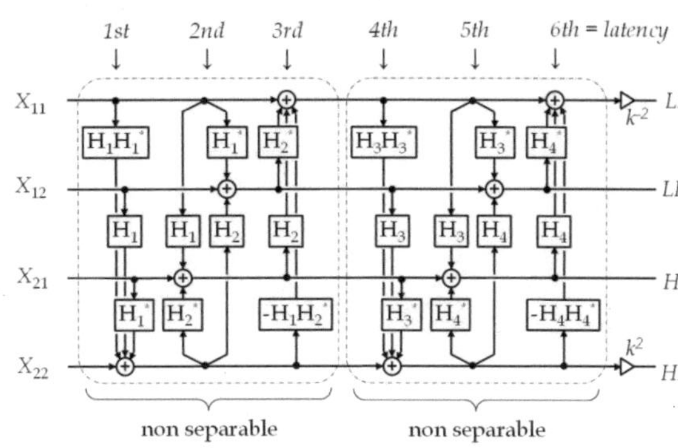


**Figure 14.** Derivation of double non separable 2D 9/7 DWT (step 2/2).

### 3.4. Lifting Implementation of Scaling for Lossless Coding

Due to the scaling pair $\{k^{-2}, k^2\}$, the DWT in Fig.14 can't be lossless, and therefore it is utilized for lossy coding. However, as explained in subsection 2.4, it becomes lossless when all the scaling pairs are implemented in lifting form with rounding operations in Fig.8. For example, the scaling pair $K_k$ in equation (30) is factorized into lifting steps as

$$\boldsymbol{K}_k^{(L)}=\begin{bmatrix}1 & s_4\\0 & 1\end{bmatrix}\begin{bmatrix}1 & 0\\s_3 & 1\end{bmatrix}\begin{bmatrix}1 & s_2\\0 & 1\end{bmatrix}\begin{bmatrix}1 & 0\\s_1 & 1\end{bmatrix} \tag{37}$$

for

$$\begin{bmatrix} s_1 & s_3 \\ s_2 & s_4 \end{bmatrix} = \begin{bmatrix} k \cdot s_1 & 0 \\ 0 & (k \cdot s_1)^{-1} \end{bmatrix} \begin{bmatrix} k^{-1} & -1 \\ 1-k & 1-k^{-1} \end{bmatrix} \tag{38}$$

Similarly, the scaling pair in equation (32) is also factorized as

$$J_k^{*(L)} = \begin{bmatrix} 1 & 0 & 0 & t_4 \\ 0 & 1 & 0 & 0 \\ 0 & 0 & 1 & 0 \\ 0 & 0 & 0 & 1 \end{bmatrix} \begin{bmatrix} 1 & 0 & 0 & 0 \\ 0 & 1 & 0 & 0 \\ 0 & 0 & 1 & 0 \\ t_3 & 0 & 0 & 1 \end{bmatrix} \begin{bmatrix} 1 & 0 & 0 & t_2 \\ 0 & 1 & 0 & 0 \\ 0 & 0 & 1 & 0 \\ 0 & 0 & 0 & 1 \end{bmatrix} \begin{bmatrix} 1 & 0 & 0 & 0 \\ 0 & 1 & 0 & 0 \\ 0 & 0 & 1 & 0 \\ t_1 & 0 & 0 & 1 \end{bmatrix} \tag{39}$$

for

$$\begin{bmatrix} t_1 & t_3 \\ t_2 & t_4 \end{bmatrix} = \begin{bmatrix} k^2 t_1 & 0 \\ 0 & (k^2 t_1)^{-1} \end{bmatrix} \begin{bmatrix} k^{-2} & -1 \\ 1-k^2 & 1-k^{-2} \end{bmatrix} \tag{40}$$

as illustrated in Fig.15. In the equation above, $t_1$ can be set to 1 [15].

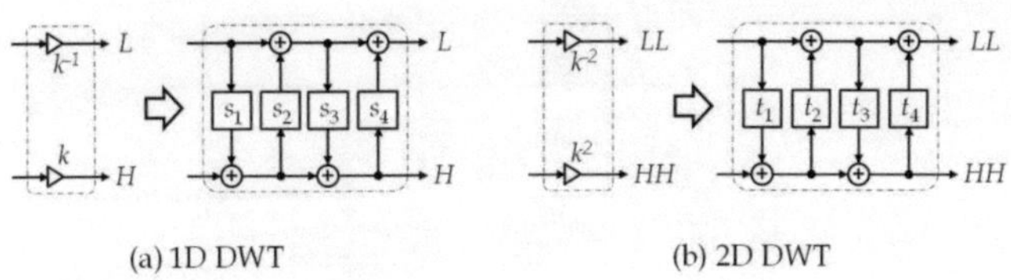


**Figure 15.** Lifting implementation of scaling pairs.

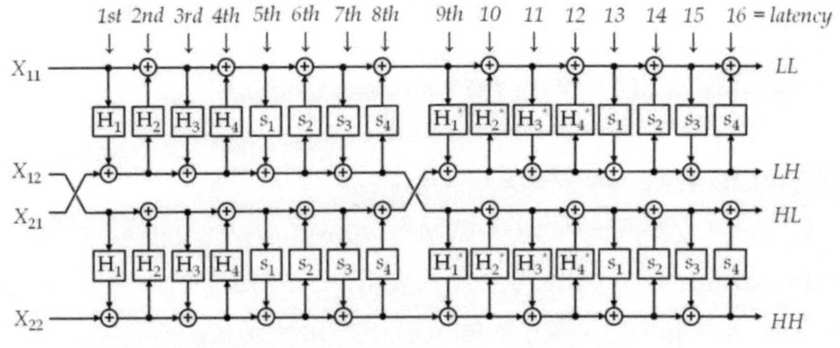


**Figure 16.** Separable 2D 9/7 DWT for lossless coding (9/7 Sep).

Fig.16, Fig.17 and Fig.18 illustrate 2D 9/7 DWTs for lossless coding. As summarized in table 1, it is indicated that the total number of lifting steps is reduced from 16 (100%) in Fig.16 to 11 (69%) in Fig.17 and 10 (63%) in Fig.18. Furthermore, the total number of rounding operations is also reduced from 32 (100%) in Fig.16 to 16 (50%) in Fig.17 and 12 (38%) as summarized in table 2.

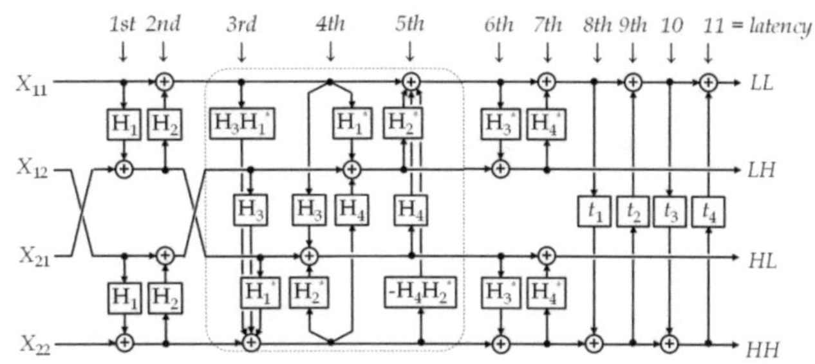

**Figure 17.** Single non separable 2D 9/7 DWT for lossless coding (9/7 Ns1).

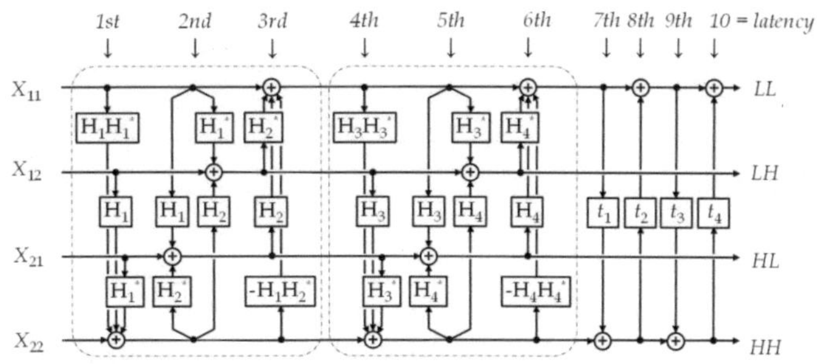

**Figure 18.** Double non separable 2D 9/7 DWT for lossless coding (9/7 Ns2).

| | | lossy | | lossless | |
|---|---|---|---|---|---|
| | | 5/3 | 9/7 | 5/3 | 9/7 |
| separable | | 4 (100%) | 8 (100%) | 4 (100%) | 16 (100%) |
| non separable | single | 3 ( 75%) | 7 ( 88%) | 3 ( 75%) | 11 ( 69%) |
| | double | --- | 6 ( 75%) | --- | 10 ( 63%) |

**Table 1.** Total number of lifting steps

## 4. Performance Evaluation

In this section, all the DWTs summarized in table 3 are compared in respect of lossless coding performance first. Lossy coding performance is evaluated next and a problem due to finite word length implementation is pointed out. This problem is avoided by compensating word length at the minimum cost.

| | | lossless | |
|---|---|---|---|
| | | 5/3 | 9/7 |
| separable | | 8 (100%) | 32 (100%) |
| non separable | single | 4 ( 50%) | 16 ( 50%) |
| | double | --- | 12 ( 38%) |

**Table 2.** Total number of rounding operations

| | | lossless | |
|---|---|---|---|
| | | 5/3 | 9/7 |
| separable | | 5/3 Sep (Fig.3) | 9/7 Sep (Fig.16) |
| non separable | single | 5/3 Ns1 (Fig.6) | 9/7 Ns1 (Fig.17) |
| | double | --- | 9/7 Ns2 (Fig.18) |

**Table 3.** DWTs discussed in this chapter

### 4.1 Lossless Coding Performance

Table 4 summarizes lossless coding performance of the DWTs in table 3 at different number of stages in octave decomposition. The EBCOT is applied as an entropy coder without quantization or bit truncation. Results were evaluated in bit rate (= average code length per pixel) in [bpp]. Fig.19 illustrates the bit rate averaged over images. It indicates that '5/3 Ns1' is the best followed by '5/3 Sep'. The difference between them is only 0.01 to 0.02 [bpp]. Among 9/7 DWTs, '9/7 Ns1' is the best followed by '9/7 Sep'. The difference is 0.03 to 0.04 [bpp]. As a result of this experiment, it was found that there is no significant difference in lossless coding performance.

| Image | DWT | Number of Stages | | | | | |
|---|---|---|---|---|---|---|---|
| 1 | 2 | 3 | 4 | 5 | 6 | | |
| Couple | 5/3 Sep | 4.74 | 4.65 | 4.63 | 4.62 | 4.62 | 4.62 |
| | 5/3 Ns1 | 4.73 | 4.64 | 4.62 | 4.61 | 4.61 | 4.61 |
| | 9/7 Sep | 4.91 | 4.83 | 4.81 | 4.80 | 4.80 | 4.80 |
| | 9/7 Ns1 | 4.89 | 4.80 | 4.79 | 4.78 | 4.78 | 4.77 |
| | 9/7 Ns2 | 4.93 | 4.84 | 4.82 | 4.81 | 4.81 | 4.81 |
| Boat | 5/3 Sep | 4.78 | 4.70 | 4.69 | 4.69 | 4.69 | 4.69 |
| | 5/3 Ns1 | 4.77 | 4.69 | 4.69 | 4.68 | 4.68 | 4.68 |

| Image | DWT | Number of Stages | | | | | |
|---|---|---|---|---|---|---|---|
| | 9/7 Sep | 4.87 | 4.80 | 4.80 | 4.79 | 4.79 | 4.79 |
| | 9/7 Ns1 | 4.85 | 4.78 | 4.77 | 4.77 | 4.77 | 4.77 |
| | 9/7 Ns2 | 4.87 | 4.80 | 4.80 | 4.79 | 4.79 | 4.79 |
| | 5/3 Sep | 5.06 | 4.97 | 4.95 | 4.95 | 4.95 | 4.95 |
| | 5/3 Ns1 | 5.05 | 4.96 | 4.94 | 4.94 | 4.94 | 4.94 |
| Lena | 9/7 Sep | 5.19 | 5.09 | 5.07 | 5.07 | 5.07 | 5.07 |
| | 9/7 Ns1 | 5.17 | 5.06 | 5.05 | 5.04 | 5.05 | 5.05 |
| | 9/7 Ns2 | 5.18 | 5.07 | 5.06 | 5.05 | 5.06 | 5.06 |
| | 5/3 Sep | 4.86 | 4.77 | 4.76 | 4.75 | 4.75 | 4.75 |
| | 5/3 Ns1 | 4.85 | 4.76 | 4.75 | 4.74 | 4.74 | 4.74 |
| average | 9/7 Sep | 4.99 | 4.91 | 4.89 | 4.89 | 4.89 | 4.89 |
| | 9/7 Ns1 | 4.97 | 4.88 | 4.87 | 4.86 | 4.87 | 4.86 |
| | 9/7 Ns2 | 4.99 | 4.90 | 4.89 | 4.88 | 4.89 | 4.89 |

**Table 4.** Bit rate for each image in lossless coding [bpp].

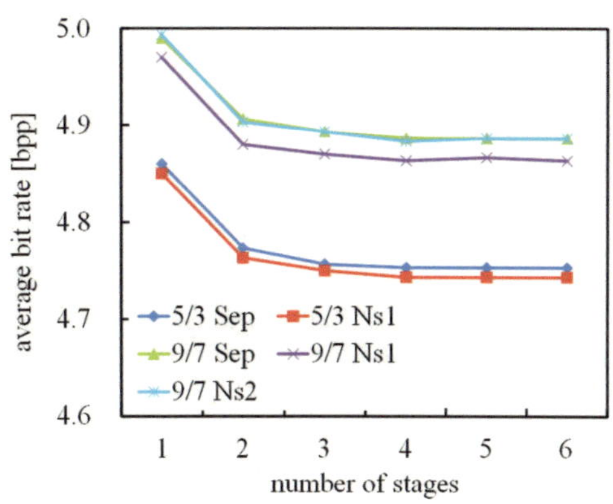


**Figure 19.** Bit rate averaged over images in lossless coding [bpp].

### *4.2. Lossy Coding Performance*

Fig.20 indicates rate distortion curves of the DWTs in table 3 for an input image 'Lena'. Five-stage octave decomposition of DWT is applied. Transformed coefficients are quantized with the optimum bit allocation and EBCOT is applied as an entropy coder. In the figure, PSNR is calculated as

$$Q = -10\log_{10}\frac{1}{255^2 N_1 N_2}\sum_{n_1=0}^{N_1-1}\sum_{n_2=0}^{N_2-1} D_{n_1,n_2}^2 \quad (41)$$

where

$$D_{n_1,n_2} = Y_{n_1,n_2} - X_{n_1,n_2} \quad (42)$$

From an input image $X_{n1,n2}$, a reconstructed image $Y_{n1,n2}$ is generated through the forward transform of the 5/3 (or 9/7) DWTs in table 3, and the backward transform of the standard 5/3 (or 9/7) DWT defined by JPEG 2000. This is to investigate compatibility between the non-separable DWTs for lossless coding, and the separable DWTs in JPEG 2000 for lossy coding.

As indicated in Fig.20, there is no difference among '9/7 Sep', '9/7 Ns1' and '9/7 Ns2'. All of them have the same rate-distortion curve. There is also no difference between '5/3 Sep' and '5/3 Ns1'. It indicates that the non-separable DWTs in table 3 have perfect compatibility with the standard DWTs defined by JPEG 2000. Note that this is true under long enough word length. In this experiment, word length of signals $F_s$ of both of the forward and the backward transform is set to 64 [bit].

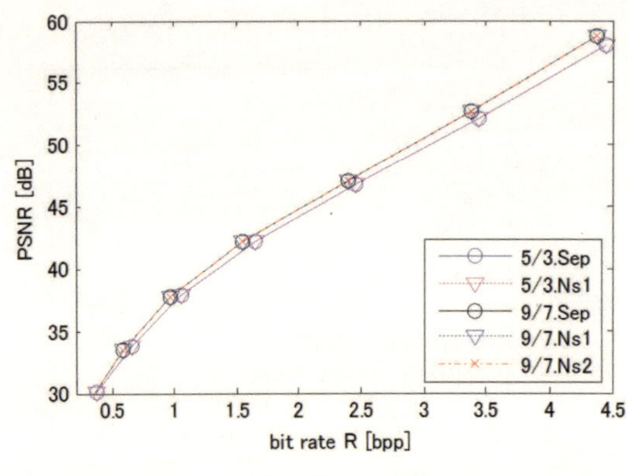


**Figure 20.** Rare distortion curves at $F_s$=64 [bit] word length of signals.

### 4.3. *Finite Word Length Implementation*

Fig.21 indicates rate distortion curves for the same image but word length of signals in the forward transform is shortened just after each of multiplications. Signal values are multiplied by $2^{-Fs}$, floored to integers and then multiplied by $2^{Fs}$. As a result, all the signals have the word length $F_s$ [bit] in fraction. According to the figure, it was observed that '9/7 Ns1' is slightly worse than '9/7 Sep', and '9/7 Ns2' is much worse. It was found that the NS DWTs have quality deterioration problem at high bit rates in lossy coding, even though they have less lifting steps.

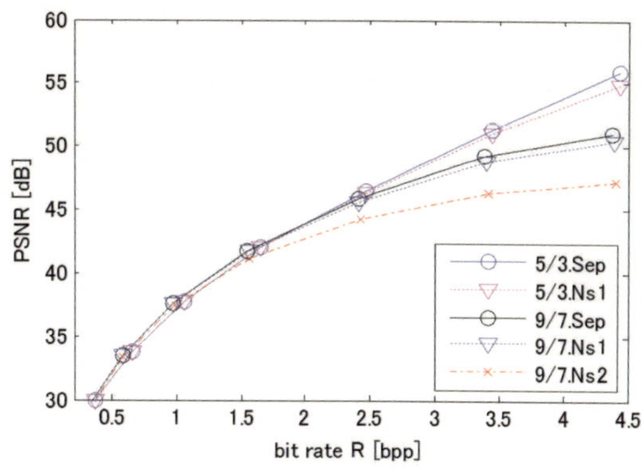


**Figure 21.** Rare distortion curves at $F_s$=2 [bit] word length of signals.

To cope with this problem, word length is compensated for '9/7 Ns2' at the minimum cost of word length. In case of finite word length implementation, the distortion $D_{n1,n2}$ in (42) contains two kinds of errors; a) quantization noise $q$ for rate control in lossy coding and b) truncation noise $c$ due to finite word length expression of signals inside the forward transform. Namely, $D_{n1,n2}=q+c$. Assuming that $q$ and $c$ are uncorrelated and both of them has zero mean, variance of the distortion is approximated as

$$Var[D]=\begin{cases}Var[q](qc)\\ Var[c](qc)\end{cases} \tag{43}$$

where *Var* denotes variance. This implies that PSNR in (41) becomes

$$Q=\begin{cases}6.02R + D_0(qc)\\ C(qc)\end{cases} \tag{44}$$

where $R$ denotes the bit rate and $D_0$ is related to the coding gain [16].

It means that finite word length noise $c$ is negligible at lower bit rates comparing to the quantization noise $q$ in respect of $L_2$ norm. However, variance of $c$ dominates over that of $q$ at high bit rates. Therefore the quality deterioration problem can be avoided by increasing the word length $F_s$. We utilize the fact that $C$ (compatibility) is a monotonically increasing function of $F_s$. Their relation is approximately described as

$$C=[p_0 \quad p_1][1 \quad F_s]T \tag{45}$$

with parameters $p_0$ and $p_1$. We compensate $F_s$ at the minimum cost of word length by $\Delta F_s$ so that

$$[p_0 \quad p_1][1 \quad F_s+\Delta F_s]^T \geq [p'_0 \quad p'_1][1 \quad F_s]^T \tag{46}$$

is satisfied where $\{p_0, p_1\}$ are parameters of the corresponding NS DWT, and $\{p'_0, p'_1\}$ are those of the separable DWT. As a result, the minimum word length for compensation is clarified as

$$\begin{aligned} &\Delta F_s \geq a + bF_s \cong a, \\ &a=(p'_0-p_0)/p_1, \; b=p'_1/p_1-1. \end{aligned} \tag{47}$$

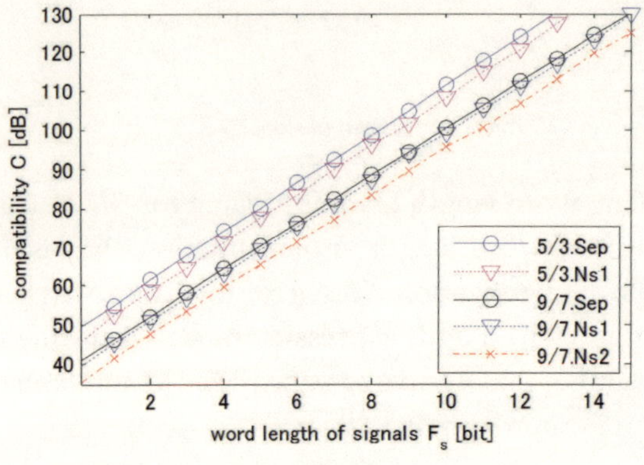


**Figure 22.** Compatibility versus word length.

| | 5/3 Sep | 5/3 Ns1 | 9/7 Sep | 9/7 Ns1 | 9/7 Ns2 |
|---|---|---|---|---|---|
| | 48.78 | 47.23 | 40.13 | 39.11 | 35.31 |
| | 6.27 | 6.24 | 6.01 | 6.01 | 5.99 |

**Table 5.** Parameters in the rate distortion curves.

Fig.22 indicates experimentally measured relations between the compatibility $C$ and the word length $F_s$. Table 5 summarizes the parameters $p_0$ and $p_1$ calculated from this figure. Table 6 summarizes two parameters $a$ and $b$ in (47) which were calculated from $p_0$ and $p_1$. It indicates that $F_s$ of '9/7 Ns1' and '9/7 Ns2' should be compensated by more than 0.17 and 0.81 [bit], respectively so that these NS DWTs have the compatibility greater than that of '9/7 Sep'. Similarly, it also indicates that '5/3 Ns1' should be compensated by more than 0.25 [bit]. As a result, the minimum word length for compensation is found to be 1 bit at maximum as summarized in table 7.

Fig.23 illustrates rate distortion curves for the compensated NS DWTs. It is confirmed that the deterioration problem observed in Fig.21 is recovered to the same level of the standard separable DWTs of JPEG 2000. It means that the finite word length problem peculiar to the non-separable 2D DWTs can be perfectly compensated by adding only 1 bit word length, in case of implementation with very short word length, i.e. $F_s$=2 [bit].

| | 5/3 Sep | 5/3 Ns1 | 9/7 Sep | 9/7 Ns1 | 9/7 Ns2 |
|---|---|---|---|---|---|
| $a$ | 0 | 0.248 | 0 | 0.170 | 0.805 |
| $b$ | 0 | 0.0048 | 0 | 0.0000 | 0.0033 |

**Table 6.** Parameters for word length compensation.

| | 5/3 Sep | 5/3 Ns1 | 9/7 Sep | 9/7 Ns1 | 9/7 Ns2 |
|---|---|---|---|---|---|
| $\Delta F_S$ | 0.000 | 0.248 | 0.000 | 0.170 | 0.805 |
| $\lceil \Delta F_s \rceil$ | 0 | 1 | 0 | 1 | 1 |

**Table 7.** The minimum word length for compensation.

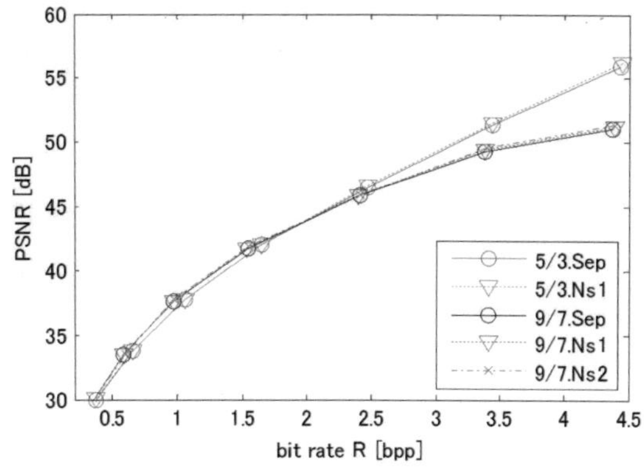


**Figure 23.** Rare distortion curves in lossy coding mode with $F_s$=2+$\Delta F_s$

## 5. Conclusions

In this chapter, 'separable' 2D DWTs defined by JPEG 2000 and its latency due to the total number of lifting steps were discussed. To reduce the latency, a 'non-separable' 2D DWTs were introduced for both of 5/3 DWT and 9/7 DWT. It was confirmed that the total number of lifting steps is reduced by the 'non-separable' DWT maintaining good compatibility with the 'separable' DWT. Performance of these DWTs were evaluated in lossless coding mode, and no significant difference was observed. A problem in finite word length implementation in lossy coding mode was discussed. It was found that only one bit compensation guarantees good compatibility with the 'separable' DWTs.

In the future, execution time of the DWTs on hardware or software platform should be investigated.

## Author details

Masahiro Iwahashi[1] and Hitoshi Kiya[2]

1 Nagaoka University of Technology, Niigata, 980-2188, Japan

2 Tokyo Metropolitan University, Tokyo, 191-0065, Japan

## References

[1] ISO / IEC FCD 15444-1, Joint Photographic Experts Group. (2000). *"JPEG2000 Image Coding System"*.

[2] Descampe, F., Devaux, G., Rouvroy, J. D., Legat, J. J., Quisquater, B., & Macq, . (2006). A Flexible Hardware JPEG 2000 Decoder for Digital Cinema". *IEEE Trans. Circuits and Systems for Video Technology*, 16(11), 1397-1410.

[3] Chrysafis, A.O. (2000). Line-based, Reduced Memory, Wavelet Image Compression". *IEEE Trans. Image Processing*, 9(3), 378-389.

[4] Jiang, W., & Ortega, A. (2001). Lifting Factorization-based Discrete Wavelet Transform Architecture Design", IEEE Trans. *Circuits and Systems for Video Technology*, 11(5), 651-657.

[5] Guangming, S., Weifeng, L., & Li, Zhang. (2009). An Efficient Folded Architecture for Lifting-based Discrete Wavelet Transform". *IEEE Trans. Circuits and Systems II express briefs*, 56(4), 290-294.

[6] Bing-Fei, W., & Chung-Fu, L. (2005). A High-performance and Memory-efficient Pipeline Architecture for the 5/3 and 9/7 Discrete Wavelet Transform of JPEG2000 Codec". *IEEE Trans. Circuits and Systems for Video Technology*, 15(12), 1615-1628.

[7] Iwahashi, M., Fukuma, S., & Kambayashi, N. (1997). Lossless Coding of Still Images with Four Channel Prediction". *IEEE International Conference Image Processing (ICIP)* [2], 266-269.

[8] Komatsu, K., & Sezaki, K. (2003). Non Separable 2D Lossless Transform based on Multiplier-free Lossless WHT". *IEICE Trans. Fundamentals*, E86-A(2).

[9] Britanak, V., Yip, P., & Rao, K. R. (2007). Discrete Cosine and Sine Transform, General properties, Fast Algorithm and Integer Approximations". *Academic Press*.

[10] Taubman, D. (1999). Adaptive, Non-separable Lifting Transforms for Image Compression". *IEEE International Conference on Image Processing (ICIP)*, 3, 772-776.

[11] Kaaniche, M., Pesquet, J. C., Benyahia, A. B., & Popescu, B. P. (2010). Two-dimensional Non Separable Adaptive Lifting Scheme for Still and Stereo Image Coding". *IEEE Proc. International Conference on Acoustics, Speech and Signal Processing (ICASSP)*, 1298-1301.

[12] Chokchaitam, S., & Iwahashi, M. (2002). Lossless, Near-Lossless and Lossy Adaptive Coding Based on the Lossless DCT". *IEEE Proc. International Symposium Circuits and Systems (ISCAS)* [1], 781-784.

[13] Iwahashi, M., & Kiya, H. (2009). Non Separable 2D Factorization of Separable 2D DWT for Lossless Image Coding". *IEEE Proc. International Conference Image Processing (ICIP)*, 17-20.

[14] Iwahashi, M., & Kiya, H. (2010). A New Lifting Structure of Non Separable 2D DWT with Compatibility to JPEG 2000". *IEEE International Conference on Acoustics, Speech, and Signal Processing (ICASSP), IVMSP, P9.*, 7, 1306-1309.

[15] Daubechies, W.S. (1998). Factoring Wavelet Transforms into Lifting Steps". *Journal of Fourier Analysis and Applications*, 4(3).

[16] Jayant, N. S., & Noll, P. (1984). Digital Coding of Waveforms- Principles and applications to speech and video". *Prentice Hall.*

Chapter 2

# A Pyramid-Based Watermarking Technique for Digital Images Copyright Protection Using Discrete Wavelet Transforms Techniques

Awad Kh. Al-Asmari and Farhan A. Al-Enizi

Additional information is available at the end of the chapter

http://dx.doi.org/10.5772/50280

## 1. Introduction

With the growth and advances in digital communication technologies, digital images have become easy to be delivered and exchanged. These forms of digital information can be easily copied and distributed through digital media. These concerns motivated significant researches in images watermarking [1]. New progress in digital technologies, such as compression techniques, has brought new challenges to watermarking. Various watermarking schemes that use different techniques have been proposed over the last few years [2-10]. To be effective, a watermark must be imperceptible within its host, easily extracted by the owner, and robust to intentional and unintentional distortions [7]. In specific, discrete wavelet transforms (DWT) has wide applications in the area of image watermarking. This is because it has many specifications that make the watermarking process robust. Some of these specifications are [4]: Space-frequency localization, Multi-resolution representation, Superior Human Visual system (HVS) modeling, and adaptively to the original image. A wavelet-based watermarking technique for ownership verification is presented by Y. Wang [11]. It uses orthonormal filter banks that are generated randomly to decompose the host image and insert the watermark in it.

Another transform technique that is used extensively in image coding is the pyramid transform which was first introduced by Burt and Adelson [12]. It can provide high compression rates and at the same time low complexity encoding. Like the DWT, pyramid transform provides multi-resolution representation of the images. These properties can be used in watermarking to establish a robust data hiding system.

In this chapter, our target is to develop an algorithm using optimal pyramid decomposition technique, and combine it with wavelet decompositions. The algorithm will be used for data hiding in digital images to meet the requirements of imperceptibility, robustness, storage requirements, security, and complexity.

## 2. Wavelet and Pyramid Transforms

The wavelet transform has the advantage of achieving both spatial and frequency localizations. Wavelet decomposition depends mainly on filter banks, typically the wavelet decomposition and reconstruction structures consist of filtering, decimation, and interpolation. Figure 1. shows two-channel wavelet structure [11].

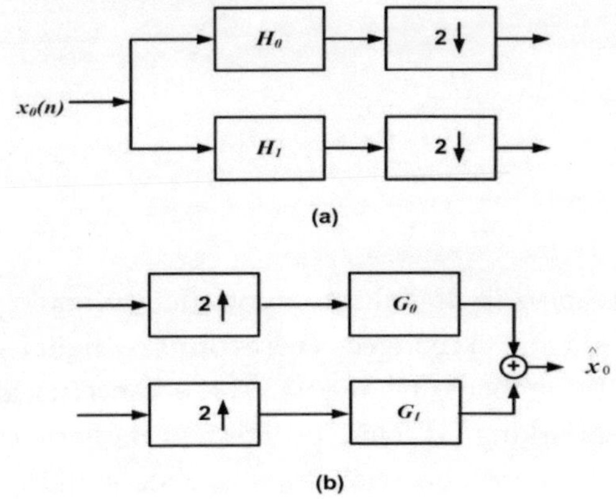


**Figure 1.** Two-channel wavelet transform structure: (a) decomposition, (b) reconstruction.

Where $H_0$, $H_1$, $G_0$, and $G_1$ are the low decomposition, high decomposition, low reconstruction and high reconstruction filters, respectively. For the perfect reconstruction (i.e. $x_0 = \hat{x}_0$), these filters should be related to each other according to the relations given below:

$$H_0(z)G_0(z) + H_1(z)G_1(z) = 2 \tag{1}$$

$$H_0(-z)G_0(z) + H_1(-z)G_1(z) = 0 \tag{2}$$

Special type of wavelet filters is the orthonormal filters. These filters can be constructed in such a way that they have large side-lobes. This makes it possible to embed more watermarks in the lower bands to avoid the effect of the different images processing techniques. These filter banks can be generated randomly depending on the generating polynomials.

For two-channel orthonormal FIR real coefficient filter banks, the following relations shall be applied [11]:

$$G_0(z)G_0(z^{-1}) + G_0(-z)G_0(-z^{-1}) = 2 \tag{3}$$

$$G_1(z) = -z^{-2k+1}G_0(-z^{-1}); k \in Z \tag{4}$$

$$H_i(z) = G_i(z^{-1}),\ i \in \{0,1\} \tag{5}$$

If $P(z)$ was defined as a polynomial, where

$$P(z) = G_0(z).G_0(z^{-1}) \tag{6}$$

Then it can be written as:

$$P(z) = 1 + \sum_{k=odd} a_k z^{-k},\ a_k = a_{-k} \tag{7}$$

Depending on the factorization of the polynomials given in equation (7), analysis and synthesis filters can be generated. If $k = 5$, then we can get four filters each of length six which constitute the two-dimensional analysis and synthesis filters. A decomposition structure can be applied as shown in Figure 2 where sub-band ca1 (the blue square) is chosen for further decompositions.

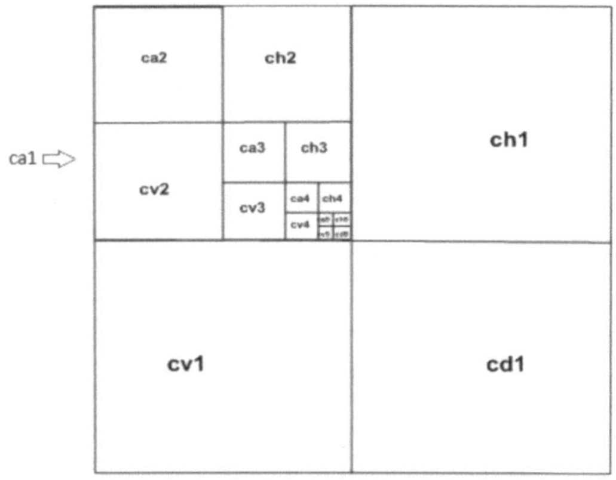


**Figure 2.** Five-level wavelet decomposing structure.

This decomposing structure is applied to King Saud University (KSU book) image of size 512×512 pixels shown in Figure 3. The resulting wavelet sub-bands are shown in Figure 4.

**Figure 3.** KSU book image.

**Figure 4.** Five-level discrete-wavelet decomposition of KSU book image.

To have a good understanding of the DWT and its effects on the image, it is better to study this decomposition technique in the frequency domain. Frequency spectrum of the original KSU image (the book) is shown in Figure 5, and frequency responses of the four sub-bands that result from the first level decomposition are shown in Figure 6. The spectrums of the four bands show the effect of the filtering process, and the shapes of these filters. From these two figures it can be seen that the spectrum of sub-band *ca1* is very close to the shape of the original image because it is only a decimated version of KSU image, whereas the other sub-bands represent the details of the test image. This is the reason why the visual perception is more sensitive to low-frequency variations than to high-frequency variations.

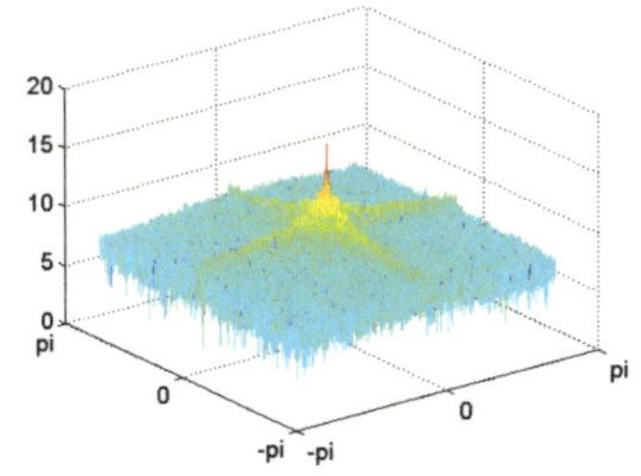


**Figure 5.** Spectrum decomposition of KSU image.

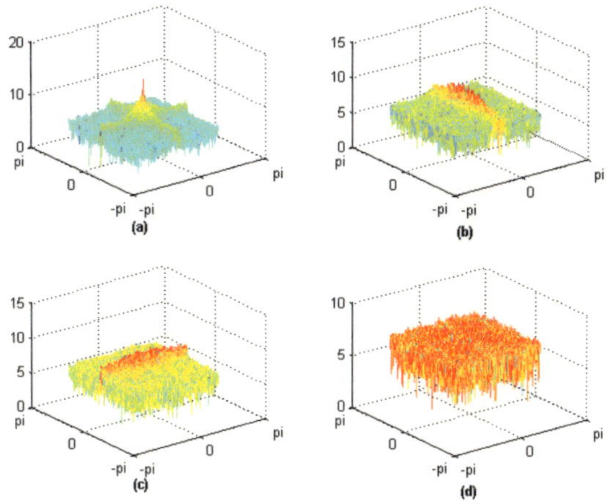


**Figure 6.** Spectrums of the 1st-level wavelet decomposition sub-bands of KSU image (the book) (a) *ca1*, (b) *ch1*, (c) *cv1*, and (d) *cd1*.

Pyramid transform was first introduced by Burt and Adelson [12]. It was used mainly for image compression. Like the DWT, pyramid transform provides the multi-resolution structure. If $x_0(n_1,n_2)$ is the original image of size $L_1 \times L_2$ pixels, then its pyramid structure can be done as shown in Figure 7.

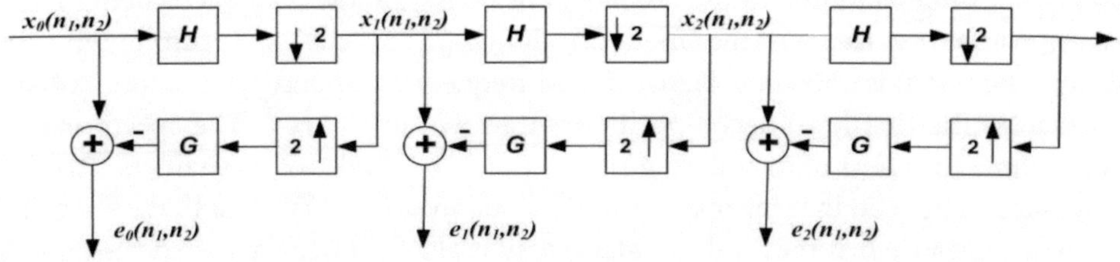


**Figure 7.** Three-level pyramid decomposition of an image $x_0(n_1,n_2)$.

For decimation by a factor of 2, the image will be filtered using analysis lowpass filter $H$, and then it will be decimated by a factor of two. This results in an image $x_1(n_1,n_2)$ which is 1/4 of the size of $x_0(n_1,n_2)$ and it is called the first-level image of the pyramid. The second level image $x_2(n_1,n_2)$ can be obtained from $x_1(n_1,n_2)$ by the same process, and this process is completed for the higher levels. The image $x_1(n_1,n_2)$ can be interpolated by a factor of 2 and then filtered using synthesis filter G. The resulting image will be $I[x_1(n_1,n_2)]$. Where $I[.]$ is the spatial interpolation and filtering operation. The synthesis filter G is a time reversal version of the analysis filter $H$. The difference (error image) $e_0(n_1,n_2)$ is given by:

$$e_0(n_1, n_2) = x_0(n_1, n_2) - I[x_1(n_1, n_2)] \tag{8}$$

This process can be done for the higher levels and we will have the error images $e_1(n_1,n_2)$, $e_2(n_1,n_2)$...etc. The optimizing of the analysis and synthesis filters plays the major role in the perfect reconstruction of the images. For watermarking purposes, random filters will be used. The error images $e_0$, $e_1$, and $e_2$ and the decimated image $d_3$ in space domain are shown in Figures [8-11]. Frequency responses of the error images $e_0$, $e_1$, $e_2$ and decimated image $d_3$ for KSU image (the book) are shown in Figure 12. The frequency response of the original image indicates that most of the energy is concentrated in the low frequency bands, mainly around the zero frequency. High frequency bands contain less energy. This results in limitations on the hiding capacity in these regions. These facts have a great effect in watermarking algorithm. So that normally high-pass bands are avoided in watermarking due to the compression effects, and low-pass bands are also avoided because there will be huge artifacts on the visual quality of the images. To perform the watermarking in the pyramid and the wavelet transforms, two requirements should be met. First, the filter banks should be generated randomly, and the decomposition structure and the bands being used for watermarking must be determined by the owner. This requires the storage of the coefficients that are used for generating these filters, and the decomposition structure of the host image. The second requirement for practical watermarking system is to perform the hiding and the extracting processes in minimum time. Storage requirements as seen before are not that large. The filters can be generated by changing only three coefficients. The running time is related directly to the computational complexity of the pyramid and wavelet transforms.

**Figure 8.** Pyramid decomposed KSU book image in space domain, $e_0$ image.

**Figure 9.** Pyramid decomposed KSU book image in space domain, $e_1$ image.

**Figure 10.** Pyramid decomposed KSU book image in space domain, $e_2$ image.

**Figure 11.** Pyramid decomposed KSU book image in space domain, $d_3$ image.

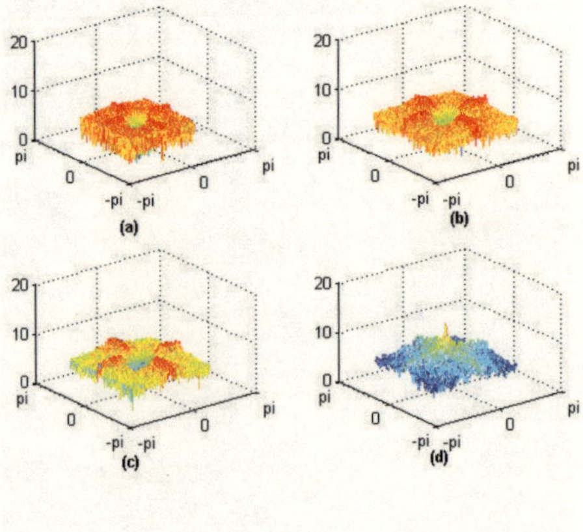


**Figure 12.** Frequency responses of the pyramidal components of KSU image (a) $e_0$ image, (b) $e_1$ image, (c) $e_2$ image, (d) decimated image $d_3$.

Computational complexity depends on the number of operations (here multiplications) required to transform an image for a number of levels $N$. A mathematical derivation of this complexity for pyramid transform is introduced in [13]. The derivation assumes that circular convolution based on fast Fourier transform (FFT) and inverse fast Fourier transforms (IFFT) is used for transforming an image pyramidally. This derivation is summarized below.

For an image $x_0(n_1,n_2)$ of size $L_1 \times L_2$, the number of multiplications needed for the first level $x_1(n_1,n_2)$ with decimation factor $M$ will be

$$L_1 L_2 \log_2 L_1 + \frac{L_1 L_2}{M} \log_2 L_2 \tag{9}$$

The first part of equation (9) results from horizontal filtering and the second part is the number of multiplications needed for vertical filtering after decimated by $M$. Let

$$\begin{gathered} K_1 = L_1 \log_2 L_1 \\ \text{And} \\ K_2 = L_2 \log_2 L_2 \end{gathered} \tag{10}$$

Then equation (9) can be applied for higher levels. In general, the total number of multiplications needed to get the decimated images $x_1(n_1,n_2)$, $x_2(n_1,n_2)$,..., $x_{N-1}(n_1,n_2)$ and the difference images $e_0(n_1,n_2)$, $e_1(n_1,n_2)$,..., $e_{N-2}(n_1,n_2)$ can be written as follows in equations (11) and (12) [13]:

$$2\left(L_2 K_1 + \frac{L_1}{M} K_2\right) \qquad N = 1 \tag{11}$$

http://dx.doi.org/10.5772/50280

$$2\left[\sum_{i=0}^{N-1}\frac{L_2K_1}{(M)^{2i}}+\frac{L_1K_2}{(M)^{2i+1}}-L_1L_2\sum_{i=0}^{N-2}(i+1)\frac{M+1}{(M)^{2i+3}}\right]\qquad N\geq 2 \tag{12}$$

Where $N$ is number of decomposition levels, $M$ is the decimation factor.

The above analysis can be extended to the wavelet transform taking into account that there are four filters for each stage of decompositions and four filters for each stage of reconstructions, and the decimation factor is $M = 2$. Numbers of multiplications in the wavelet transform are shown in equations (13) and (14).

$$8\left(L_2K_1+\frac{L_1}{M}K_2\right)\qquad N=1 \tag{13}$$

$$8\left[\sum_{i=0}^{N-1}\frac{L_2K_1}{(M)^{2i}}+\frac{L_1K_2}{(M)^{2i+1}}-L_1L_2\sum_{i=0}^{N-2}(i+1)\frac{M+1}{(M)^{2i+3}}\right]\qquad N\geq 2 \tag{14}$$

Our algorithm performance will be measured in terms of peak signal-to-noise ratio (PSNR) between the original image and the watermarked one, and the correlation between the original watermark and the extracted one. False alarm probability $P_f$ is an important aspect in the watermarking systems. It is the probability that the extracted pattern from unwatermarked image or an image watermarked with another pattern, has a correlation with the original watermark greater than the threshold value $T$, or the probability that the extracted pattern from our watermarked image has a correlation with the original one less than the threshold value. This probability is related to the threshold that is chosen.

The watermark extraction is similar to determining a signal in a noisy environment [11]; since the watermark is of size $n$ by $n$ and the energy of the extracted pattern is normalized before computing the correlation, then, all the possible patterns are lying on a sphere of dimension $n^2$ with radius one. If we define $m = n^2$, the surface area of a $m$-dimensional sphere of radius $\rho$ is given in equation (15):

$$S=mV_m\rho^{m-1} \tag{15}$$

Where $V_m=\pi^{m/2}/(m/2)!$. All the patterns are assumed to have equal probabilities. Then, the false alarm probability $P_f$ equals to the fraction of two areas $A_1/A$. $A$ is the area of the whole sphere, while $A_1$ contains all points on the sphere whose inner products with the point corresponding to the rotated watermark pattern are larger than $T$. By rotating the coordinate axes to make the rotated watermark pattern correspond to point $[1,0,\ldots,0]^T$, then, $A_1$ can be calculated as follows:

$$A_1 = \int_T^1 (m-1)V_{m-1}\left(\sqrt{1-x^2}\right)^{m-2} \frac{dx}{\sqrt{1-x^2}} \qquad (16)$$

And $A = mV_m$. Therefore, $P_f$ can be calculated as given below [11]:

$$P_f = \frac{\int_T^1 (m-1)V_{m-1}\left(\sqrt{1-x^2}\right)^{m-3} dx}{mV_m} \qquad (17)$$

As the threshold value of the correlator increases, then the false alarm probability decreases which indicates more reliability. Accepted false alarm probability depends on the requirements, for example a $P_f$ less than $1.35\times10^{-11}$, corresponds to a correlation threshold value that should be greater than 0.40.

## 3. Proposed Watermarking Technique

In this section, we introduce our digital image watermarking technique. The technique consists of two stages: first stage is the pyramid transform and the second stage is the DWT. The watermark can be a logo image of size $n\times n$ pixels. If $x_0(n_1, n_2)$ was the original image of size $L_1\times L_2$ pixels, then the pyramid structure for three levels can be done as shown in Figure 7, where $H$ and $G$ are the analysis and synthesis filters respectively, $e_0(n_1,n_2)$, $e_1(n_1,n_2)$, and $e_2(n_1,n_2)$ are the error images, and $d_3$ is the decimated image.

Our proposed algorithm will use one of the error images resulting from the pyramid decomposition as a host image for the wavelet watermarking process. That is, the watermark will be inserted in one of the error images using wavelet decomposition. A method for wavelet image watermarking is proposed by Y. Wang [11]. It uses FIR, real-coefficients, randomly generated orthonormal filter banks. The watermark will replace the coefficients of one of the higher sub-bands. Then, the watermarked image will be reconstructed. However, a method for generating optimal pyramid transform filters has been introduced by F. Chin [14]. Therefore, The original image can be pyramidally decomposed using random analysis filters for three levels resulting in three error images $e_0$, $e_1$, and $e_2$ of sizes $L_1\times L_2$, $(L_1/2)\times(L_2/2)$, and $(L_1/4)\times(L_2/4)$ pixels respectively. Each of these error images can be used for wavelet watermarking process that will be interpreted in three methods.

Method that depends on decomposing $e_0$ will increase the computational complexity. Furthermore, the visual quality of the reconstructed image is found to be affected when the difference image $e_2$ is decomposed. This is due to the fact that the watermark is hidden in the lower frequency bands, which will affect the significant coefficients of the decomposed image. The method that depends on decomposing $e_1$ will provide a trade-off between imperceptibility, robustness, and computational complexity. These observations will be presented in the simulation results. Therefore, $e_1$ can be wavelet decomposed using the analysis filter banks that were generated according to a structure chosen by the owner and guarantees imperceptibility and robustness. A possible structure is shown in Figure 2. Then, the watermark which is $16\times16$ pixels image will be scrambled, rotated, and then it will replace the black sub-band shown in Figure 13. Wavelet and pyramid reconstructions using the synthesis filters will then be performed. The proposed watermarking algorithm using $e_1$ is shown in Figure 14.

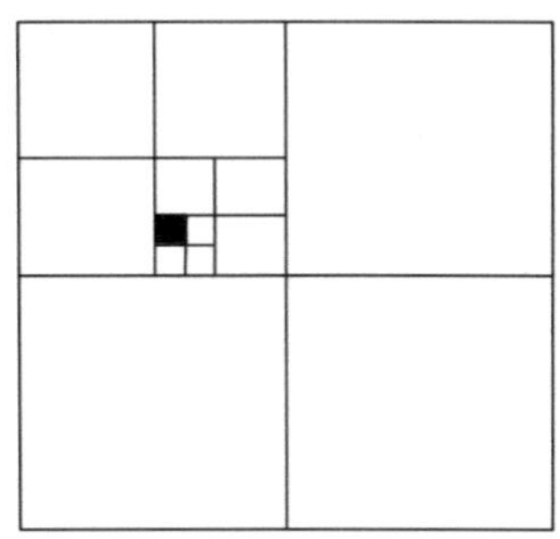

**Figure 13.** Wavelet decomposition structure for the error image $e_1$.

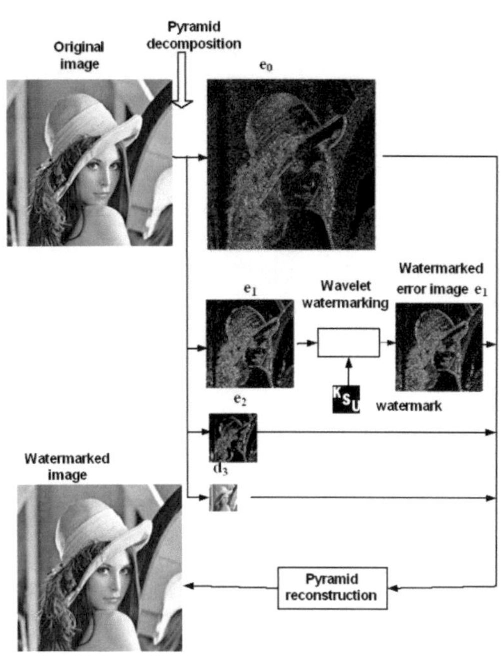


**Figure 14.** Proposed Pyramid-Wavelet watermarking algorithm using $e_1$.

## 4. Experimental Results

In this section we demonstrate the performance of our algorithm using our proposed method on grayscale test images of sizes 512×512 pixels, and compare it with method of Y. Wang [11]. The test images are Lena, Baboon, Peppers, Goldhill, and Barbara. The original and watermarked images of Lena are shown in figure 15. Our algorithm performance will be measured in terms of peak signal-to-noise ratio (PSNR) between the original image and the watermarked one, and the correlation between the original watermark and the extracted one. For accepted false alarm probability $P_f$ (i.e. less than $1.35\times10^{-11}$), correlation threshold value should be greater than 0.40 [11]. For comparison, the average values over the five test images are computed. Table 1 shows the average PSNR and the average correlation values for our method and method of Y. Wang [11]. Our proposed method gives higher average values for both the PSNR and the correlation. This guarantees good perceptual transparency and reliability.

(a) Original image (b) Watermarked image

**Figure 15.** Original and watermarked images.

| | Proposed method | Y. Wang [11] |
|---|---|---|
| Average PSNR | 46.52 | 42.14 |
| Average correlation | 0.992 | 0.986 |

**Table 1.** Average PSNR and correlation of proposed method and Y. Wang method [8].

http://dx.doi.org/10.5772/50280

To see the robustness of our algorithm, the watermarked images were subjected to certain common attacks. These attacks are JPEG compression, median filters, histogram equalization, zero mean 100 variance Gaussian noise, and 1% salt-and-pepper noise. The average compression over the five test images is 0.328 bpp. Table 2 shows the average correlation values for the five test images with these attacks. It can be seen that our proposed algorithm provides higher values with two of the attacks. These attacks are the median filter and the JPEG compression. However, for the additive noise and the histogram equalization, it gives approximately the same average values. Importance of this result is that median filters and JPEG attacks are among the worst attacks in watermarking systems. They are able to destroy many watermarking systems without affecting the visual quality. Surviving them gives the used algorithm high robustness.

The other important advantage of our proposed algorithm is the savings in the computational complexity. Normally, DWT and pyramid transform use the fast Fourier transform (FFT). Computational complexity depends on the number of multiplications being performed [13]. Table 3 shows the number of multiplications and savings for our method and method of Y. Wang [11]. It can be shown that our method achieves a saving of 54%. This is due to the fact that the wavelet decomposition was performed on a smaller image $e_1$ of size 256×256 pixels rather than performing it on the original image of 512×512 pixels.

| Type of Attack | Average Correlations | |
|---|---|---|
| | **Proposed method** | **Y. Wang [11]** |
| JPEG compression (average: 0.328 bpp) | 0.602 | 0.562 |
| Median filter | 0.909 | 0.430 |
| Histogram equalization | 0.965 | 0.963 |
| Gaussian noise | 0.967 | 0.974 |
| 1% Salt-and-pepper noise | 0.948 | 0.956 |

**Table 2.** Average correlations of proposed method and Y. Wang method [11] upon some common attacks.

| Hiding technique | Proposed method | Y. Wang [11] |
|---|---|---|
| Number of multiplications | 16,687,104 | 36,347,904 |
| Savings in computational complexity (%) | 54.09 | 0 |

**Table 3.** Computational complexity and savings with respect to method of Y. Wang [11].

## 5. Application on Digital Color Images

The proposed Pyramid-Based Watermarking Technique can also be applied on the digital color images. In this section, we demonstrate the performance of our algorithm using the proposed method on standard RGB color test images of sizes 512×512 pixels and the watermark was inserted in the green component. The test images are Lena, Baboon, and Peppers. The original and watermarked images of Lena are shown in Figure 16. Table 4 shows the correlation values of the watermarking process for the images. To ensure the robustness of our method, it was subjected to attacks of Gaussian noise of zero mean and variance of 100, 1% salt-and-pepper noise, and JPEG compression. Tables 5 and 6 show the correlation values when adding the two types of noise. It can be seen that our proposed algorithm is robust to these kinds of noise. Table 7 shows the correlation values when our watermarked images were compressed using JPEG compression at quality factors of 50,60,70,80, and 90 to different bit rates. It can be seen that for an average bit rate of 1.67 bpp, the normalized correlation is 0.50. This value is above the threshold mentioned in reference [10] which is 0.23. So, our algorithm is robust against JPEG compression at quality factors greater than 50.

(a) Original Lena image (b) Watermarked Lena image

**Figure 16.** a). The original standard 512×512 RGB color image. (b) Watermarked color image.

| Image | Correlation |
|---|---|
| Lena | 1 |
| Baboon | 1 |
| Peppers | 1 |

**Table 4.** Correlation values of watermarking process of color images using our proposed method.

http://dx.doi.org/10.5772/50280

| Image | Correlation |
|---|---|
| Lena | 0.90 |
| Baboon | 0.98 |
| Peppers | 0.77 |

**Table 5.** Correlation values of watermarking process of color images using our proposed method upon attack of Gaussian noise.

| Image | Correlation |
|---|---|
| Lena | 0.91 |
| Baboon | 0.98 |
| Peppers | 0.70 |

**Table 6.** Correlation values of watermarking process of color images using our proposed method upon attack of 1% salt-and-pepper noise.

| Image | Quality factor | Bitrate (bpp) | Correlation Proposed method |
|---|---|---|---|
| Lena | 50 | 0.74 | 0.29 |
| | 60 | 0.85 | 0.30 |
| | 70 | 1.03 | 0.41 |
| | 80 | 1.34 | 0.44 |
| | 90 | 2.11 | 0.74 |
| Baboon | 50 | 1.54 | 0.50 |
| | 60 | 1.78 | 0.54 |
| | 70 | 2.13 | 0.65 |
| | 80 | 2.71 | 0.75 |
| | 90 | 4.06 | 0.91 |
| Peppers | 50 | 0.80 | 0.23 |
| | 60 | 0.93 | 0.29 |
| | 70 | 1.13 | 0.35 |
| | 80 | 1.47 | 0.42 |
| | 90 | 2.45 | 0.67 |
| Average | | 1.67 | 0.50 |

**Table 7.** Correlation values of watermarking process of color images using our proposed method upon attack of JPEG compression.

## 6. Conclusions

In this chapter, we proposed a pyramid-wavelet watermarking technique. The technique uses the spatial-frequency properties of the pyramid and wavelet transforms to embed a watermark in digital images. From the results, the proposed algorithm achieved a trade-off between the perceptual invisibility and the robustness. However, it enhanced the performance of the wavelet-based watermarking algorithm of Y. Wang [11] in many aspects such as compression and median filter attacks. The security issues were addressed extensively in the design, where the filter banks being used are generated randomly. The owner has full control on the filter banks, the decomposition structure, and the band being used for embedding. On the other hand, the watermark can be also controlled by the owner; he can rotate and scramble it. The proposed algorithm provided savings in the computational complexity which is a significant aspect in watermarking systems design. The filters being used for pyramid and wavelet transform should be optimized for perfect reconstruction, and this will help in designing robust watermarking systems to get the best performance.

## Author details

Awad Kh. Al-Asmari[1,2*] and Farhan A. Al-Enizi[3]

*Address all correspondence to: alasmari@ksu.edu.sa

1 College of Engineering, King Saud University, Riyadh, Saudi Arabia

2 Salman bin Abdulaziz University, Saudi Arabia

3 College of Engineering, Salman bin Abdulaziz University, Saudi Arabia

## References

[1] Langelaar, G. C., Setyawan, I., & Lagendijk, R. L. (2000, Sept.) Watermarking digital image and video data. A state-of-the-art overview. *IEEE Signal Processing Magazine*, 17, 20-46.

[2] Aboofazeli, M., Thomas, G., & Moussavi, Z. (2004, May). A wavelet transform based digital image watermarking scheme. *Proc. IEEE CCECE*, 2, 823-826.

[3] Al-Asmari, Awad Kh., & Al-Enizi, Farhan A. (2006). A Pyramid-Based Watermarking Technique for Digital Images Ownership Verification. Paper presented at First National Information Technology Symposium (NITS 2006), Feb. 5-7, King Saud University, Saudi Arabia.

[4] Meerwald, P., & Uhl, A. (2001). A survey of wavelet-domain watermarking algorithms. *Proc. SPIE*, 4314, 505-516.

[5] Mong-Shu, L. (2003). Image compression and watermarking by wavelet localization. *Intern. J. Computer Math.*, 80(4), 401-412.

[6] Al-Enizi, Farhan A., & Al-Asmari, Awad Kh. (2006). A Pyramid-Based Watermarking Technique for Secure Fingerprint Images Exchange. The International Conference on Computer & Communication 2006 (ICCC06), International Islamic University Malaysia.

[7] Kundur, D., & Hatzinakos, D. (1998, May). Digital watermarking using multiresolution wavelet decomposition. *Proc. IEEE ICASSP*, 5, 2969-2972.

[8] Guzman, V. H., Miyatake, M. N., & Meana, H. M. P. (2004). Analysis of a wavelet-based watermarking algorithm. *Proc. IEEE CONIELECOMP*, 283-287.

[9] Al-Asmari, Awad Kh., & Al-Enizi, Farhan A. (2009). Watermarking Technique for Digital Color Images Copyright Protection. International Conference of Computing in engineering, science and information 2009 (HPCNCS-09) Florida, USA.

[10] Shih-Hao, W., & Yuan-Pei, L. (2004, Feb.) Wavelet tree quantization for copyright protection watermarking. *IEEE Transactions on Image Processing*, 13, 154-165.

[11] Wang, Y., Doherty, J. F., & Van Dyck, R. E. (2002). A wavelet-based watermarking algorithm for ownership verification of digital images. *IEEE Trans. Image Processing*, 11, 77-88.

[12] Burt, P. J., & Adelson, E. H. (1983). The Laplacian pyramid as a compact image code. *IEEE Trans. Communication*, 31, 532-540.

[13] Al-Asmari, A. Kh. (1995). Optimum bit rate pyramid coding with low computational and memory requirements. *IEEE trans. Circuits Syst. Video Technol.*, 5, 182-192.

[14] Chin, F., Choi, A., & Luo, Y. (1992). Optimal Generating Kernels for Image Pyramids by Piecewise Fitting. *IEEE trans. Pattern Anal. Machine Intell.*, 14, 1190-1198.

Chapter 3

# DWT Based Resolution Enhancement of Video Sequences

Sara Izadpanahi, Cagri Ozcinar,
Gholamreza Anbarjafari and Hasan Demirel

Additional information is available at the end of the chapter

http://dx.doi.org/10.5772/48827

## 1. Introduction

Mobile phones are one of the most commonly used tools in our daily life and many people record videos of the various events by using the embedded cameras, and usually due to low resolution of the cameras, reviewing the videos on the high resolution screens is not very pleasant. That is one of the reasons that nowadays resolution enhancements of low resolution video sequences are at the centre of interest of many researchers. There are two main approaches in the literature for performing the resolution enhancement. The first approach is multi-frame super resolution based on the combination of image information from several similar images taken from a video sequence (M. Elad and A. Feuer, PAMI, 1999). The second approach is referred as single-frame super resolution, which uses prior training data to enforce super resolution over a single low resolution input image. In this work we are following the first approach which is multi frame resolution enhancement taken from low resolution video sequences.

Tsai and Huang are the pioneers of super resolution idea (1984). They used the frequency domain approach. Further work has been conducted by Keren et al. (1988) describing a spatial domain procedure by using a global translation and rotation model in order to perform image registration. Furthermore, Reddy and Chatterji (1996) introduced a frequency domain approach for super resolution. Later on, Cortelazzo and Lucchese (2000) presented a method for estimating planar roto-translations that operates in the frequency domain. Irani and Peleg (1991) have developed a motion estimation algorithm, which considers translations and rotations in spatial domain. Meanwhile, further researches have been conducted on developing on resolution enhancement of low resolution video sequences (Demirel and Izadpanahi, 2008, B. Marcel, M. Briot, and R. Murrieta, 1997, Demirel et al. [EUSIPCO] 2009, N. Nguyen and P. Milanfar, 2000, Robinson et al 2010). Vandewalle et al. (2006) considered a frequency domain technique to specifically register a set of aliased images. In their method images were differently considered by a planar motion method. Their proposed algorithm used low-frequency information which has the highest signal-to-noise ratio (SNR), and in their setup, the aliasing-free part of the images.

Wavelet transform is also being widely used in many image processing applications, especially in image and video super resolution techniques (Piao et al. 2007, Demirel et al. [IEEE Geoscience and Remote Sensing Letter] 2010, Temizel and Vlachos 2005, Demirel and Anbarjafari 2010, Anbarjafari and Demirel [ETRI], 2010 ). A one-level discrete wavelet transform (DWT) of a single frame of a video sequence produces a low frequency subband, and three high frequency subbands oriented at 0 , 45 , and 90 (Mallat,1999).

In this work, we have proposed a new video resolution enhancement technique which generates sharper super resolved video frames. The proposed technique uses DWT to decompose low resolution frames of the video sequences into four subbands, namely, low-low (LL), low-high (LH), high-low (HL), and high-high (HH). Then the three high frequency subbands (LH, HL, and HH subbands) of the respective frames have been enlarged by using bicubic interpolation. In parallel, the input low resolution frames have been super resolved by using Irani and Peleg technique separately (Irani and Peleg, 1991). Illumination inconsistence can be attributed to uncontrolled environments. Because Irani and Peleg registration technique is used, it is an advantage that the frames used in the registration process have the same illumination. In this paper, we have also proposed a new illumination compensation method by using singular value decomposition (SVD). The illumination compensation technique is performed on the frames before the implementation of Irani and Peleg resolution enhancement technique. Finally, the interpolated high frequency subbands, obtained from DWT of the corresponding frames, and their respective super resolved input frames have been combined by using inverse DWT (IDWT) to reconstruct a high resolution output video sequence. The proposed technique has been compared with several state-of-art image resolution enhancement techniques. The following registration techniques are used for comparison purposes:

- Cortelazzo and Lucchese registration technique (2000)
- Marcel et al., registration technique (1997)
- Vandewalle et al., registration technique (2006)
- Keren et al., registration technique (1988),

The reconstruction techniques used in this work for comparison are:

- Bicubic interpolation
- Iterated Back Projection (1991)

http://dx.doi.org/10.5772/48827

- Robust super resolution technique (Zomet et al., 2001)
- Structure Adaptive Normalized Convolution (Pham et al., 2006)

The experimental results are showing that the proposed method overcomes the aforementioned resolution enhancement techniques. Also as it will be shown in the experimental section, the proposed illumination compensation improves the quality of the super resolved sequence (the PSNR) by 2.26 dB for Akiyo video sequence.

## 2. State-of-art super resolution methods

In this section a brief introduction of four super resolution methods, which have been used to compare the performance of the proposed super resolution technique, are reviewed.

### 2.1. L. Lucchese et al. super resolution method

Lucchese et al. super resolution method operates in the frequency domain. The estimation of relative motion parameters between the reference image and each of the other input images is based on the following property: The amplitude of the Fourier transform of an image and the mirrored version of the amplitude of the Fourier transform of a rotated image have a pair of orthogonal zero-crossing lines. The angle that these lines make with the axes is identical to half the rotation angle between the two images. Thus the rotation angle will be computed by finding these two zero crossings lines. This algorithm uses a three-stage coarsest to finest procedure for rotation angle estimation with a wide range of degree accuracy. The shift is estimated afterwards using a standard phase correlation method.

### 2.2. Reddy et al. super resolution method

In this method a registration algorithm that uses the Fourier domain approach to align images which are translated and rotated with respect to one another, was proposed. Using a log-polar transform of the magnitude of the frequency spectra, image rotation and scale can be converted into horizontal and vertical shifts. These can therefore also be estimated using a phase correlation method. Their method utilizes reparability of rotational and translational components property of the Fourier transform. According to this property, the translation only affects the phase information, whereas the rotation affects both phase and amplitude of the Fourier transform. One of the properties of the 2D Fourier Transform is that if we rotate the image, the spectrum will rotate in the same direction. Therefore, the rotational component can first be estimated. Then, after compensating for rotation, and by using phase correlation techniques, the translational component can be estimated easily.

### 2.3. Irani et al. super resolution method

Irani et al. have developed a motion estimation algorithm. This algorithm considers translations and rotations in spatial domain. The motion parameters which are unknown can be computed from the set of approximation that can be derived from the following equation (1), where the horizontal shift $a$, vertical shift $b$, and rotation angle $\theta$ between two images $g_1$ and $g_2$ can be expressed as:

$$g_2(x, y)=g_1(x\cos\theta - y\sin\theta + a,\ y\cos\theta + x\sin\theta + b) \tag{1}$$

Finally, after determining and applying the results, the error measure between images g1 and g2 is approximated by (1) where this summation is counted over overlapping areas of both images.

$$\begin{aligned} E(a, b, \theta)=&\sum [g_1(x, y) + \left(a - y\theta - \frac{x\theta^2}{2}\right)\frac{\partial g_1}{\partial x} \\ &+\left(a + x\theta - \frac{y\theta^2}{2}\right)\frac{\partial g_1}{\partial y} - g_2(x, y)]^2 \end{aligned} \tag{2}$$

For reducing E to its minimal value and obtaining more accurate result, the linear system in (5) is applied. By solving the following matrix, the horizontal shift $a$, vertical shift $b$, and rotation angle $\theta$ will be computed as follows.

$$M = \begin{bmatrix} a \\ b \\ c \end{bmatrix},\ B = \begin{bmatrix} \sum \frac{\partial g_1}{\partial x}(g_1 - g_2) \\ \sum \frac{\partial g_1}{\partial y}(g_1 - g_2) \\ \sum R(g1 - g2) \end{bmatrix} \tag{3}$$

$$A = \begin{bmatrix} \sum\left(\frac{\partial g_1}{\partial x}\right)^2 & \sum\left(\frac{\partial g_1}{\partial x}\frac{\partial g_1}{\partial y}\right) & \sum\left(R\frac{\partial g_1}{\partial x}\right) \\ \sum\left(\frac{\partial g_1}{\partial x}\frac{\partial g_1}{\partial y}\right) & \sum\left(\frac{\partial g_1}{\partial y}\right)^2 & \sum\left(R\frac{\partial g_1}{\partial y}\right) \\ \sum\left(R\frac{\partial g_1}{\partial x}\right) & \sum\left(R\frac{\partial g_1}{\partial y}\right) & \sum R^2 \end{bmatrix}_{3x3} \tag{4}$$

$$AM = B \Rightarrow A^{-1}AM = A^{-1}B \Rightarrow M = A^{-1}B \tag{5}$$

Fig. 1 (a-d) shows the four low resolution consecutive frames, where (e), (f) and (g) shows super resolved high resolution images by using Cortelazzo et al., Reddy et al., and Irani et. al methods respectively.

http://dx.doi.org/10.5772/48827

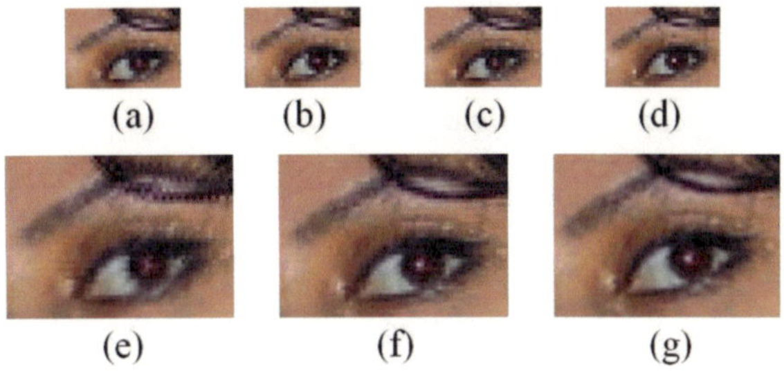


**Figure 1.** a) through (d) are four low resolution images taken from a video sequence. (e) High resolution image of (a) through (d) using Cortelazzo et al. (f), Reddy et al. (g) and Irani et al. methods.

### 2.4. Motion-based localized super resolution technique by using discrete wavelet transform

The main loss of an image or a video frame after being super resolved is on its high frequency components (i.e. edges), which is due to the smoothing caused by super resolution techniques. Hence, in order to increase the quality of the super resolved image, preserving the edges is essential. Hence, DWT has been employed in order to preserve the high frequency components of the image by decomposing a frame into different subband images, namely Low-Low (LL), Low-High (LH), High-Low (HL), and High-High (HH).

LH, HL, and HH subband images contain the high frequency components of the input frame. The DWT process for each frame of the input video generates 4 video sequences in each subband (i.e. LL, LH, HL and HH video sequences). Then, the Irani et al. super resolution method in (1991) is applied to all subband video sequences separately. This process results in 4 super resolved subband video sequences. Finally, IDWT is used to combine the super resolved subbands to produce the high resolution video sequence.

By super resolving the LL, LH, HL and HH video sequences and then by applying IDWT, the output video sequence would contain sharper edges than the super resolved video sequence obtained by any of the aforementioned super resolution techniques directly. This is due to the fact that, the super resolution of isolated high frequency components in HH, HL and LH will preserve more high frequency components after the super resolution of the respective subbands separately than super resolving the low resolution image directly.

In this technique, the moving regions are extracted to be super resolved with the proposed super resolution technique explained above. The static regions are similarly transformed into wavelet domain and each static subband sequence is interpolated by bicubic interpolation. The high resolution sequence of the static region is generated by composing the interpolated frames using the IDWT. Eventually, the super resolved sequence is achieved by combining the super resolved moving sequence and the interpolated static region sequence.

The method can be summarized with the following steps:

1. Acquire frames from video and extract motion region(s) using frame subtraction.
2. Determine the significant local motion region(s) by applying connected component labeling.
3. Apply DWT to decompose the static background region into different subbands.

4. Apply bicubic interpolation for enhancing resolution of each subband obtained from step 3.

5. Use IDWT to reconstruct the super resolved static background.

6. Apply DWT to decompose the moving foreground region(s) into different subbands.

7. Super resolve the extracted subbands by applying Irani et al. super resolution method.

8. Use IDWT to reconstruct the super resolved moving region(s).

9. Combine the sequences obtained from steps (5) and (8) to generate the final super resolved vide sequence.

In the first step, four consecutive frames are used where each frame is subtracted from the reference frame so the differences between frames are extracted. After applying OR operation for all subtracted images local motion(s) will appear.

In the second step, the area of local motion(s) can be determined by using connected component labeling. In the third, fourth, and fifth steps the rest of the frames which does not include any motion and it is static, will be decomposed by DWT, interpolated with the help of bicubic interpolation, and composed by IDWT.

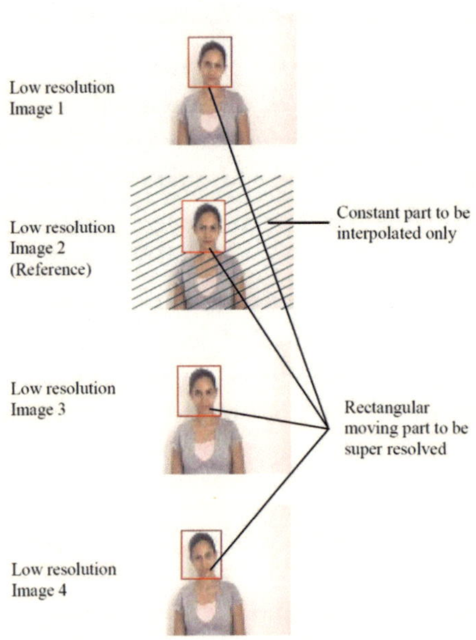


**Figure 2.** First four consecutive frames taken from a video sequence with one moving region. The rectangular moving part for each four frames is changing adaptively.

Fig. 2 shows four consecutive frames taken from a video sequence. The second frame is used as the reference frame. The rectangular part shown in each frame corresponds to the moving part. The rest of the reference frame is the static part. In every four frame the rectangular moving part will change according to the moving part in those frames.

In the sixth, seventh and eighth steps, motion parts will be decomposed into different subbands by DWT, super resolved by using Irani et al. super resolution technique, and all subbands will be composed by IDWT.

In the final step, we combine super resolved motion frames with the interpolated background to achieve the final high resolution video sequence. The algorithm is shown in Fig. 3.

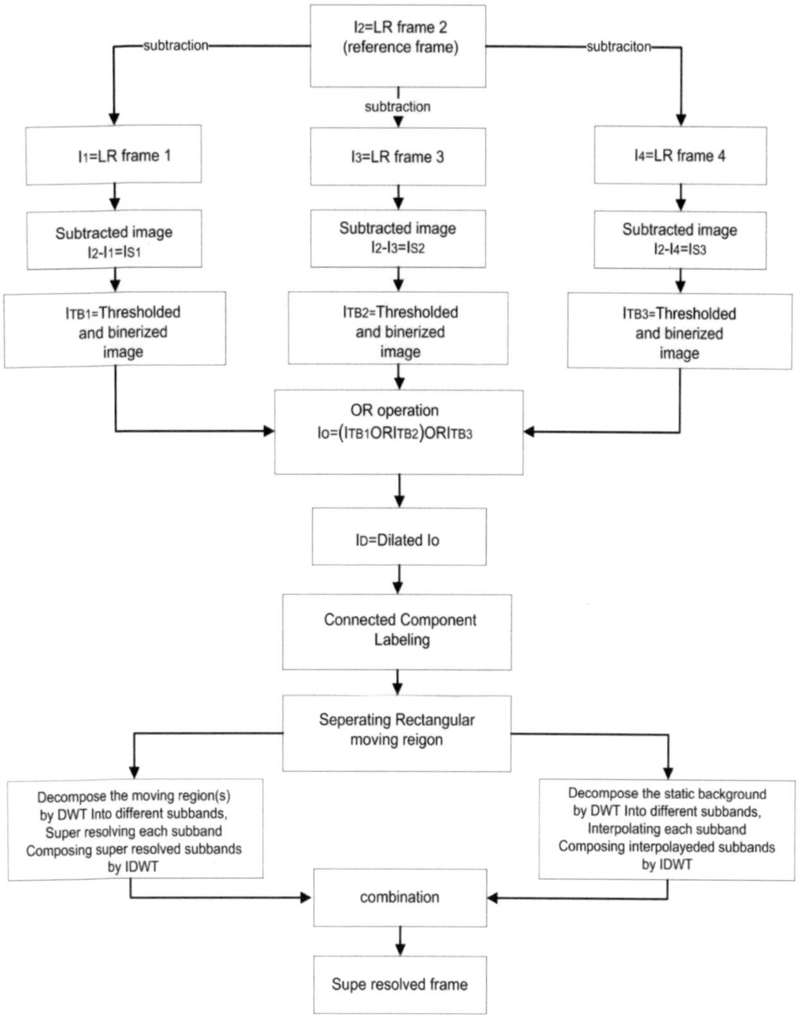


**Figure 3.** The algorithm of the proposed super resolution method for video enhancement.

## 3. Proposed Resolution Enhancement Technique

As mentioned in the introduction, there are many super resolution techniques for enhancing the resolution of the video sequences. The main loss of a video frame after being super resolved is on its high frequency components (i.e. edges), which is due to the smoothing caused within the super resolution processes. Also in many video resolution enhancement techniques due to slight changes in illumination of the successive frames, registration will be done poorly which causes drop in the quality of the super resolved sequence. Therefore, in order to increase the quality of the super resolved video sequence, preserving the edges (high frequencies) of each frame and correcting the slight illumination differences can increase the quality of the super resolved sequence.

In the present work, the Irani and Peleg registration technique is used for registration in which at each stage four successive frames are used. The frames can be named as $f_0$, $f_1$, $f_2$, and $f_3$ in which $f_1$ is the reference frame (subject to resolution enhancement). The illumination compensation is applied in order to reduce the illumination difference between $f_0$, $f_2$, and $f_3$ and $f_1$ for better registration. The illumination compensation is obtained by applying illumination enhancement using singular value decomposition (SVD) (Demirel et al. [ISCIS], 2008) iteratively. The number of iteration depends on the threshold, τ, value which is equalled to the difference between the mean of the reference frame and the mean of the corresponding frame and is chosen according to the application. In this paper, the threshold value has been heuristically chosen to be 0.2. The aim of illumination correction technique is to enhance the illumination of frames $f_0$, $f_2$, and $f_3$ in order to have the same illumination as the reference frame. For this purpose each frame has been decomposed into three matrices by using SVD:

$$f_i = U_i \Sigma_i V_i^T \quad i = 0,1,2,3 \tag{6}$$

in which $U$ and $V$ are two orthogonal square matrices known as hanger and aligner respectively, and Σ is a matrix containing the sorted eigenvalues of $f$ on its main diagonal. As it is reported in (Demirel et al. [IEEE Geoscience and Remote Sensing Letter] 2010, Demirel et al. [ISCIS], 2008), Σ contains the intensity information of the given frame. The first singular value, $\sigma_1$, is usually much bigger than the other singular values. That is why manipulating the $\sigma_1$ will affect the illumination of the image significantly. Hence our aim will be correcting the illumination of the frames in the way that the biggest singular value of the enhanced frame is close enough to the highest singular value of the reference frame. For this purpose a correction coefficient is calculated by using:

$$\xi_{f_j} = \frac{\max(\Sigma_{f_1})}{\max(\Sigma_{f_j})} \quad j = 0,2,3 \tag{7}$$

Then the enhanced frame is constructed by using:

$$f_{\text{enhanced}_j} = U_j(\xi_j \Sigma_j) V_j^T \quad j = 0,2,3 \tag{8}$$

Because after obtaining the enhanced frame, it will be converted into 8-bit representation (quantization will take the place), therefore highest singular value obtained from the repetition of equation (8) will slightly differ from the highest singular value in the right hand side of equation (10). The algorithm of the illumination enhancement technique is shown in Fig. 4.

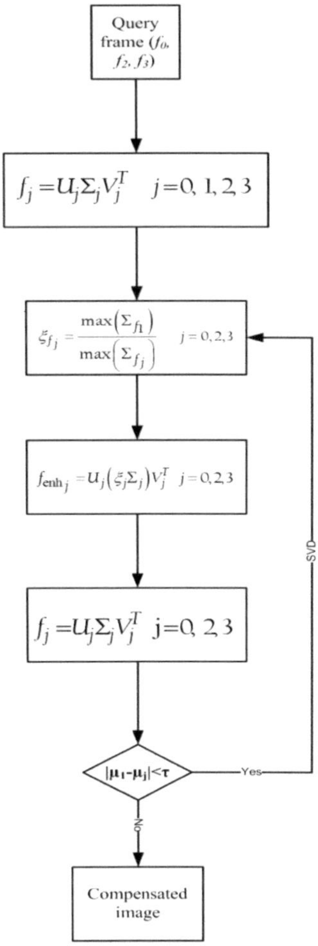


**Figure 4.** The illumination compensation technique used before the registration.

Fig. 5 is showing the convergence of pixel average of two of the frames towards the reference frame for Akiyo video sequence in progressive iterations.

In this work, discrete wavelet transform (DWT) (Mallat, 1999) has been applied in order to preserve the high frequency components of each frame. The one level DWT process for each frame of the input video generates four video sequences (i.e. LL subband sequences and three high frequency subband sequences with 0 , 45 , and +90 orientations known as LH, HL, and HH subbands). In parallel to DWT process, the Irani and Peleg super resolution technique is applied to video sequences in spatial domain. This process results in super resolved frame which can be regarded as a LL subband of a higher (target) resolution frame. The LH, HL, and HH subbands of the higher (target) resolution frames are generated by interpolation of the previously extracted LH, HL, and HH subbands from the input reference frames. Finally, Inverse DWT (IDWT) is used to reconstruct the super resolved subbands to produce the resolution enhanced frame, resulting in a high resolution video sequence.

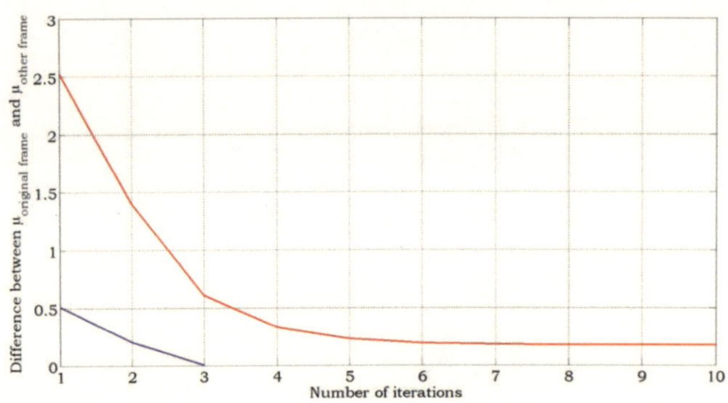


**Figure 5.** The convergence of the mean of the first (blue) and the third (red) frames of the Akiyo sequence to the mean of the second frame (reference).

By super resolving the different subbands of video sequences and then by applying IDWT, the output video sequence contains sharper edges. This is due to the fact that, the proposed super resolution technique isolates high frequency components and preserves more high frequency components after the super resolution of the respective subbands separately than other super resolution technique.

The proposed method can be summarized with the following steps:

10. Acquire frames from a video.

11. Apply the proposed illumination compensation technique before registration.

12. Apply DWT to decompose the low resolution input video sequence into different subband sequences.

13. Super resolve the original corresponding frame by applying Irani and Peleg super resolution technique.

14. Apply bicubic interpolation to the extracted high frequency subbands (LH, HL, and HH).

15. Apply IDWT to the output of step 4 and three outputs of step 5 in order to reconstruct the high resolution super resolved sequence.

In the fourth step, four illumination compensated consecutive frames are used for registration in implementation of Irani and Peleg super resolution technique. Fig. 6 illustrates the block diagram of the proposed video resolution enhancement technique.

A possible application of the proposed resolution enhancement technique is that if someone is holding his/her digital camera while taking a series of four shoots of a scene within a short period of time. The small translation of the person's hands during capturing the snapshots which may cause some illumination changes is sufficient to reconstruct the high resolution image.

In all steps of the proposed technique db.9/7 wavelet function and bicubic interpolation are used. In the next section, the result of comparison between the proposed technique with the conventional and state-of-art techniques mentioned in the introduction is reported. The quantitative results are showing the superiority of the proposed method over the other techniques.

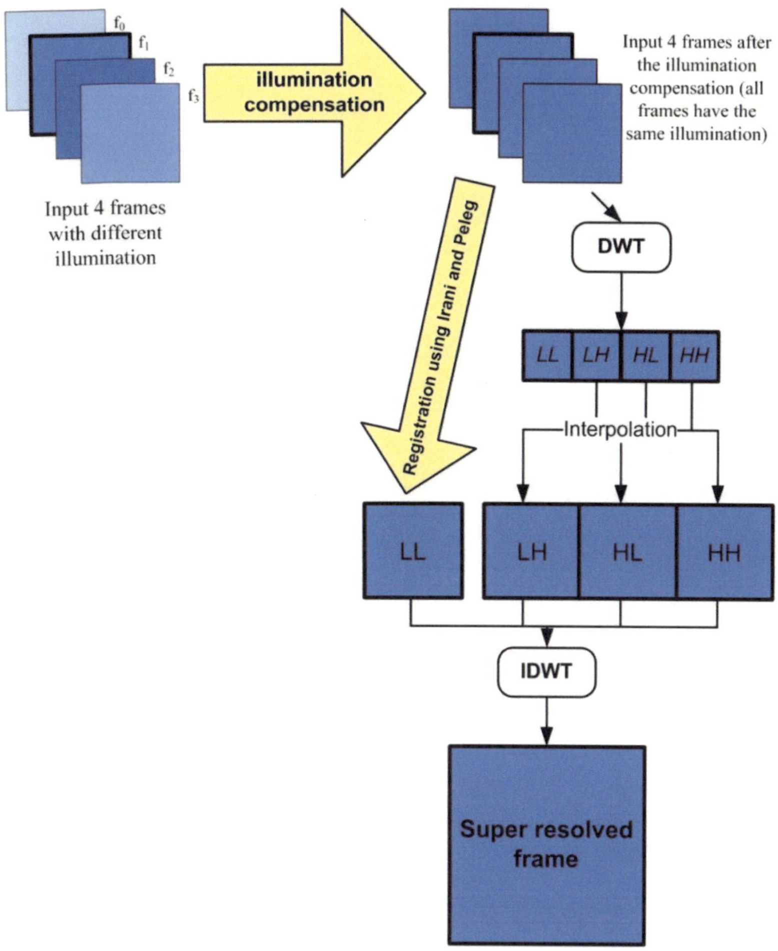


**Figure 6.** The block diagram of the proposed video resolution enhancement technique.

## 4. Results and Discussions

Super resolution method proposed in this paper is compared with the state-of-art super resolution techniques using Vandewalle (2006), Marcel (1997), Lucchese (2000), and Keren (1988) registration followed by interpolation, iterated back projection, robust super resolution, and structure adaptive normalized convolution techniques for reconstruction. The proposed method has been tested on four well known video sequences (Xiph.org Test Media, 2010), namely Mother daughter, Akiyo, Foreman, and Container. Table 1 is showing the PSNR value of the aforementioned super resolution techniques for the above video sequences.

| RESOLUTION ENHANCEMENT TECHNIQUE | | PSNR (dB) VALUE FOR DIFFERENT SEQUENCES | | | |
|---|---|---|---|---|---|
| REGISTRATION | RECONSTRUCTION | MOTHER DAUGHTER | AKIYO | FOREMAN | CONTAINER |
| Vandewalle | Interpolation | 24.29 | 29.45 | 28.01 | 23.6 |
| | Iterated Back Projection | 27.1 | 31.49 | 30.17 | 24.3 |
| | Robust SR | 27.15 | 31.5 | 30.24 | 24.46 |
| | Structure Adaptive Normalized Convolution | 28.95 | 32.98 | 33.46 | 26.38 |
| Marcel | Interpolation | 24.44 | 29.6 | 28.16 | 24.96 |
| | Iterated Back Projection | 27.12 | 31.52 | 29.84 | 25.2 |
| | Robust SR | 27.18 | 31.54 | 30.24 | 25.25 |
| | Structure Adaptive Normalized Convolution | 28.66 | 33.16 | 33.25 | 26.28 |
| Lucchese | Interpolation | 24.1 | 29.62 | 28.19 | 24.53 |
| | Iterated Back Projection | 27.06 | 31.52 | 29.88 | 25.28 |
| | Robust SR | 27.13 | 31.55 | 30.29 | 25.31 |
| | Structure Adaptive Normalized Convolution | 29.01 | 32.8 | 33.3 | 26.36 |
| Keren | Interpolation | 23.16 | 29.6 | 28.17 | 24.78 |
| | Iterated Back Projection | 27.17 | 31.53 | 29.87 | 25.31 |
| | Robust SR | 27.2 | 31.55 | 30.29 | 25.46 |
| | Structure Adaptive Normalized Convolution | 28.63 | 32.97 | 33.25 | 26.15 |
| Proposed resolution enhancement technique without illumination compensation | | 31.53 | 34.07 | 35.87 | 28.94 |
| Proposed resolution enhancement technique with illumination compensation | | 32.17 | 35.24 | 36.52 | 30.07 |

**Table 1.** The average PSNR (dB) values of different resolution enhancement techniques on the test video sequences.

The low resolution video sequences are generated by downsampling and lowpass filtering each frame of the high resolution video sequence (Temizel, 2007). In this way we keep the original high resolution video sequences for comparison purposes as a ground truth. All video sequences have 300 frames and the reported average PSNR values in Table 1 are the average of 300 PSNR values. The low resolution video sequences have the size of 128x128 and the super resolved sequences have the size of 256x256.

Fig. 7 is demonstrating the visual result of the proposed method for proposed method compared with other state-of-art techniques for 'mother-daughter' video sequences. As it is observable from Fig. 4, the proposed method is results in a sharper image compared with the other conventional and state-of-art video super resolution techniques.

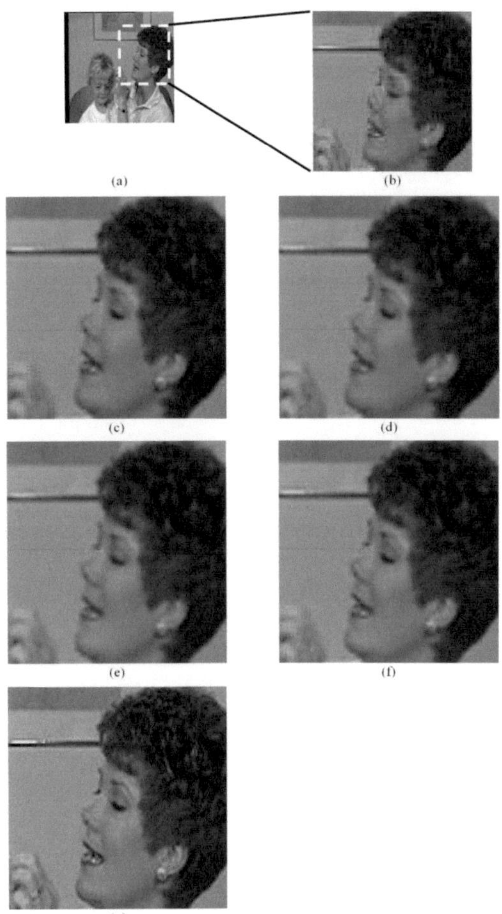


**Figure 7.** The visual representation of a frame of low resolution of 'mother-daughter' video sequence (a) and a zoomed segment of the frame (b), and the super resolved frame by using: Keren (c), Lucchese (d), Marcel (e), Vandewalle (f) registration technique with Structure Adaptive Normalized Convolution reconstruction technique, and the proposed technique (g).

## 5. Conclusion

This paper proposes a new video resolution enhancement technique by applying an illumination compensation technique based on SVD before registration process and using DWT in order to preserve the high frequency components of the frames. The output of the Irani and Peleg technique is used as LL subband in which LH, HL, and HH subbands are obtained by using bicubic interpolation of the former high frequency subbands. Afterwards all these subbands have been combined using IDWT to generate respective super resolved frame. The proposed technique has been tested on various well known video sequences, where the quantitative results show the superiority of proposed technique over the conventional and state-of-art video super resolution techniques.

## Acknowledgements

Authors would like to thank Prof. Dr. Ivan Selesnick from Polytechnic University for providing the DWT codes in MATLAB.

## Author details

Sara Izadpanahi[1], Cagri Ozcinar[2], Gholamreza Anbarjafari[3*] and Hasan Demirel[1]

*Address all correspondence to: sjafari@ciu.edu.tr

1 Department of Electrical and Electronic Engineering, Eastern Mediterranean University, Gazimağusa, via Mersin-10, Turkey

2 Department of Electronics Engineering, University of Surrey, GU2 7XH, Surrey, UK

3 Department of Electrical and Electronic Engineering, Cyprus International University, Lefkoşa, Kuzey Kıbrıs Türk Cumhuriyeti, via Mersin 10, Turkey

## References

[1] Anbarjafari, G., & Demirel, H. (2010). Image Super Resolution Based on Interpolation of Wavelet Domain High Frequency Subbands and the Spatial Domain Input Image. *ETRI Journal*, 32(3), Jun 2010, 390-394.

[2] Cortelazzo, L., & Lucchese, G. M. (2000). A noise-robust frequency domain technique for estimating planar roto translations. *IEEE Transactions on Signal Processing*, 48(6), June 2000, 1769-1786.

[3] Demirel, H., Anbarjafari, G., & Jahromi, M. N. S. (2008). Image Equalization Based on Singular Value Decomposition. *The 23rd International Symposium on Computer and Information Sciences, ISCIS 2008*, Istanbul, Turkey.

[4] Demirel, H., Anbarjafari, G., & Izadpanahi, S. (2009). Improved Motion-Based Localized Super Resolution Technique Using Discrete Wavelet Transform for Low Resolution Video Enhancement. *17th European Signal Processing Conference (EUSIPCO-2009)*, Glasgow, Scotland, Aug. 2009, 1097-1101.

[5] Demirel, H., & Anbarjafari, G. (2010). Satellite Image Super Resolution Using Complex Wavelet Transform. *IEEE Geoscience and Remote Sensing Letter*, 7(1), Jan 2010, 123-126.

[6] Demirel, H., & Izadpanahi, S. (2008). Motion-Based Localized Super Resolution Technique for Low Resolution Video Enhancement. *16th European Signal Processing Conference (EUSIPCO-2008)*, Lausanne, Switzerland, Aug. 2008.

[7] Demirel, H., Ozcinar, C., & Anbarjafari, G. (2010). Satellite Image Contrast Enhancement Using Discrete Wavelet Transform and Singular Value Decomposition. *IEEE Geoscience and Remote Sensing Letter*, 7(2), April 2010, 334-338.

[8] Elad, M., & Feuer, A. (1999). Super-resolution reconstruction of image sequences. *IEEE Trans. On Pattern Analysis and Machine Intelligence (PAMI)*, 21(9), September 1999, 817-834.

[9] Irani, M., & Peleg, S. (1991). Improving resolution by image registration. *CVGIP: Graphical Models and Image Processing*, 53(3), May 1991, 231-239.

[10] Keren, D., Peleg, S., & Brada, R. (1988). Image sequence enhancement using subpixel displacements. *IEEE Computer Society Conference on Computer Vision and Pattern Recognition*, June 1988, 742-746.

[11] Mallat, S. (1999). A wavelet tour of signal processing. Published by Academic Press, 1999, 2nd edition ISBN 012466606X, 9780124666061.

[12] Marcel, B., Briot, M., & Murrieta, R. (1997). Calcul de Translation et Rotation par la Transformation de Fourier. *Traitement du Signal*, 14(2), 135-149.

[13] Nguyen, N., & Milanfar, P. (2000). A wavelet-based interpolation-restoration method for superresolution (wavelet superresolution). *Circuits Systems, Signal Process*, 19(4), 321-338.

[14] Pham, T. Q., van Vliet, L. J., & Schutte, K. (2006). Robust Fusion of Irregularly Sampled Data Using Adaptive Normalized Convolution. *EURASIP Journal on Applied Signal Processing*, 2006, Article ID 83268.

[15] Piao, Y., Shin, L., & Park, H. W. (2007). Image Resolution Enhancement using Inter-Subband Correlation in Wavelet Domain. *International Conference on Image Processing (ICIP 2007)*, 1, I-445-448.

[16] Reddy, B. S., & Chatterji, B. N. (1996). An fft-based technique for translation, rotation and scale-invariant image registration. *IEEE Transactions on Image Processing*, 5(8), August 1996, 1266-1271.

[17] Robinson, M. D., Toth, C. A., Lo, J. Y., & Farsiu, S. (2010). Efficient Fourier-wavelet Super-resolution. *IEEE Transactions on Image Processing*, 19(10), 2669-2681.

[18] Temizel, A. (2007). Image resolution enhancement using wavelet domain hidden Markov tree and coefficient sign estimation. *International Conference on Image Processing (ICIP2007)*, 5, V-381-384.

[19] Temizel, A., & Vlachos, T. (2005). Wavelet domain image resolution enhancement using cycle-spinning. *Electronics Letters*, 41(3), Feb. 2005, 119-121.

[20] Tsai, R. Y., & Huang, T. S. (1984). Multiframe image restoration and registration. *Advances in Computer Vision and Image Processing*, T. S. Huang, Ed. JAI Press, 1, 317-339.

[21] Vandewalle, P., Süsstrunk, S., & Vetterli, M. (2006). A Frequency Domain Approach to Registration of Aliased Images with Application to Super-Resolution. *EURASIP Journal on Applied Signal Processing*, (special issue on Super-resolution), 2006, Article ID 71459.

[22] Xiph.org Test Media, Retrieved on October 2010, from the World Wide Web on http://media.xiph.org/video/derf/.

[23] Zomet, A., Rav-Acha, A., & Peleg, S. (2001). Robust super-resolution. *Proceedings on international conference on computer vision and pattern recognition (CVPR)*, I-645-I-650.

Section 2

# Recent Applications of DWT

Chapter 4

# An Adaptive Resolution Method Using Discrete Wavelet Transform for Humanoid Robot Vision System

Chih-Hsien Hsia, Wei-Hsuan Chang and
Jen-Shiun Chiang

Additional information is available at the end of the chapter

http://dx.doi.org/10.5772/55114

## 1. Introduction

The RoboCup (Kitano et al., 1995) is an international joint project to stimulate research efforts in the field of artificial intelligence, robotics, and related fields. According to the rules for the 2009 RoboCup, in the league for kid-sized robots (Avalable, 2009), the competitions were to take place on a rectangular field with an area of 600 × 400 $cm^2$ containing two goals and two landmark poles, as shown in Fig. 1. A goal was placed in the middle of each goal line, with one of the goals colored yellow and the other colored blue. As shown in Fig. 2, each goal for the kid-sized robot field had a crossbar height of 90 cm, a goal wall height of 40 cm, a goal wall width of 150 cm, and a 50 cm depth for the goal wall. The two landmark poles were placed on each side of the two intersection points between the touch line and the middle field line. The landmark pole was a cylinder with a diameter of 20 cm. It consisted of three segments, each 20 cm in height, stacked on top of each other. The lowest and the highest segments have the same color as the goal on its left side, as shown in Fig. 3. The ball is the standard size orange tennis ball. All of the above objects are the most critical characteristics in the field, and they are also the key features which we have to pay attention to.

The functions of humanoid robot vision system include image capturing, image analyses, and digital image processing by using visual sensors. For digital image processing, it is to transform the image into the analyzable digital pattern by digital signal processing. We can further use image analysis techniques to describe and recognize the image content for the robot vision. The robot vision system can use the environment information captured in front of the robot to recognize the image by means of the technique of human vision system. An object recognition algorithm is thus proposed to the humanoid robot soccer competition.

Generally speaking, object recognition uses object features to extract the object out of the picture frame, and thus shape (Chaumette, 1994) and (Jean & Wu, 2004), contour (Sun et al, 2003), (Kass et al., 1988), and (Canny, 1986), color (Herodotou et al., 1998) and (Ikeda, 2003), texture, and sizes of object features are commonly used. It is important to extract the information in real-time because the moving ball is one of the most critical object in the contest field. The complex feature such as contour is not suited to recognize in our application. The objects don't have the obvious texture which is not suited to use in the contest field. However the object color is distinctive in the contest field, we mainly choose the color information to determine the critical objects.

Although this approach is simple, the real-time efficiency is still low. Because there is a lot of information to be processed in every frame for real-time consideration, Sugandi et al. (Sugandi et al, 2009) proposed a low resolution method to reduce the information. It can speed up the processing time, but the low resolution results in a shorter recognizable distance and it may increase the false recognition rate. In order to improve the mentioned drawbacks, we propose a new approach, adaptive resolution method (ARM), to reduce the computation complexity and increase the accuracy rate.

The rest of this study is organized as follows. Section 2 presents the related background such as the general color based object recognition method, low resolution method, and encountered problems. Section 3 describes the proposed approach, ARM. The experimental results are shown in Section 4. Finally, the conclusions are outlined in Section 5.

**Figure 1.** The field for the competitions.

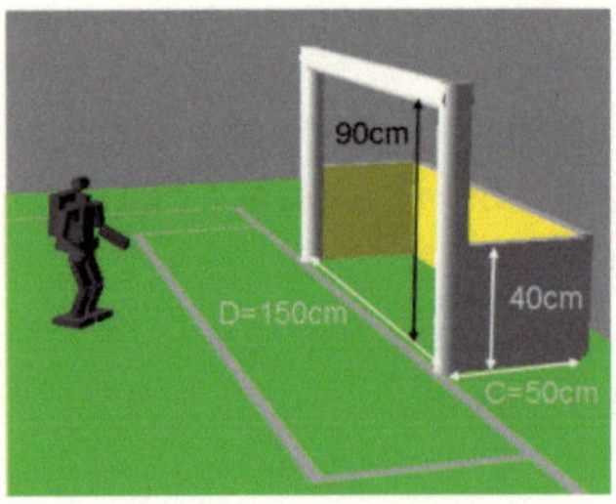


**Figure 2.** The goal information.

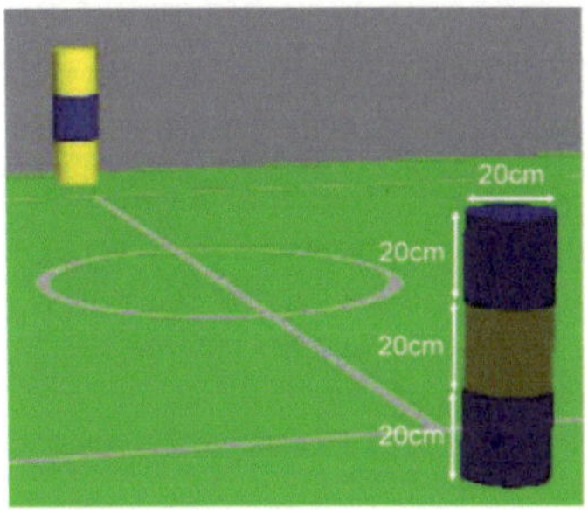


**Figure 3.** The landmark information.

## 2. Background

### 2.1. Color based object recognition method

An efficient vision system plays an important role for the humanoid robot soccer players. Many robot vision modules have provided some basic color information, and it can extract the object by selecting the color threshold. The flow chart of a traditional color recognition method is shown in Fig. 4. The RGB color model comes from the three additive primary colors, red, green, and blue. The main purpose of the RGB color model (Gonzalez & Woods, 2001) is for the sensing, representation, and display of images in electronic systems, such as televisions and computers, and it is the basic image information format. The X, Y, and Z axes represent the red, green, and blue color components respectively, and it can describe all colors by different proportion combinations. Because the RGB color model is not explicit, it can be easily influenced by the light illumination and make people select error threshold values.

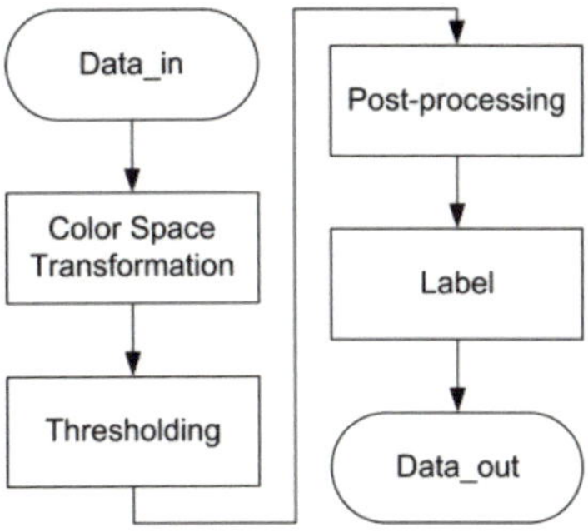


**Figure 4.** The flow chart of the traditional color recognition method.

An HSV (HSV stands for hue, saturation, and value) color model relates the representations of pixels in the RGB color space, which attempts to describe perceptual color relationships more accurately than RGB. Because the HSV color model describes the color and brightness component respectively, the HSV color model is not easily influenced by the light illumination. The HSV color model is therefore extensively used in the fields of color recognition. The HSV transform function is shown in eqs. (1)-(3) as follows:

$$H = \begin{cases} \left(6 + \dfrac{G-B}{\max - \min}\right) \times 60°, \ if\ R = \max \\ \left(2 + \dfrac{B-R}{\max - \min}\right) \times 60°, \ if\ G = \max \\ \left(4 + \dfrac{R-G}{\max - \min}\right) \times 60°, \ if\ B = \max \end{cases} \tag{1}$$

$$S = \begin{cases} 0 & , \ if\ \max = 0 \\ \dfrac{\max - \min}{\max} & , \ otherwise \end{cases} \tag{2}$$

$$V = max \tag{3}$$

In (1), (2), and (3), the range of $H$, hue, is 0°~360°; the range of $S$, is 0~1, and the range of $V$, value, is 0~255. The RGB values are confined by (4):

$$\begin{aligned} \max &= MAX(R,G,B) \\ \min &= MIN(R,G,B) \end{aligned} \tag{4}$$

where "max" indicates the maximum value in the RGB color components and "min" indicates the minimum value in the RGB color components. Hence, we can directly make use of $H$ and $S$ to describe a color range of high environmental tolerance. It can help us to obtain the foreground objects mask, $M$(x,y), by the threshold value selection as shown in (5).

$$M(x,y) = \begin{cases} 1, \ if\ T_{H1} < H(x,y) < T_{H2} \cap S(x,y) > T_s \\ 0, \ otherwise \end{cases} \tag{5}$$

where $T_{H1}$, $T_{H2}$, and $T_S$ are the thresholds of hue and threshold of saturation by manual setting. The foreground object mask usually accompanies with the noise, and we can remove the noise by the simple morphological methods, such as dilation, erosion, opening, and closing. It needs to separate the objects by labeling when many objects with the same colors are existed in the frame. The following procedure is the flow for labeling (Gonzalez & Woods, 2001):

Step 1: Scan the threshold image $M$(x,y); Step 2: Give the value $Label_{color}^{i}$ to the connected component $Q$\{n\} of pixel(x,y); Step 3: Give the same value to the connected component of $Q$\{n\};

Step 4: Until no connected component can be found; Step 5: Update, $i = i+1$. Then go to Step 1 and repeat Steps 2~4; Step 6: Completely scan the image.

By using the above-mentioned procedure, the objects can be extracted. Although this method is simple, it is only suitable for low frame rate sequences. For a high resolution or noisy sequence, this approach may need very high computation complexity.

### 2.2. Low resolution method

To overcome the above-mentioned problems, several approaches of low resolution method were proposed (Sugandi et al., 2009), (Cheng & Chen et al., 2006). The flow chart of a general low resolution method is shown in Fig. 5. Several low resolution methods, such as the approach of applying 2-D discrete wavelet transform (DWT) and the using of 2×2 average filter (AF), were discussed. (Cheng & Chen, 2006) applied the 2-D DWT for detecting and tracking moving objects and only the $LL_3$-band image is used for detecting motion of the moving object (It is suggested that the $LL_3$-band is a good candidate for noise elimination (the user can choose a suited decomposition level according to the requirement, and actually there is no need to do the reconstruction for these applications). Because noises are preserved in high-frequency, it can reduce computing cost for post-processing by using the $LL_3$-band image. This method can be used for coping with noise or fake motion effectively, however the conventional DWT scheme has the disadvantages of complicated calculation when an original image is decomposed into the LL-band image. Moreover if it uses an $LL_3$-band image to deal with the fake motion, it may cause incomplete moving object detecting regions. In (Sugandi et al., 2009) proposed a simple method by using the low resolution concept to deal with the fake motion such as moving leaves of trees. The low resolution image is generated by replacing each pixel value of an original image with the average value of its four neighbor pixels and itself as shown in Fig. 6. It also provides a flexible multi-resolution image like the DWT. Nevertheless, the low resolution images generated by using the 2×2 AF method are more blurred than that by using the DWT method. It may reduce the preciseness of post-processing (such as object detection, tracking, and object identification), because the post-processing depends on the correct location of the moving object detecting and accuracy moving object.

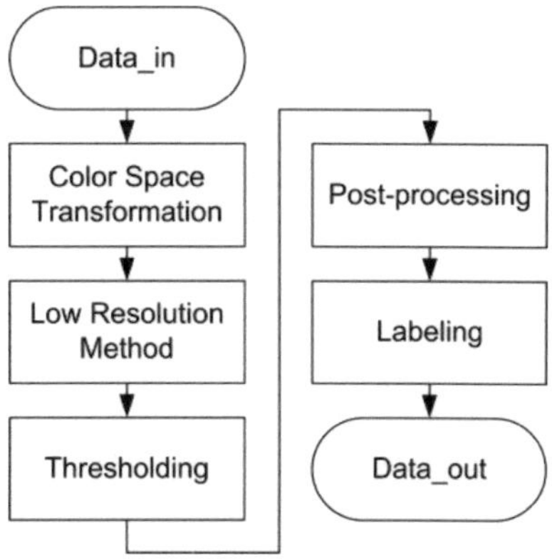


**Figure 5.** The flow chart of a general low resolution method.

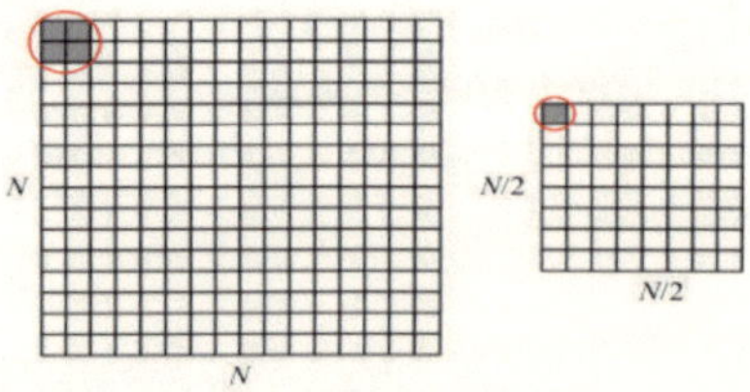


**Figure 6.** Diagram of the 2×2 AF method

In order to detect and track the moving object more accurately, we propose a new approach, adaptive resolution method (ARM), which is based on the 2-D integer symmetric mask-based discrete wavelet transform (SMDWT) (Hsia et al, 2009). It does not only retain the features of the flexibilities for multi-resolution, but also does not cause high computing cost when using it for finding different subband images. In addition, it preserves more image quality of the low resolution image than that of the average filter approach (Sugandi et al., 2009).

### *2.2.1. Symmetric Mask-Based Discrete Wavelet Transform (SMDWT)*

In 2-D DWT, the computation needs large transpose memory and has a long critical path. On the other hand SMDWT has many advanced features such as short critical path, high speed operation, regular signal coding, and independent subband processing (Hsia et al, 2009). The derivation coefficient of the 2-D SMDWT is based on the 2-D 5/3 integer lifting-based DWT. For computation speed and simplicity considerations, four-masks, 3×3, 5×3, 3×5, and 5×5, are used to perform spatial filtering tasks. Moreover, the four-subband processing can be further optimized to speed up and reduce the temporal memory of the DWT coefficients. The four-matrix processors consist of four-mask filters, and each filter is derived from one 2-D DWT of 5/3 integer lifting-based coefficients.

In the ARM approach, we can select only the LL-band mask of SMDWT (The moving object is low-frequency energy). Unlike the conventional DWT method to process row and column dimensions respectively by low-pass filter and down-sampling, the LL-mask band of SMDWT can be used to directly calculate the LL-band image. The matrix function of the LL-mask is shown in (6) and the coefficients of the LL-mask are shown in Fig. 7 (Hsia et al, 2009). SMDWT (using the LL-band mask only) can reduce the image transfer computing cost and remove the noise. Besides, this approach can have accurate object tracking for various types of occlusions.

$$\begin{aligned}
LL(i,j) &= (9/16)x(2i,2j) + (1/64)\Sigma^1_{u=0}\Sigma^1_{v=0}x(2i-2+4u,2j-2+4v) + \\
&+ (1/16)\Sigma^1_{u=0}\Sigma^1_{v=0}x(2i-1+2u,2j-1+2v) + (-1/32)\Sigma^1_{u=0}\Sigma^1_{v=0}x(2i-1+2u,2j-2+4v) + \\
&+ (-1/32)\Sigma^1_{u=0}\Sigma^1_{v=0}x(2i-2+4u,2j-1+2v) + (3/16)\Sigma^1_{u=0}\left[x(2i-1+2u,2j) + x(2i,2j-1+2u)\right] + \\
&+ (-3/32)\Sigma^1_{u=0}\left[x(2i-2+4u,2j) + x(2i,2j-2+4u)\right].
\end{aligned} \tag{6}$$

| | | | | |
|---|---|---|---|---|
| 1/64 | -1/32 | -3/32 | -1/32 | 1/64 |
| -1/32 | 1/16 | 3/16 | 1/16 | -1/32 |
| -3/32 | 3/16 | 9/16 | 3/16 | -3/32 |
| -1/32 | 1/16 | 3/16 | 1/16 | -1/32 |
| 1/64 | -1/32 | -3/32 | -1/32 | 1/64 |

**Figure 7.** The subband masks coefficients of the LL-mask.

# 3. The proposed method

## 3.1. Adaptive Resolution Methos (ARM)

ARM takes advantage of the information obtained from the image to know the area of the ball and chooses the most suitable resolution. The operation flow chart is shown in Fig. 8. After HSV color transformation, ARM chooses the most proper resolution by the situation at this moment in time. The high resolution approach brings a longer recognizable distance but with a slower running speed. On the other hand, the low resolution approach brings a lower recognizable distance but with a faster running speed. When we got the area information of the ball from the image last time, we could convert it as the "sel" signal through the adaptive selector to choose the appropriate resolution. The "sel" condition is shown in (7):

$$\text{sel} = \begin{cases} 0(\text{original size}),\ if\ 0 \le A_{ball} < A_{thd1} \\ 1(\text{1-level SMDWT}),\ if\ A_{thd1} \le A_{ball} < A_{thd2} \\ 2(\text{2-level SMDWT}),\ if\ A_{ball} \ge A_{thd2} \end{cases} \tag{7}$$

In (7), $A_{thd1}$ and $A_{thd2}$ are the threshold values for the area of ball. The relationship between the resolution and the distance of the ball is described in Table 1. According to Table 1, we can conclude that $A_{thd1}$ and $A_{thd2}$ are set to 54 and 413, respectively. The threshold selection is performed for each different resolution of working environment. The threshold value is used to produce the recognizable distance. If the ball disappears in the frame, the frame will change into the original size to have a higher probability to find out the ball. Since the sizes of other critical objects (such as goal and landmark) in the field are larger than the ball, they can be recognized easily. Fig. 9 shows the results of different resolutions after the HSV transformation.

## 3.2. Sample object recognition method

According to the above-mentioned color segmentation method, it can fast and easily extract the orange ball in the field, but it is not enough to recognize the goals and landmarks. The colors of the goals and landmarks are yellow and blue, and by color segmentation the extraction of goals and landmarks may not be correct as shown in Fig. 10. Therefore we have to use

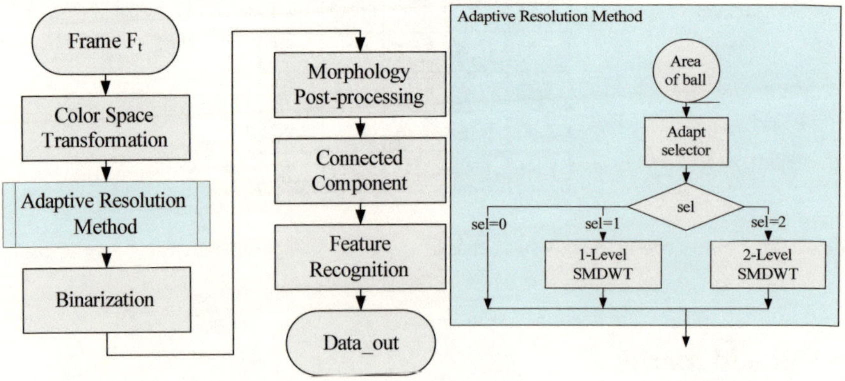


**Figure 8.** The flow chart of ARM.

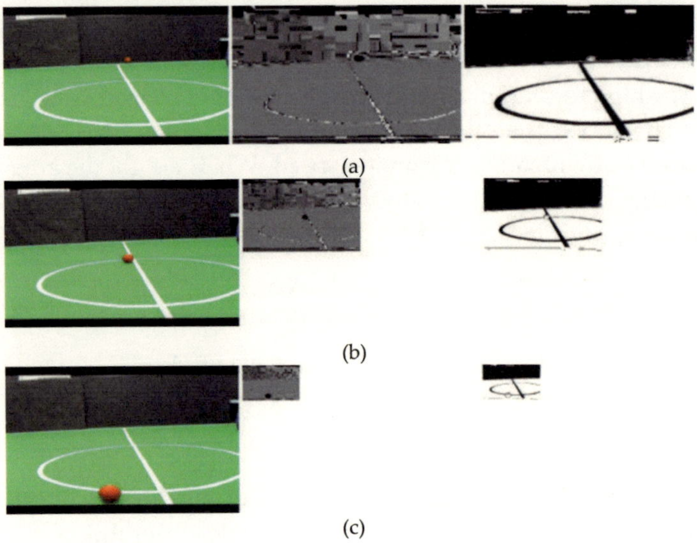


**Figure 9.** The results after the HSV transformation under the resolutions of video. (a) Recognizable max distance of ball in 320×240; (b) Recognizable max distance of ball in 160×120; (c) Recognizable max distance of ball in 80×60

more features and information to extract them. Since the contest field is not complicated, a simple recognition method can be used to reduce the computation complexity. The landmark is a cylinder with three colors. Let us look at one of the landmark with the upper and bottom layers in yellow, and the center layer in blue; this one is defined as the YBY-landmark. The diagram is shown in Fig. 11. The color combinations of the other one are in contrast of the previous one, and the landmark is defined as the BYB-landmark. The labels of the YBY-landmark can be calculated by (8). The BYB landmark is in the same manner as the YBY-landmark.

| Resolution | Level of DWT | Recognizable max distance of ball | *Area of ball |
|---|---|---|---|
| 320×240 | 0(original) | 404.6 cm | 18 pixels |
| 160×120 | 1 | 322.8 cm | 54 pixels |
| 80×60 | 2 | 121.3 cm | 413 pixels |

*The area means the pixel number in the original resolution.

**Table 1.** The relationship between the resolution and the distance of the ball.

$$\begin{aligned} &P_{YBY}(x,y) = L_Y^i(x,y) \cup L_Y^j(x,y) \cup L_B^k(x,y) \\ &\text{if } \left\{ \left| L_Y^i(x_c) - L_Y^j(x_c) \right| < \beta_Y \right\} \cap \left\{ L_Y^i(y_{\max}) < L_B^k(y_c) < L_Y^j(y_{\min}) \right\} \end{aligned} \tag{8}$$

**Figure 10.** False segmentation of the landmark

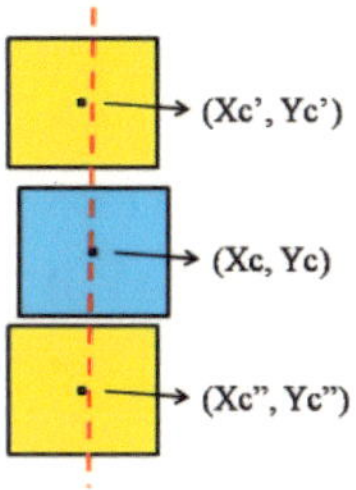


**Figure 11.** The diagram of the landmark.

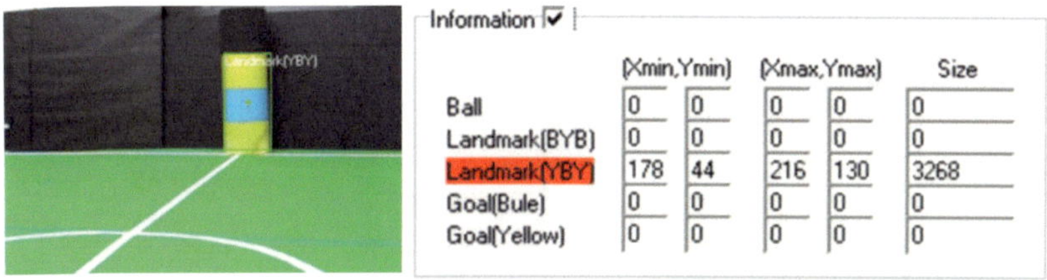


**Figure 12.** The result of landmark recognition.

According to the above-mentioned labeling procedure, we labeled all of the yellow and blue components in the frame and assigned the numbers to those components. Where $L_Y^i$ is defined the pixels of the *i*-th yellow component (Y), $y_{min}$ and $y_{max}$ the minimum value and the maximum value for the object *i* at *y* direction respectively, $x_c$ and $y_c$ the center point of the object at the horizontal and vertical direction respectively. The vertical bias value $\beta_Y$ is set as 15. The landmark is composed of two same color objects in the vertical line, and the center is in different color. If it can find an object with this feature, the system can treat this object as the landmark and outputs the frame coordinate data.

The result of landmark recognition is shown in Fig.12. Eq. (9) is used to define the label of the ball:

$$B(x,y) = L_O^s(x,y),\ if\ \alpha_1 \le \frac{L_O^s(x_{max}) - L_O^s(x_{min})}{L_O^s(y_{max}) - L_O^s(y_{min})} \le \alpha_2 \cap A_s \text{ is the maxaimum} \tag{9}$$

where is the pixel of the *s*-th orange component in a frame. Since the ball is very small in the picture frame, in order to avoid noise, the ball is treated as the maximum orange object and with a shape ratio of height to width approximately equal to 1. Here $\alpha_1$ and $\alpha_2$ are set to 0.8 and 1.2, respectively. The result of ball recognition is shown in Fig. 13. The goal recognition is defined in (10).

$$\begin{aligned} &G_B(x,y) = L_B^m(x,y), \\ &if\ L_B^m(x,y) \notin P_{BYB}(x,y) \cap L_B^m(x,y) \notin P_{YBY}(x,y) \cap A_B^m > \gamma_B \end{aligned} \tag{10}$$

where is the pixel of the *m*-th blue component in a picture frame. Since the blue goal is composed of the blue object, it is not a part of the YBY-landmark and BYB-landmark. The size of the goal in the field is the largest object, and therefore we set the parameter $\gamma$ as 50. The result of goal recognition is shown in Fig. 14. The yellow goal is in the same manner as the blue goal.

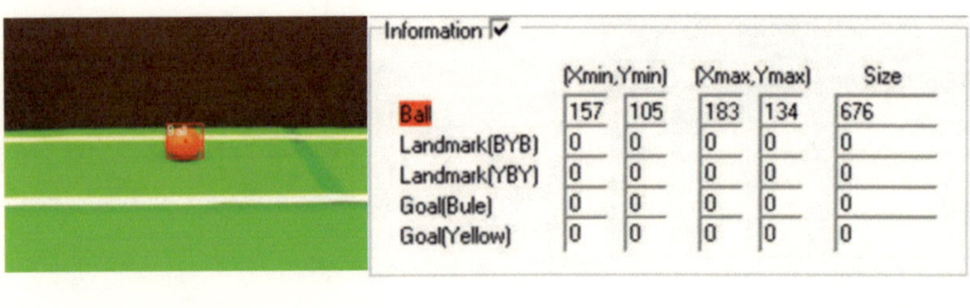


**Figure 13.** The result of ball recognition.

http://dx.doi.org/10.5772/55114

**Figure 14.** The result of goal recognition.

### 3.3. Coordinate transformation

Because our proposed approach, ARM is using the different resolutions in the object recognition, we transform the coordinate into the original resolution by level-based of DWT when the object information is outputted. The transform equation is defined in (11).

$$O(x,y) = LL_n\left(x \times 2^n, y \times 2^n\right) \tag{11}$$

where $O$ is the original image, $LL_n$ is the LL-band iamge after transformation, and n is the transformation level.

## 4. Experimental results

In this work, the environment information is extracted by the Logitech QuickCam Ultra Vision (Using the monocular vision technique). The image resolution is 320×240, and the frame rate is 30 FPS (frame per second). For the simulation computer, the CPU is Intel Core 2 Duo CPU 2.1GHz, and the development tool is Borland C++ Builder 6.0. The graphical interface is shown in Fig. 15.

This work is dedicated to the RoboCup soccer humanoid league rules of the 2009 competition. In order to prove the robustness of the proposed approach, many scenes of various situations are simulated to verify the high recognition accuracy rate and fast processing time. For the analyses of recognition accuracy rate, it is classified as a correct recognition if the critical object is labeled completely and named correctly such as the objects of Goal[B] and Ball shown in Fig. 16(a). On the other hand there are two categories for false recognition, "false positive" and "false negative". "False positive" means that the system recognizes the irrelevant object as the critical object, such as the Goal[Y] shown in Fig. 16(b). "False negative" means the system cannot label or name the critical object, such as those balls shown in Figs. 16(c) and 16(d).

### 4.1. Low resolution analysis

Several low resolution methods, such as down-sampling (DS), AF, and SMDWT, were implemented and simulated in this experiment and the noise removing capabilities with these

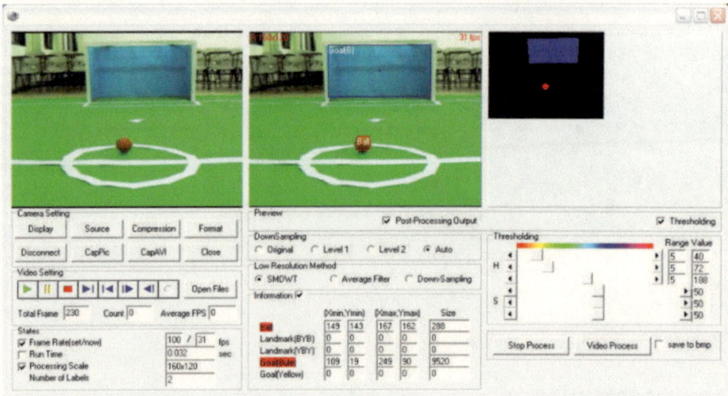

**Figure 15.** The graph interface for simulation.

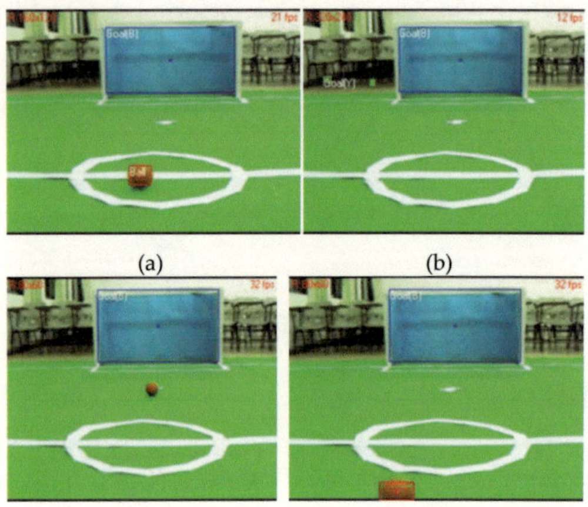

(a) (b) (c) (d)

**Figure 16.** The determination of recognition accuracy. (a) correct recognition. (b) false positive. (c) false negative. (d) false negative.

methods were analyzed. The flow chart of noise removing for the low resolution approaches is shown in Fig. 17. The input frame resolution is 320×240, and the resolution turns to be 160×120 after the low resolution processing. The noise numbers under different low resolution methods were counted. The contents of the simulated scene are obtained by turning the camera to left to see the YBY-landmark and keeping turning until the YBY-landmark disappeared from the camera scope. In this situation the background of the scene produces noise very easily. The hue threshold values of the orange, yellow, and blue colors are set as 35~45, 70~80, and 183~193, respectively, and the saturation threshold of the orange, yellow, and blue colors values are all set as 70. The experimental results under different low resolution methods, DS, AF, and SMDWT, are shown in Figs. 18-20, respectively.

The experiment data are listed in Table 2. According to Table 2, the DS approach has the worst noise removing capability; the 2×2 AF approach also has a bad noise removing capability for big noise block even though this method can make the image smoother. On the other hand, the SMDWT approach (using LL-mask only) has a better noise removing capability than the other methods, and it can retain the information of low-frequency component and remove the noise of high-frequency component in the image.

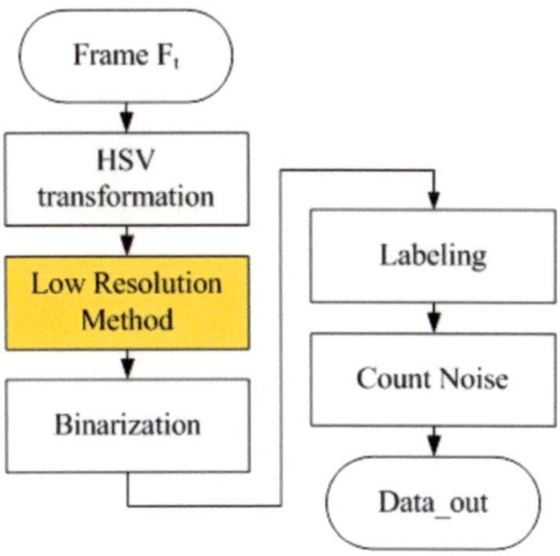


**Figure 17.** The flow chart of noise removing capability.

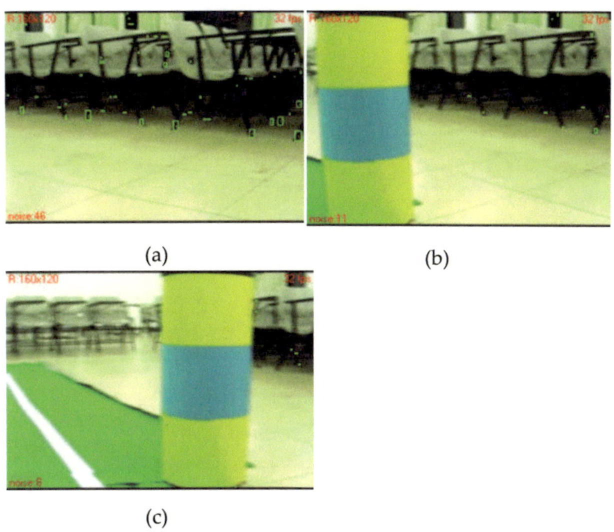

**Figure 18.** Fig. 18. The noise removing capability by using DS. (a) frame 37. (b) frame 67. (c) frame 97.

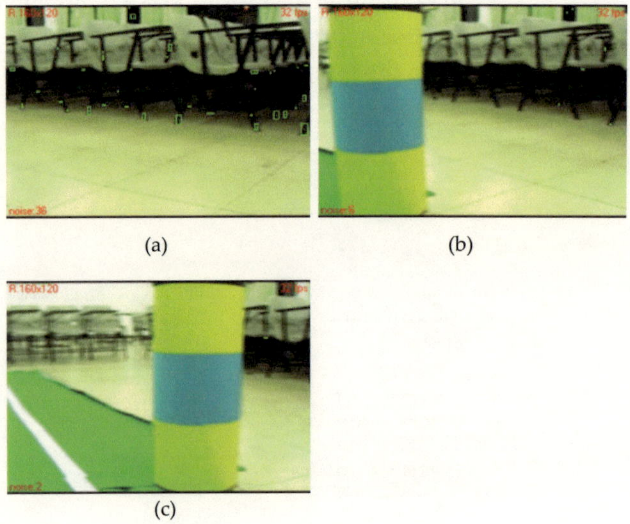


**Figure 19.** The noise removing capability by using 2×2 AF method. (a) frame 37. (b) frame 67. (c) frame 97.

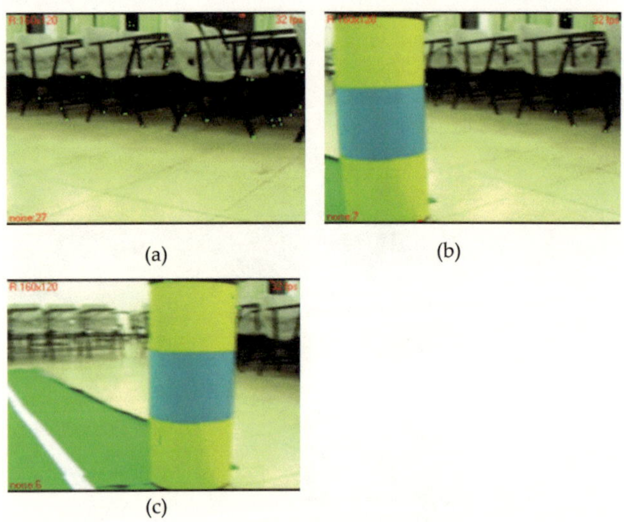


**Figure 20.** The Gaussian noise removing capability by using SMDWT. (a) frame 37. (b) frame 67. (c) frame 97.

In order to improve the noise removing capability of the whole system, we added the opening operator (OP) of mathematical morphology after labeling in the flow chart of Fig. 17. The results after adding the opening operator are shown in Figs. 21-23.

http://dx.doi.org/10.5772/55114

| Method | Total frame | Total noise number | *Average noise number | Average frame rate |
|---|---|---|---|---|
| DS | 153 | 4,133 | 27.01 | 42.24 FPS |
| AF | | 3,191 | 20.86 | 41.03 FPS |
| SMDWT | | 2,670 | 17.45 | 38.13 FPS |

*Average noise number = (Total noise number) / (Total frame)

**Table 2.** The noise counts under different low resolution methods.

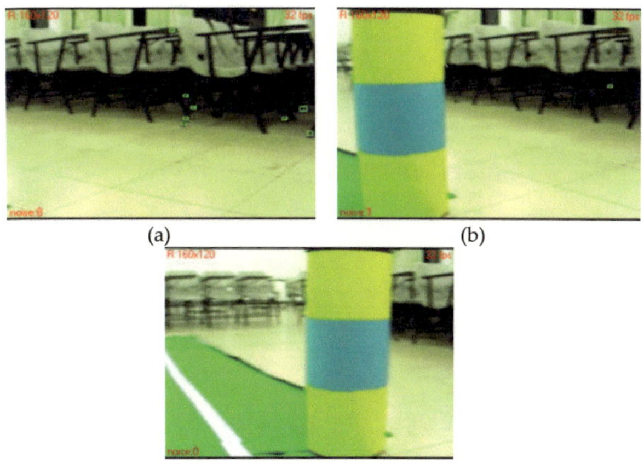

(a) (b) (c)

**Figure 21.** The noise removing capability by using DS and opening operator. (a) frame 37. (b) frame 67. (c) frame 97.

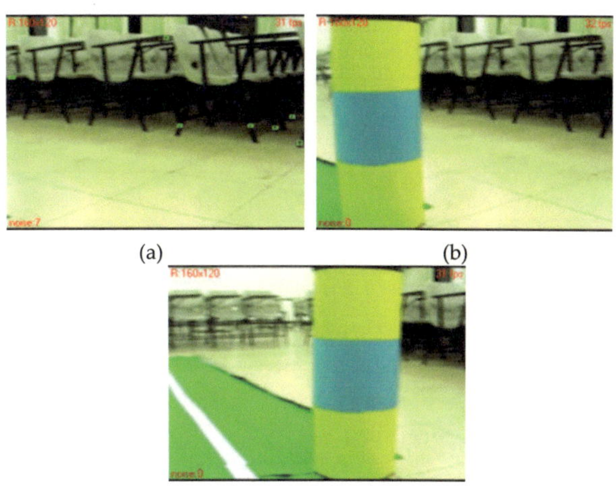

(a) (b) (c)

**Figure 22.** The noise removing capability by using 2×2 AF method and opening operator. (a) frame 37. (b) frame 67. (c) frame 97.

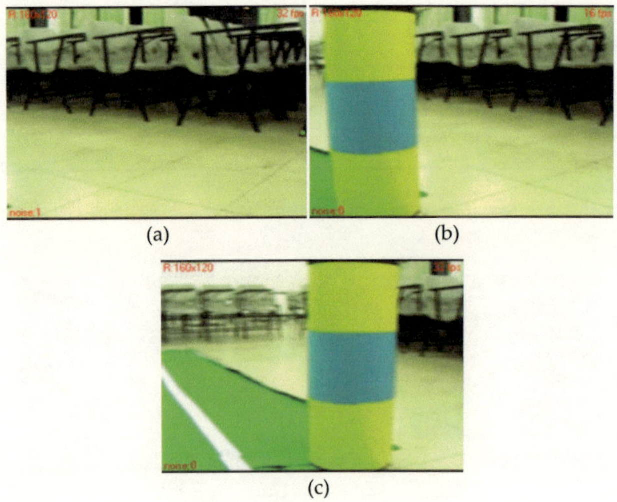

**Figure 23.** The noise removing capability by using SMDWT and opening operator. (a) frame 37. (b) frame 67. (c) frame 97

The experiment data after adding the opening operator are shown in Table 3. Compared with the results of Table 2, the noise numbers are reduced significantly after adding the opening operator, and it can reduce the unnecessary computation. The SMDWT approach has the best performance and the frame rate can be as high as 30 FPS. Therefore this work adopts the SMDWT approach as the low resolution method.

| Method | Total frame | Total noise number | Average noise number | Average frame rate |
|---|---|---|---|---|
| DS + OP | 153 | 408 | 2.67 | 38.01 FPS |
| AF + OP | | 334 | 2.18 | 37.73 FPS |
| SMDWT + OP | | 60 | 0.39 | 30.95 FPS |

**Table 3.** The noise counts under different low resolution methods with opening operator

## 4.2. Adaptive Resolution Method (ARM) analyses

In this experiment, we try to verify that ARM does not only retain high recognition accuracy rate, but also can raise the system processing efficiency. The hue threshold values of the orange, yellow, and blue colors are set as 35~45, 70~80, and 183~193, respectively. The saturation threshold values of the orange, yellow, and blue colors are all set as 70. To verify the ARM approach, the camera is set in the center of the contest field. The scene tries to simulate that the robot kicks ball into the goal and the vision system will track the ball. The results under resolutions of 320×240, 160×120, 80×60, and ARM are shown in Figs. 24-27, respectively.

http://dx.doi.org/10.5772/55114

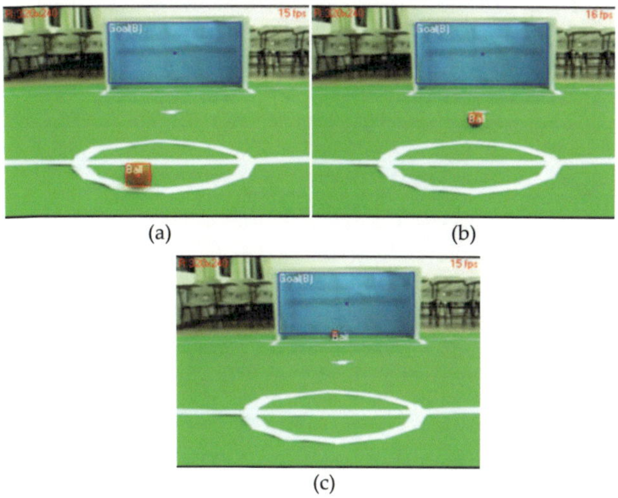


**Figure 24.** The result of object recognition under resolution 320×240. (a) frame 20. (b) frame 35. (c) frame 110.

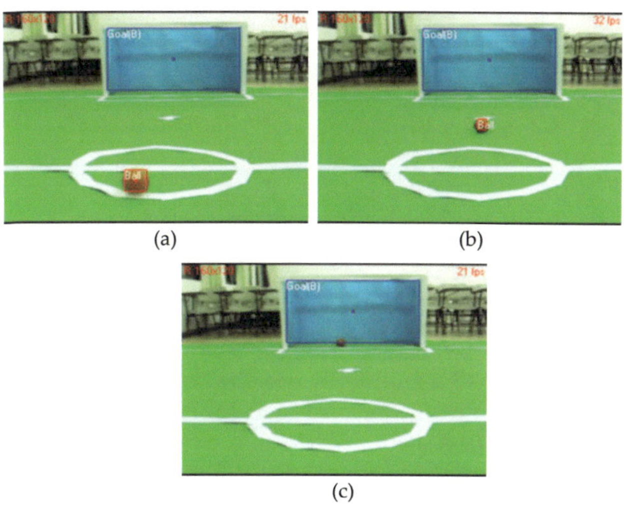


**Figure 25.** The result of object recognition under resolution 160×120. (a) frame 20. (b) frame 35. (c) frame 110.

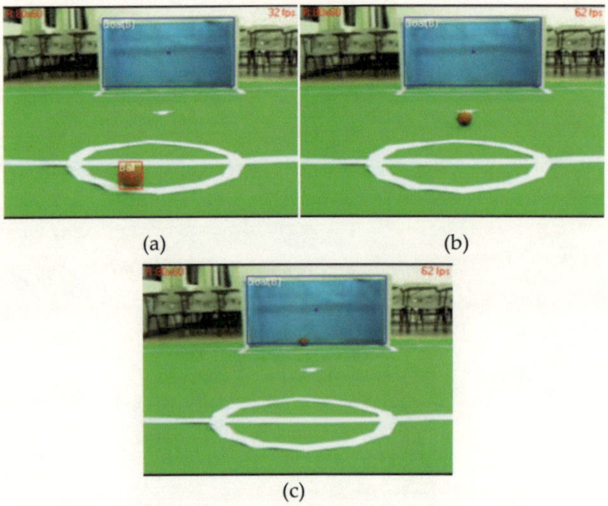


**Figure 26.** The result of object recognition under resolution 80×60. (a) frame 20. (b) frame 35. (c) frame 110.

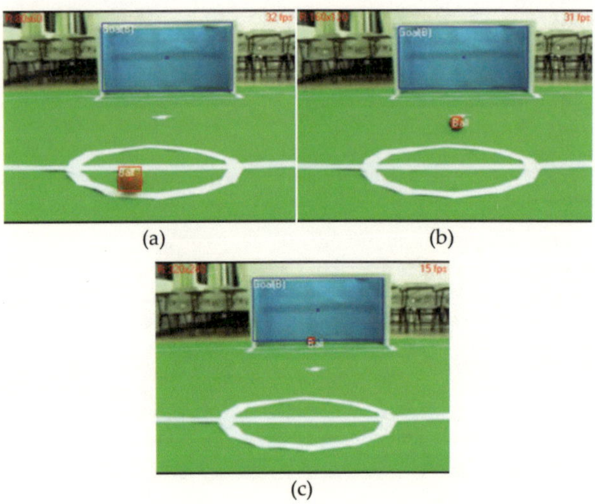


**Figure 27.** The result of object recognition under the ARM approach. (a) frame 20. (b) frame 35. (c) frame 110.

The experiment data of the accuracy rate and average FPS under different resolutions and ARM are shown in Table 4 and Fig. 28. According to Table 4, although the 320×240 resolution has a high accuracy rate, the processing speed is slow. The 80×60 resolution has the highest processing speed, but it has the lowest accuracy rate. By this approach, it gets high accuracy rate only when the object is close to the camera. On the other hand, the proposed ARM approach does not only have a high accuracy rate, but also keeps high processing speed. According to Fig. 28, the result shows that ARM selects the most proper resolution when the ball is in different distances. ARM uses the 80×60 resolution when the level is equal to 2 and uses the 160×80 resolution when the scale level is equal to 1. As the scale level is equal to 0, ARM selects the original input frame size (320×240).

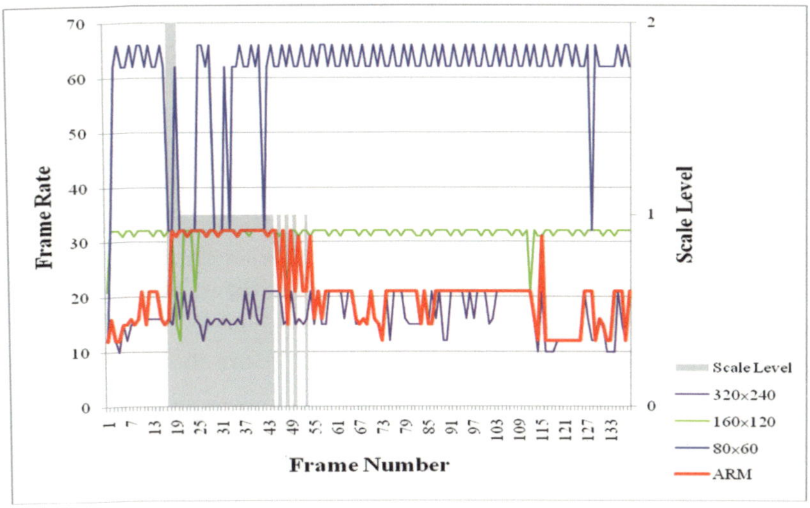


**Figure 28.** The relationship between frame number and frame rate under different resolutions and ARM.

| Resolution | Total frame | Object frame | False positive | False negative | Accuracy rate | Average frame rate |
|---|---|---|---|---|---|---|
| 320×240 | 138 | 138 | 0 | 6 | 95.65% | 16.93 FPS |
| 160×120 | | | 0 | 52 | 62.32% | 31.46 FPS |
| 80×60 | | | 0 | 109 | 21.01% | 59.84 FPS |
| ARM | | | 0 | 7 | 94.93% | 21.17 FPS |

**Table 4.** The experimental results of the accuracy rate and average FPS under different resolutions and ARM.

### 4.3. The critical objects recognition analysis

In this experiment, several scenes were simulated to improve the robustness of feature recognition approaches proposed in this work.

#### *4.3.1. Landmark recognition analysis*

According to (8), the landmark is composed of two same color objects in the vertical line, and the bias value $\beta$ is the key point to make sure whether this block is a landmark or not. A small bias value $\beta$ will cause the missing recognition, however a large $\beta$ may recognize an irrelevant block as a landmark, and these two situations are shown in Fig. 29.

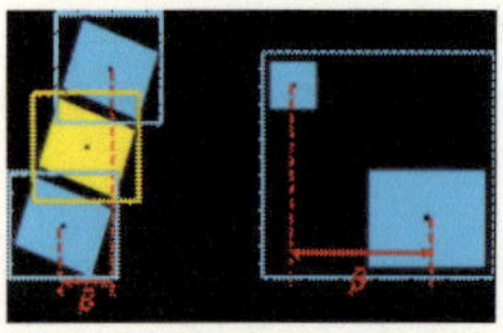

(a) (b)

**Figure 29.** The diagram of false recognition of landmark. (a) the case of small $\beta$. (b) the case of large $\beta$.

In this experiment, different values of $\beta$ were set to test the effects. The scene is used for simulating that the camera captures a slantwise landmark when the robot is walking. The hue threshold values of the orange, yellow, and blue colors are set as 35~45, 65~75, and 175~185, respectively. The saturation threshold values of the orange, yellow, and blue colors are all set as 60. The results under values of $\beta$ equal to 5, 10, 15, and 20 are shown in Figs. 30-33, respectively.

The experiment data of landmark recognition is shown in Table 5. According to this table, we can have a higher recognition accuracy rate when $\beta$ is greater than 15. Generally speaking, the vibration of robot walking is not more intense than the simulation, and therefore $\beta$ is set as 15 in this work. It will increase the chance of false recognition as a larger $\beta$ is used.

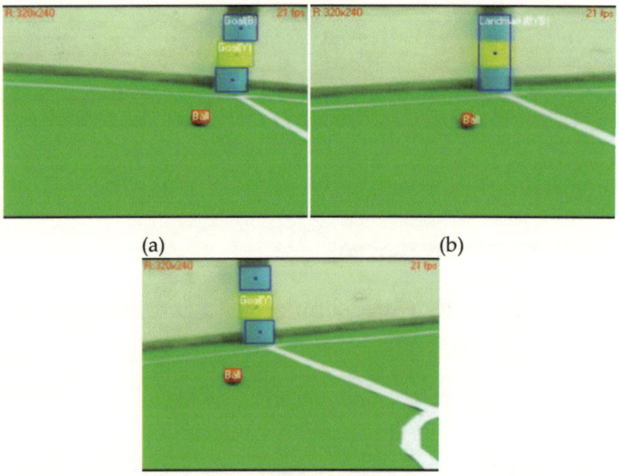

(a) (b)

(c)

**Figure 30.** The result of object recognition with $\beta$ equal to 5. (a) frame 246. (b) frame 253. (c) frame 260.

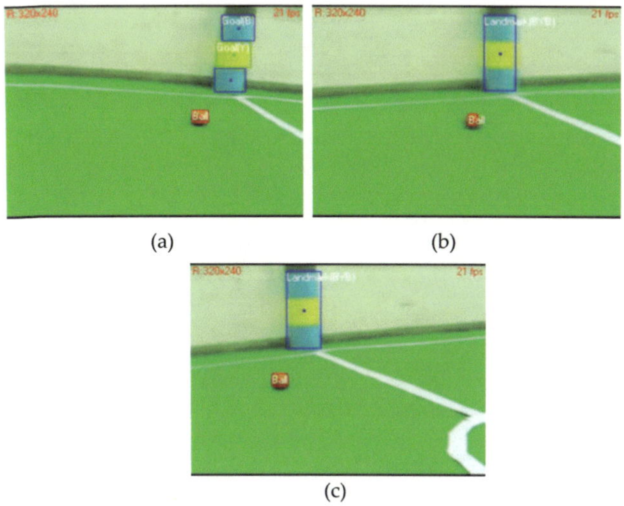


**Figure 31.** The result of object recognition with $\beta$ equal to 10. (a) frame 246. (b) frame 253. (c) frame 260.

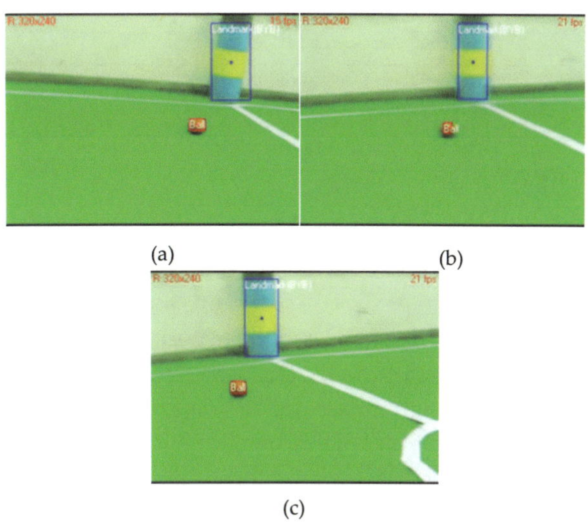


**Figure 32.** The result of object recognition with $\beta$ equal to 15. (a) frame 246. (b) frame 253. (c) frame 260.

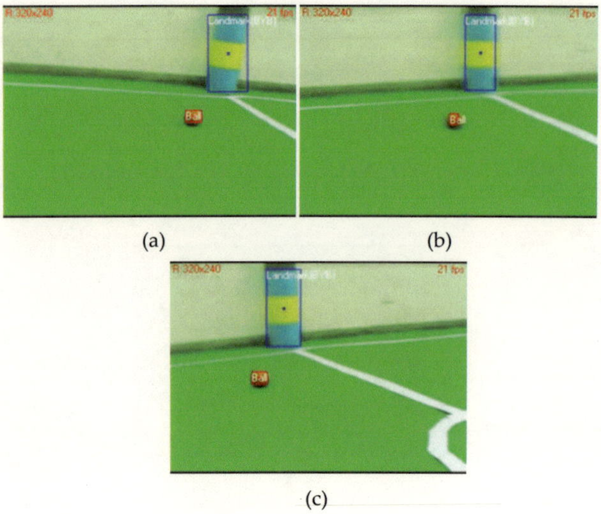


**Figure 33.** The result of object recognition with $\beta$ equal to 20. (a) frame 246. (b) frame 253. (c) frame 260.

| β | Total frame | Object frame | Correct recognition | Accuracy rate | Average frame rate |
|---|---|---|---|---|---|
| 5 | 664 | 664 | 304 | 45.78% | 20.02 FPS |
| 10 | | | 545 | 82.08% | 20.07 FPS |
| 15 | | | 637 | 95.93% | 20.15 FPS |
| 20 | | | 631 | 95.03% | 20.18 FPS |

**Table 5.** The experimental results under different values of $\beta$.

### *4.3.2. Goal recognition analysis*

The goal is the largest critical object in the field, and hence the camera always captures the incomplete goal in the frame when the robot is walking in the field. It causes a false recognition easily by using the feature of the shape ratio to recognize the goal. We improve this drawback by using the proposed method in Section 3.2 and the experimental results are shown here. The camera is set in the center of the contest field. The scene tries to simulate that the robot raises its head to see the goal and turns right to see the YBY-landmark and then turns left to see the BYB-landmark. The hue threshold values of the orange, yellow, and blue colors are set as 35~45, 70~80, and 183~193, respectively. The saturation threshold values of the orange, yellow, and blue colors are all set as 60. The results are shown in Fig. 34 and the experiment data are listed in Table 6. According to the result, the system can make the correct recognition of goal even though the goal is occluded.

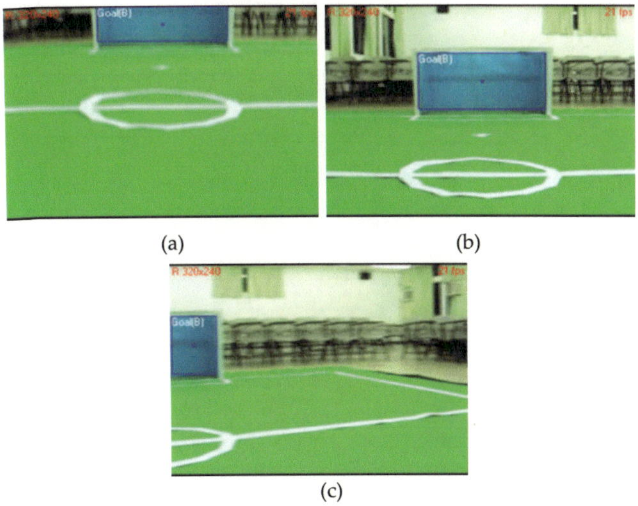

Figure 34. The results of goal recognition. (a) frame 34. (b) frame 76. (c) frame 118.

| condition | Total frame | Object frame | False positive | False negative | Accuracy rate | Average frame rate |
|---|---|---|---|---|---|---|
| Goal Recognition | 328 | 297 | 0 | 7 | 97. 64% | 21.98 FPS |

Table 6. The experiment data of goal recognition.

### 4.3.3. Ball recognition analysis

For the ball recognition, the system determines the orange block which has the maximum pixels as a ball for preventing the influence of noise. In this experiment, two balls are used in the scene. One ball is static in the field, and the other one moves into the frame and then moves away from the camera. The hue threshold values of the orange, yellow, and blue colors are set as 35~45, 70~80, and 183~193, respectively. The saturation threshold values of the orange, yellow, and blue colors are all set as 60. The result is shown in Fig. 35 and the experiment data are shown in Table 7. The static ball is labeled absolutely if only one ball is in the field, and the result is shown in Fig. 35(a). Because another ball has a bigger area when it is moving into the frame, the system will label the moving ball and determine the static ball as noise, and the result is shown in Fig. 35(b). When the moving ball is distant from the camera, the static ball is labeled again, and the result is shown in Fig. 35(c).

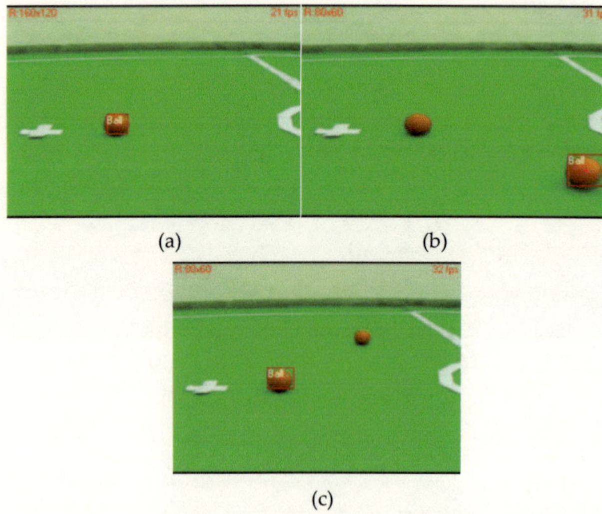


**Figure 35.** The result of ball recognition. (a) frame 124. (b) frame 131. (c) frame 156.

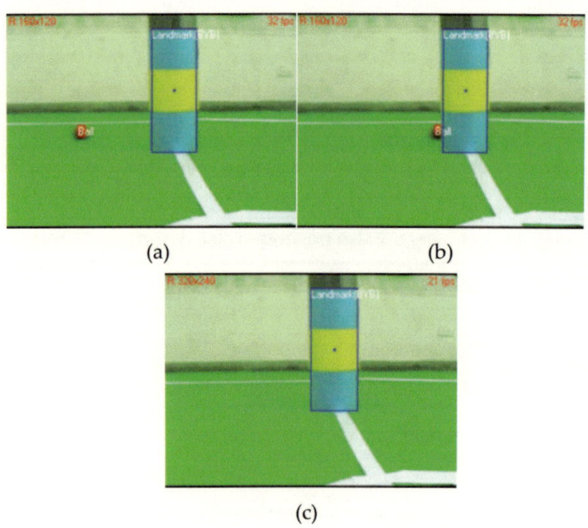


**Figure 36.** The result of ball recognition. (a) frame 145. (b) frame 151. (c) frame 153.

| condition | Total frame | Object frame | False positive | False negative | Accuracy rate | Average frame rate |
|---|---|---|---|---|---|---|
| Ball Recognition | 274 | 274 | 0 | 0 | 99.99% | 30.93 FPS |
| Ball Occlusion | 289 | 289 | 3 | 0 | 98.96% | 20.69 FPS |

**Table 7.** The experiment data of ball recognition.

Besides, it can also handle the situation when the ball is occluded partially by using the feature recognition proposed. We use the scene that the ball is occluded by the landmark during the ball moving in the frame from left to right. The hue threshold values of the orange, yellow, and blue colors are set as 35~45, 70~80, and 175~185, respectively. The saturation threshold values of the orange, yellow, and blue colors are all set as 50. The results are shown in Fig. 36 and the experiment data are shown in Table 7.

### 4.4. Environmental tolerance analysis

The color deviation by luminance variation has the most influence to the result of the color-based recognition method proposed in this work. Before the robot soccer competition we usually have one day to prepare for the contest, and therefore we can regulate the threshold values easily by the graph interface according to the luminance of the field. The results under different luminance are shown in Fig. 37. The reference threshold values are shown in Table 8.

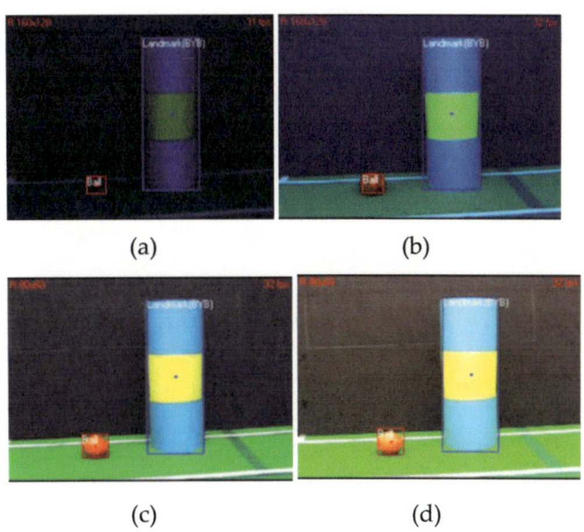


**Figure 37.** The results of object recognition under different luminance. (a) 16 lux. (b) 178 lux. (c) 400 lux. (d) 893 lux.

| Luminance | Hue_O | Sat_O | Hue_Y | Sat_Y | Hue_B | Sat_B |
|---|---|---|---|---|---|---|
| 16 lux | 3~13 | 10 | 118~128 | 50 | 220~230 | 96 |
| 178 lux | 13~23 | 60 | 119~129 | 60 | 205~215 | 96 |
| 400 lux | 17~27 | 50 | 61~71 | 50 | 190~200 | 50 |
| 596 lux | 17~27 | 50 | 57~67 | 50 | 180~190 | 50 |
| 893 lux | 23~33 | 50 | 57~67 | 45 | 180~190 | 50 |

**Table 8.** The threshold values used under different luminance.

The system cannot only recognize the critical objects under different luminance, but it can also accommodate the light changing suddenly. This experiment simulates that the robot recognizes the BYB-landmark and ball in the field under the light changing suddenly. The hue threshold values of the orange, yellow, and blue colors are set as 33~43, 67~77, and 175~185, respectively. The saturation threshold values of the orange, yellow, and blue colors are all set as 50. The results are shown in Fig. 38 and the experiment data are listed in Table 9. According to the result, the proposed method has a good performance about environmental tolerance.

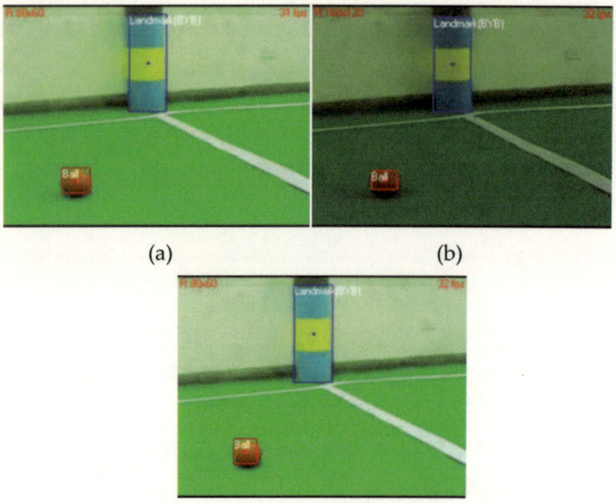

(a) (b) (c)

**Figure 38.** The result of object recognition under the light changing suddenly. (a) frame 388. (b) frame 440. (c) frame 535.

| condition | Total frame | Object frame | False positive | False negative | Accuracy rate | Average frame rate |
|---|---|---|---|---|---|---|
| Light Influence | 1,219 | 1,219 | 0 | 0 | 99.99% | 31.14 FPS |

**Table 9.** The experiment data of light influence.

### 4.5. Synthetic analyses

In this experiment, several scenes were simulated to compare the recognition accuracy rate and processing time between the 320×240 resolution and ARM. Scene 1: the ball is approach it to the camera slowly. Scene 2: the robot is approaching the ball after shooting the ball to the goal. Scene 3: the robot finds the ball and then tries to get approaching and kick it. Scene 4: the camera captures a blurred image when the head motor of the robot is rotating very fast. Scene 5: the robot localizes itself by seeing the landmarks. The hue threshold values of the orange, yellow, and blue colors are set as 35~45, 70~80, and 185~190, respectively. The saturation threshold values of the orange, yellow, and blue colors are all set as 50. The experiment data of these scenes are shown in Table 10 and the experimental results are shown in Figs. 39-43, respectively. According to the simulation results, our proposed method accommodates many kinds of scenes. It has the accuracy rate of more than 93% on average and the average frame rate can reach 32 FPS. It does not only maintain the high recognition accuracy rate for the high resolution frames, but also increases the average frame rate for about 11 FPS compared to the conventional high resolution approach. Furthermore, all of the experimental result videos mentioned in this section are appended in.

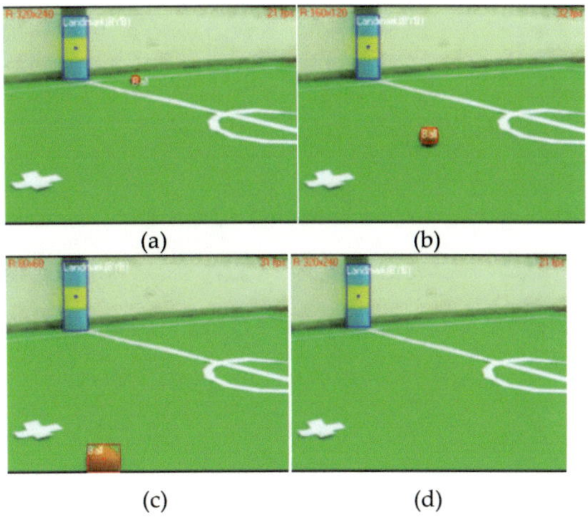


**Figure 39.** The result of Scene 1. (a) frame 11. (b) frame 46. (c) frame 63. (d) frame 65.

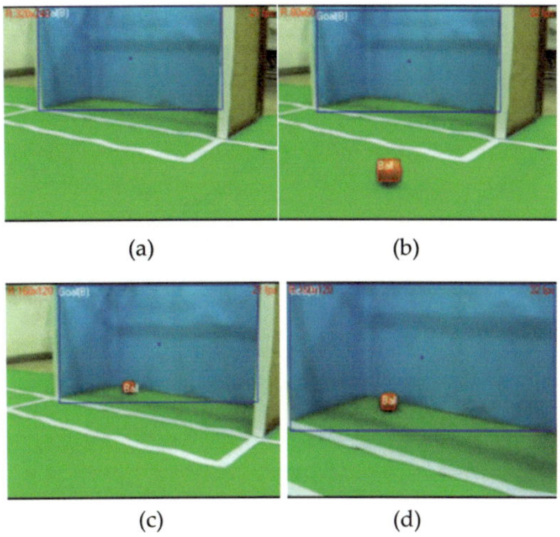


**Figure 40.** The result of Scene 2. (a) frame 89. (b) frame 98. (c) frame 240. (d) frame 347.

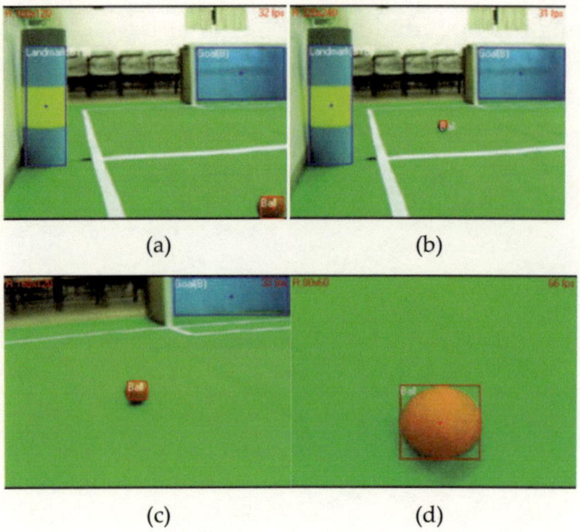

**Figure 41.** The result of Scene 3. (a) frame 81. (b) frame 159. (c) frame 456. (d) frame 793.

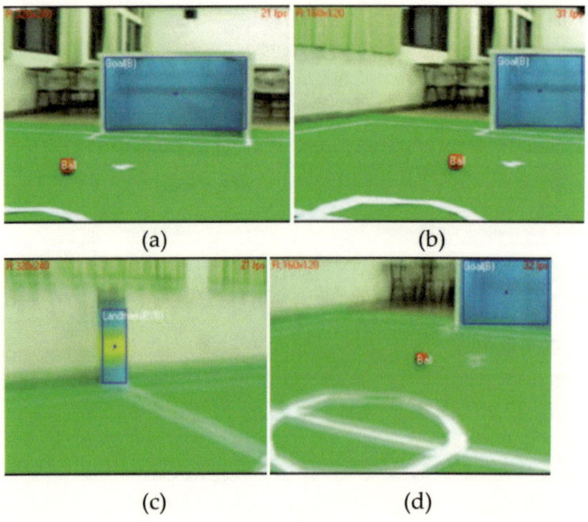

**Figure 42.** The result of Scene 4. (a) frame 81. (b) frame 162. (c) frame 273. (d) frame 620.

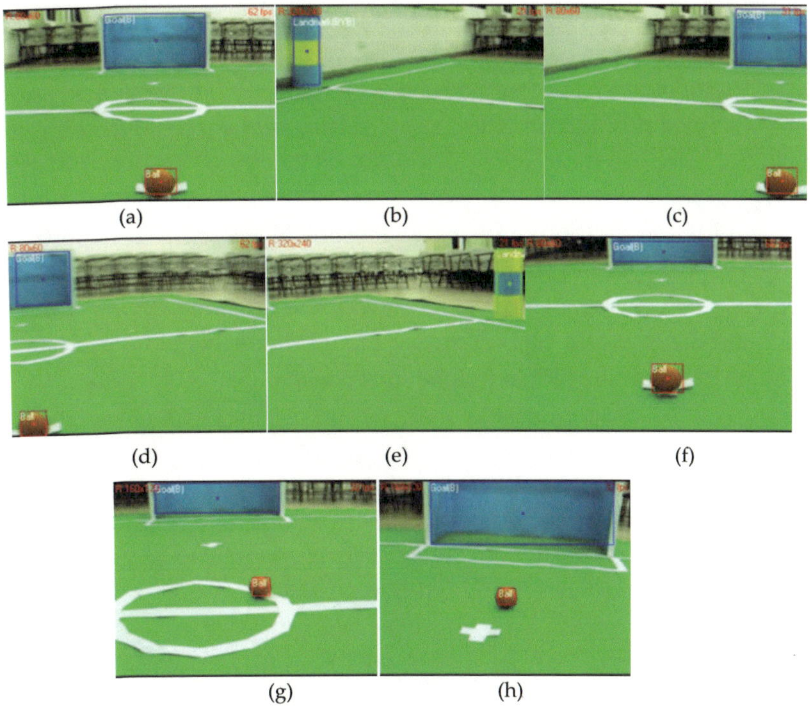


**Figure 43.** The result of Scene 5. (a) frame 106. (b) frame 211. (c) frame 347. (d) frame 372. (e) frame 434. (f) frame 581. (g) frame 748. (h) frame 954.

| Scene | Resolution | Total frame | Object frame | False positive | False negative | Accuracy rate | Average frame rate |
|---|---|---|---|---|---|---|---|
| 1 | 320×240 | 165 | 165 | 1 | 5 | 96.36% | 20.49 FPS |
| | ARM | | | 0 | 4 | 97.58% | 23.31 FPS |
| 2 | 320×240 | 409 | 409 | 27 | 1 | 93.15% | 21.36 FPS |
| | ARM | | | 11 | 2 | 96.82% | 29.88 FPS |
| 3 | 320×240 | 919 | 919 | 16 | 15 | 96.63% | 19.75 FPS |
| | ARM | | | 1 | 28 | 96.84% | 28.48 FPS |
| 4 | 320×240 | 679 | 627 | 3 | 83 | 86.28% | 19.29 FPS |
| | ARM | | | 2 | 88 | 85.65% | 27.31 FPS |
| 5 | 320×240 | 1,114 | 1,114 | 12 | 60 | 93.54% | 22.38 FPS |
| | ARM | | | 4 | 74 | 93.00% | 40.58 FPS |
| Total | 320×240 | 3,286 | 3,234 | 59 | 164 | 93.10% | 20.78 FPS |
| | ARM | | | 18 | 196 | 93.38% | 32.25 FPS |

**Table 10.** The experimental results of several kinds of scene simulation.

## 5. Conclusions

An outstanding humanoid robot soccer player must have a powerful object recognition system to fulfill the functions of robot localization, robot tactics, and barrier avoiding. In this study, we propose an HSV color based object segmentation method to accomplish object recognition. The object recognition system uses the proposed adaptive resolution method (ARM) and sample object recognition method, and it can recognize objects. The experimental results indicate that the proposed method is not only simple and capable of real-time processing but that it also achieves high accuracy and efficiency with the functions of object recognition and tracking. The method achieves a high accuracy rate of more than 93% on average, and the average frame rate can reach 32 FPS in indoor situations.

## Author details

Chih-Hsien Hsia[1], Wei-Hsuan Chang[2] and Jen-Shiun Chiang[2]

1 Department of Electrical Engineering, National Taiwan University of Science and Technology Taipei, Taiwan

2 Department of Electrical Engineering, Tamkang University Taipei, Taiwan

## References

[1] Avalable: http://www.robocup2009.org/153-0-rules.

[2] Canny, J. (1986). A computational approach to edge detection, *IEEE Transactions on Pattern Analysis and Machine Intelligence*, Vol. 8, (June 1986) pp. 679-698.

[3] Chaumette, F. (1994). Visual servoing using image features defined on geometrical primitives, *IEEE Conference on Decision and Control*, (December 1994) pp. 3782-3787.

[4] Cheng, F.-H. & Chen, Y.-L. (2006). Real time multiple objects tracking and identification based on discrete wavelet transform, Pattern Recognition, Vol. 39, No. 6, (June 2006) pp. 1126-1139.

[5] Chiang, J.-S., Hsia, C.-H., Hsu, H.-W., & Li C.-I. (2011). Stereo vision-based self-localization system for RoboCup," IEEE International Conference on Fuzzy Systems, (June 2011) pp. 2763-2770.

[6] Gonzalez, R. C. & Woods, R. E. (2001). *Digital image processing,* Addison-Wesley Longman Publish Co., Inc., Boston.

[7] Herodotou, N., Plataniotis, K. N., & Venetsanopoulos, A. N. (1998). A color segmentation scheme for object-based video coding, *IEEE Symposium on Advances in Digital Filtering and Signal Processing* (June 1998) PP. 25-29.

[8] Hsia, C.-H.; Guo, J.-M. & Chiang, J.-S. (2009). Improved low complexity algorithm for 2-D integer lifting-based discrete wavelet transform using symmetric mask-based scheme, *IEEE Transactions on Circuits and Systems for Video Technology*, Vol. 19, No 8, (August 2009) pp. 1201-1208.

[9] Ikeda, O. (2003). Segmentation of faces in video footage using HSV color for face detection and image retrieval, *International Conference on Image Processing*, Vol. 2, (September 2003) pp. III-913-III-916.

[10] Jean, J.-H. & Wu, R.-Y. (2004). Adaptive visual tracking of moving objects modeled with unknown parameterized shape contour, *IEEE International Conference on Networking, Sensing and Control*, (March 2004) pp. 76-81.

[11] Kass, M., Witkin, A., & Terzopoulos, D. (1988). Snakes: active contour models, *International Journal of Computer Vision*, Vol. 1, (January 1988) pp. 321–331.

[12] Kitano, H., Asada, M., Kuniyoshi, Y., Noda, I., & Osawa, E. (1995). Robocup: The robot world cup initiative, *IJCAI-95 Workshop on Entertainment and AI/ALife*, (1995) pp. 19-24.

[13] Sun, S. J., Haynor, D. R., & Kim, Y. M. (2003). Semiautomatic video object segmentation using VSnakes, *IEEE Transactions on Circuits System Video Technology*. Vol. 13, Vol. 1, (January 2003) pp. 75-82.

[14] Sugandi, B., Kim, H., Tan, J. K., & Ishikawa, S. (2009). Real time tracking and identification of moving persons by using a camera in outdoor environment, *International Journal of Innovative Computing, Information and Control*, Vol. 5, Vol. 5, (May 2009) pp. 1179-1188.

Chapter 5

# Modelling and Simulation for the Recognition of Physiological and Behavioural Traits Through Human Gait and Face Images

Tilendra Shishir Sinha, Devanshu Chakravarty, Rajkumar Patra and Rohit Raja

Additional information is available at the end of the chapter

http://dx.doi.org/10.5772/52565

## 1. Introduction

In the present chapter the authors have ventured to explain the process of recognition of physiological and behavioural traits of human-gait and human-face images, where a trait signifies a character on a feature of the human subject. Recognizing physiological and behavioural traits is a knowledge intensive process, which must take into account all variable information of about human gait and human face patterns. Here the trained data consists of a vast corpus of human gait and human face images of subjects of varying ages. Recognition must be done in parallel with both test and trained data sets. The process of recognition of physiological and behavioural traits involves two basic processes: *modelling* and *understanding*. Recognition of human-gait images and human-face images has been done separately. Modelling involves formation of a noise-free artificial human gait model (AHGM) of human-gait images and formation of artificial human-face model (AHFM) of human-face images. Understanding involves utilization of the hence formed models for recognition of physiological and behavioural traits. Physiological traits of the subject are the measurement of the physical features of the subject for observation of characteristics. The observable characters may be categorized into four factors: *built, height, complexion* and *hair*. Behavioural traits of the subject involve the measurement of the characteristic behaviour of the subject with relevant to four factors: *dominance, extroversion, patience* and *conformity*. Recognition in this chapter has been done in two environments: *open-air space* and *clear-under-water space.* The current chapter presents a well defined application of high-end computing techniques like soft-computing, utility computing and also some concepts of cloud computing.

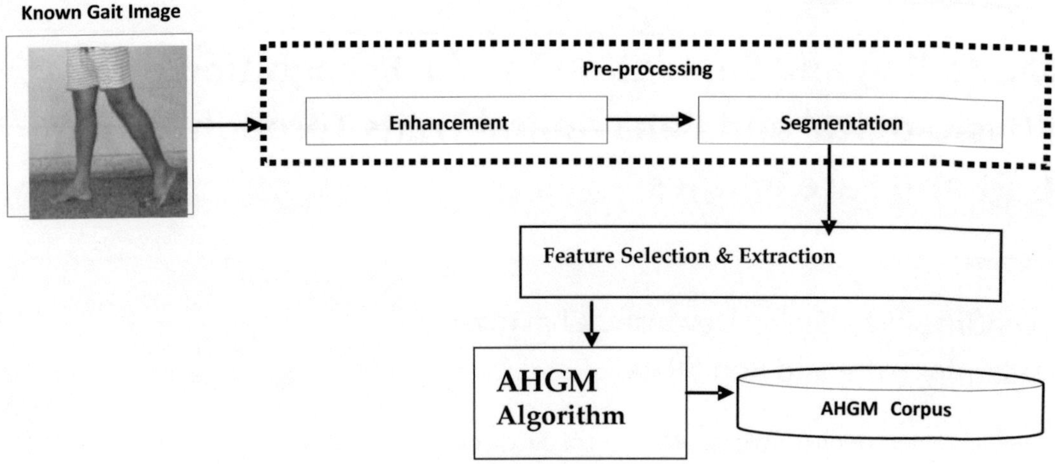


**Figure 1.** A Schematic diagram for the formation of AHGM

## 2. Modelling of AHGM and AHFM

### 2.1. Illustration of an Artificial Human-Gait Model (AHGM)

Human-gait analysis is a systematic study and analysis of human walking. It is used for diagnosis and the planning of treatment in people with medical conditions that affect the way they walk. Biometrics such as automatic face and voice recognition continue to be a subject of great interest. Human-Gait is a new biometric aimed to recognize subjects by the way they walk (Cuňado et al. 1997). However, functional assessment, or outcome measurement is one small role that quantitative human-gait analysis can play in the science of rehabilitation. If the expansion on human-gait analysis is made, then ultimate complex relationships between normal and abnormal human-gait can be easily understood (Huang et al. 1999; Huang et al. 1999). The use of quantitative human-gait analysis in the rehabilitation setting has increased only in recent times. Since past five decades, the work has been carried out for human-gait abnormality treatment. Many medical practitioners along with the help of scientists and engineers (Scholhorn et al. 2002) have carried out more experimental work in this area. It has been found from the literature that two major factors: *time* and *effort*, play a vital role. In the present chapter, a unique strategy has been adopted for further analysis of human-gait using above two factors for the recognition of physiological and behavioral traits of the subject. Many researchers from engineering field till 1980 have not carried out the work onhuman-gait analysis. In the year 1983, Garrett and Luckwill, carried the work for maintaining the style of walking through electromyography and human-gait analysis. In the year 1984, Berger and his colleagues, detected angle movement and disturbances during walking. In the year 1990, Yang and his colleagues, further carried the experimental work for the detection of short and long steps during walking. In the year 1993 Grabiner and his colleagues investigated that when an obstacle is placed in the path of a subject, how much time is taken by the subject to recover its normal walking after hitting an obstacle. In the year 1994, Eng and his colleagues, with little modifications and detection of angles, have carried out the same work. In the year 1996 again Schillings and his colleagues investigated similar type of work with little bit modifications in the mechanism as adopted by Grabiner and Eng in the year 1993 and 1994 respectively. In the year 1999 Schillings and his colleagues further carried the work that was done in the year 1996 with little modifications. In the year 2001 Smeesters and his colleagues calculated the trip duration and its threshold value by using human-gait analysis. From the literature, it has been also observed that very little amount of work has been carried out using high-end computing approach for the biometrical study through human-gait. The schematic diagram for the formation of knowledge-based model, that is, AHGM has been shown in figure 1.

Figure 1 gives an outline of the process of formation of AHGM. In this process a known human-gait image has to be fed as input. Then it has to be pre-processed for enhancement and segmentation. The enhancement is done for filtering any noise present in the image. Later on it is segmented using connected component method (Yang 1989; Lumia 1983). Discrete Cosine Transform (DCT) is employed for loss-less compression, because it has a strong energy compaction property. Another advantage in using DCT is that it considers real-values and provides better approximation of an image with fewer coefficients. Segmentation is carried out for the detection of the boundaries of the objects present in the image and also used in detecting the connected components between pixels. Hence the Region of Interest (ROI) is detected and the relevant human-gait features are extracted. The relevant features that have to be selected and extracted in the present chapter are based on the physical characteristics of human-gait of the subject. The physical characteristics that must be extracted are: foot-angle, step-length, knee-to-ankle (K-A) distance, foot-length and shank-width. These features are calculated using Euclidean distance measures. The speed of the human-gait can be calculated using Manhattan distance measures. Based on these features relevant parameters have to be extracted. The relevant parameters based on aforesaid geometrical features are: mean, median, standard deviation, range of parameter (lower and upper bound parameter), power spectral density (psd), auto-correlation and discrete wavelet transform (DWT) coefficient, eigen-vector and eigen-value. In this chapter of the book, the above parameters have been experimentally extracted after analyzing 10 frames of human-gait image of 100 different subjects of varying age groups. As the subject walks, the configuration of its motion repeats periodically. For this reason, images in a human-gait sequence tend to be similar to other images in the sequence when separated in time by the period of the human-gait. With a cyclic motion such as a human-gait, the self-similarity image has a repeating texture. The frequency of the human-gait determines the rate at which the texture repeats. Initially the subject is standing at standstill position. During this instance the features that have to be extracted are the foot-length, symmetrical measures of the knee- length, curvature measurement of the shank, maximum-shank-width and minimum-shank-width. Through the measurement of the foot-length of both the legs of the subject, the difference in the length of two feet can be detected. From the symmetrical measurement of the knee-length, the disparity in length of legs, if any, can be measured. Through curvature measurement of the shank, any departure from normal posture can be detected.

Measurement of shank-width helps in predicting probable anomalies of the subject and also will show any history of injury or illness in the past. The relevant feature based parameters that have to be extracted are fed as input to an Artificial Neuron (AN) as depicted in figure 2. Each neuron has an input and output characteristics and performs a computation or function of the form, given in equation (1):

$$O_i = f(S_i) \text{ and } S_i = W^T X \tag{1}$$

where $X = (x_1, x_2, x_3, \ldots, x_m)$ is the vector input to the neuron and W is the weight matrix with $w_{ij}$ being the weight (connection strength) of the connection between the $j^{th}$ element of the input vector and $i^{th}$ neuron. $W^T$ means the transpose of the weight matrix. The f (.) is an activation or nonlinear function (usually a sigmoid), $O_i$ is the output of the $i^{th}$ neuron and $S_i$ is the weighted sum of the inputs.

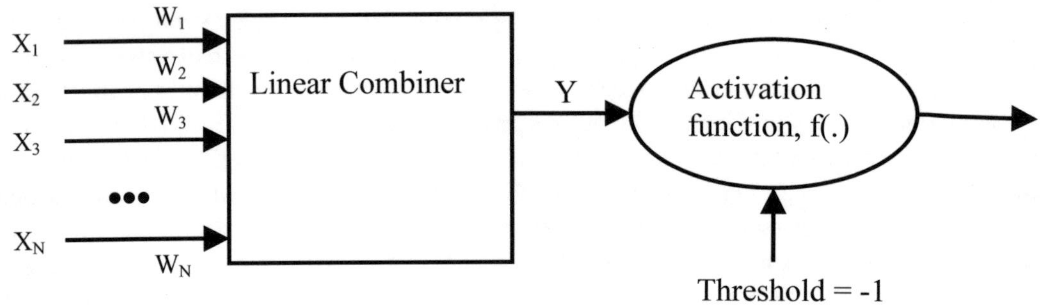


**Figure 2.** An artificial neuron

A single artificial neuron, as shown in figure 2, by itself is not a very useful tool for AHGM formation. The real power comes when a single neuron is combined into a multi-layer structure called artificial neural networks. The neuron has a set of nodes that connect it to the inputs, output or other neurons called synapses. A linear combiner is a function that takes all inputs and produces a single value. Let the input sequence be $\{X_1, X_2, \ldots, X_N\}$ and the synaptic weight be $\{W_1, W_2, W_3, \ldots, W_N\}$, so the output of the linear combiner, Y, yields to equation (2),

$$Y = \sum_{i=1}^{N} X_i W_i \tag{2}$$

An activation function will take any input from minus infinity to infinity and squeeze it into the range –1 to +1 or between 0 to 1 intervals. Usually an activation function being treated as a sigmoid function that relates as given in equation (3), below:

$$f(Y) = \frac{1}{1+e^{-Y}} \tag{3}$$

The threshold defines the internal activity of the neuron, which is fixed to –1. In general, for the neuron to fire or activate, the sum should be greater than the threshold value.

In the present chapter, feed-forward network has to be used as a topology and back propagation as a learning rule for the formation of corpus or knowledge-based model called AHGM. This model has to be optimized for the best match of features using genetic algorithm. The matching has to be done for the recognition of behavioural features of the subject, not only in open-air-space but also in under-water-space. The reason for adopting genetic algorithm is that, it is the best search algorithm based on the mechanics of natural selection, mutation, crossover, and reproduction. They combine survival of the fittest features with a randomized information exchange. In every generation, new sets of artificial features are created and are then tried for a new measure after best-fit matching. In other words, genetic algorithms are theoretically and computationally simple on fitness values. The crossover operation has to be performed by combining the information of the selected chromosomes (human-gait features) and generates the offspring. The mutation and reproduction operation has to be utilized by modifying the offspring values after selection and crossover for the optimal solution. Here in the present chapter, an AHGM signifies the population of genes or human-gait parameters.

#### 2.1.1. *Mathematical formulation for extraction of physiological traits from human-gait*

Based on the assumption that the original image is additive with noise. To compute the approximate shape of the wavelet (that is, any real valued function of time, possessing a specific structure), in a noisy image and also to estimate its time of occurrence, two methods are generally used. The first one is simple-structural-analysis method and the second one is the template-matching method.Mathematically, for the detection of wavelets in noisy image, assume a class of wavelets, $S_i(t)$, I = 0,...N-1, all possess certain common structural features. Based on this assumption that noise is additive, then the corrupted image has to be modeled by the equation,

$$\mathrm{X}(\mathrm{m,n}) = \mathrm{i}(\mathrm{m,n}) + \mathrm{G}\,\mathrm{d}(\mathrm{m,n}) \tag{4}$$

where i(m,n) is the clean image, d(m,n) is the noise and G is the term for signal-to-noise ratio control. Next windowing the image and assuming G = 1, equation (4) becomes:

$$\mathrm{x_w}(\mathrm{m,n}) = \mathrm{i_w}(\mathrm{m,n}) + \mathrm{d_w}(\mathrm{m,n}) \tag{5}$$

Fourier transform of both sides of equation (5), yields:

$$X_w\left(e^{j\omega 1}, e^{jw2}\right) = I_w\left(e^{j\omega 1}, e^{jw2}\right) + D_w\left(e^{j\omega 1}, e^{jw2}\right) \quad (6)$$

Where $X_w(e^{j\omega 1},e^{jw2})$, $I_w(e^{j\omega 1},e^{jw2})$ and $D_w(e^{j\omega 1},e^{jw2})$ are the Fourier transforms of windowed noisy, original-image and noisy-image respectively.

To de-noise this image, wavelet transform has to be applied. Let the mother wavelet or basic wavelet be $\psi(t)$, which yields to,

$$y(t) = \exp\,(j2pft - t^2/2) \quad (7)$$

Further as per the definition of Continuous Wavelet Transform CWT $(a,\tau)$, the relation yields to,

$$\text{CWT}\,(a,t) = (1/\sqrt{a}\int x(t)y\{(t-t)/a\}\,dt \quad (8)$$

The parameters obtained in equation (8) have to be discretized, using Discrete Parameter Wavelet Transform (DPWT).

This DPWT (m, n) is to be obtained by substituting $a = a_0^m$, $\tau = n\,\tau_0 a_0^m$. Thus equation (8) in discrete form results to equation (9),

$$\text{DPWT}\,(m, n) = 2^{-m/2}\sum_k \sum_l x(k,l)\Psi\left(2^{-m}k - n\right) \quad (9)$$

where 'm' and 'n' are the integers, $a_0$ and $\tau_0$ are the sampling intervals for 'a' and '$\tau$', x(k,l) is the enhanced image. The wavelet coefficient has to be computed from equation (9) by substituting $a_0 = 2$ and $\tau_0 = 1$.

Further the enhanced image has to be sampled at regular time interval 'T' to produce a sample sequence {i (mT, nT)}, for m = 0,1,2, M-1 and n=0,1,2,…N-1 of size M x N image. After employing Discrete Fourier Transformation (DFT) method, it yields to the equation of the form,

$$I(u,v) = \sum_{m=0}^{M-1} \sum_{n=0}^{N-1} i(m,n) \exp\ (-j2\pi(um/M + vn/N)) \quad (10)$$

for u=0,1,2,…,M-1 and v = 0, 1, 2, ……..,N-1

In order to compute the magnitude and power spectrum along with phase-angle, conversion from time-domain to frequency-domain has to be done. Mathematically, this can be formulated as, let R(u,v) and A(u,v) represent the real and imaginary components of I(u,v) respectively.

The Fourier or magnitude spectrum, yields to,

$$|I(u,v)| = \left[R^2(u,v) + A^2(u,v)\right]^{1/2} \tag{11}$$

The phase-angle of the transform is defined as,

$$\varphi(u,v) = \tan^{-1}\left[\frac{A(u,v)}{R(u,v)}\right] \tag{12}$$

The power-spectrum is defined as the square of the magnitude spectrum. Thus squaring equation (11) yields to,

$$P(u,v) = |I(u,v)|^2 = R^2(u,v) + A^2(u,v) \tag{13}$$

Due to squaring, the dynamic range of the values in the spectrum becomes very large. Thus to normalize this, logarithmic transformation has to be applied in equation (11). Thus it, yields,

$$|I(u,v)|_{normalize} = \log(1 + |I(u,v)|) \tag{14}$$

The expectation value of the enhanced image has to be computed and it yields to the relation as,

$$\mathrm{E}\left[\mathrm{I}(\mathrm{u,v})\right] = \frac{1}{MN}\sum_{u=0}^{M-1}\sum_{v=0}^{N-1} I(u,v) \tag{15}$$

where 'E' denotes expectation. The variance of the enhanced image has to be computed by using the relation given in equation (16),

$$\mathrm{Var}\left[\mathrm{I}(\mathrm{u,v})\right] = \mathrm{E}\{\left[\mathrm{I}(\mathrm{u,v}) - \mathrm{I}'(\mathrm{u,v})\right]^2 \tag{16}$$

The auto-covariance of an enhanced image has to be also computed using the relation given in equation (17),

$$C_{xx}(u,v) = E\{[I(u,v) - I'(u,v)][I(u,v) - I'(u,v)]\} \tag{17}$$

Also the powerspectrumdensity has to be computed from equation (17),

$$P_E(f) = \sum_{m=0}^{M-1} \sum_{n=0}^{N-1} C_{xx}(m,n)W(m,n)\exp(-j2\pi f(m+n)) \tag{18}$$

where $C_{xx}(m,n)$ is the auto-covariance function with 'm' and 'n' samples and W(m,n) is the Blackman-window function with 'm' and 'n' samples.

The datacompression has to be performed using Discrete Cosine Transform (DCT). The equation (19) is being used for the data compression.

$$DCT_c(u,v) = \sum_{m=0}^{M-1} \sum_{n=0}^{N-1} I(m,n)\cos\left(\frac{2\pi T(m+n)}{MN}\right) \tag{19}$$

Further for the computation of principal components (that is, eigen-values and the corresponding eigen-vectors), a pattern vector $\overline{p_n}$, which can be represented by another vector $\overline{q_n}$ of lower dimension, has to be formulated using (10) by linear transformation. Thus the resultant yields to equation (20),

$$\overline{p_n} = [M]\ \overline{q_n} \tag{20}$$

where $[M]=[I(m,\ n)]$ for m= 0 to M-1 and n = 0 to N-1.

and $\overline{q_n}$ = min([M]), such that $\overline{q_n} > 0$

Taking the covariance of equation (20), it yields, the corresponding eigen-vector, given in equation (21),

$$\overline{P} = \mathrm{cov}(\overline{p_n}) \tag{21}$$

and thus

$$\overline{P}\ .\ M_i = \lambda_i\ .\ M_i \tag{22}$$

where '$\lambda_i$'are the corresponding eigen-values.

Segmentation of an image has to be performed using connected-component method. For mathematical formulation, let 'pix' at coordinates (x,y) has two horizontal and two vertical neighbours, whose coordinates are (x+1,y), (x-1,y), (x,y+1) and (x,y-1). This forms a set of 4-neighbors of 'pix', denoted as $N_4$(pix). The four diagonal neighbours of 'pix' have coordinates (x+1,y+1),(x+1,y-1),(x-1,y+1) and (x-1,y-1), denoted as $N_D$(pix). The union of $N_4$(pix) and $N_D$(pix), yields 8-neighbours of 'pix'. Thus,

$$N_8(\text{pix}) = N_4(\text{pix}) \cup N_D(\text{pix}) \tag{23}$$

A path between pixels '$\text{pix}_1$' and '$\text{pix}_n$' is a sequence of pixels $\text{pix}_1$, $\text{pix}_2$, $\text{pix}_3$,.....,$\text{pix}_{n-1}$,$\text{pix}_n$, such that $\text{pix}_k$ is adjacent to $p_{k+1}$, for $1 \leq k < n$. Thus connected-component is defined, which has to be obtained from the path defined from a set of pixels and which in return depends upon the adjacency position of the pixel in that path.

From this the speed of walking has to be calculated. Mathematically, it has to be formulated as, let the source be 'S' and the destination be 'D'. Also assume that normally this distance is to achieve in 'T' steps. So 'T' frames or samples of images are required.

Considering the first frame, with left-foot ($F_L$) at the back and right-foot ($F_R$) at the front, the coordinates with (x,y) for first frame, such that $F_L(x_1,y_1)$ and $F_R(x_2,y_2)$. Thus applying the Manhattan distance measures, the step-length has to be computed as,

$$|step-length| = |x_2 - x_1| + |y_2 - y_1| \tag{24}$$

Let normally, $T_{act}$ steps are required to achieve the destination. From equation (24), $T_1$ has to be calculated for the first frame. Similarly, for 'nth' frame, $T_n$ has to be calculated. Thus total steps, calculated are,

$$T_{calc} = T_1 + T_2 + T_3 + \ldots\ldots + T_n \tag{25}$$

Thus walking-speed or walking-rate has to be calculated as,

$$walking-speed = \begin{cases} norm & ,if \quad T_{act} = T_{calc} \\ fast & ,if \quad T_{act} < T_{calc} \\ slow & ,if \quad T_{act} > T_{calc} \end{cases} \tag{26}$$

### 2.1.2. *Mathematical formulation for extraction of behavioral traits from human-gait*

Next to compute the net input to the output units, the delta rule for pattern association has to be employed, which yields to the relation,

$$y_{-inj} = \sum_{i,j=1}^{n} x_i w_{ij} \tag{27}$$

where '$y_{-inj}$' is the output pattern for the input pattern '$x_i$' and j = 1 to n.

Thus the weight matrix for the hetero-associative memory neural network has to be calculated from equation (27). For this, the activation of the output units has to be made conditional.

$$y_i = \begin{cases} +1 & if \quad y_{-inj} > 0 \\ 0 & if \quad y_{-inj} = 0 \\ -1 & if \quad y_{-inj} < 0 \end{cases} \tag{28}$$

The output vector 'y' gives the pattern associated with the input vector 'x'. The other activation function may also be used in the case where the target response of the net is binary. Thus a suitable activation function has been proposed by,

$$f(x) = \begin{cases} 1 & if \quad x > 0 \\ 0 & if \quad x <= 0 \end{cases} \tag{29}$$

Considering two measures, Accuracy and Precision has been derived to access the performance of the system, which may be formulated as,

$$\text{Accuracy} = \frac{Correctly\,\text{Re}\,cognized \quad feature}{Total\,number\,of\,\,features} \tag{30}$$

$$\text{Precision} = \frac{TPR}{TPR + FPR} \tag{31}$$

where TPR = True positive recognition and FPR = False positive recognition.

Further the analysis has to be done for the recognition of behavioral traits with two target classes (normal and abnormal). It can be further illustrated that AHGM has various states, each of which corresponds to a segmental feature vector. In one state, the segmental feature vector is characterized by eleven parameters. Considering only three parameters: the step_length: distance, mean, and the standard deviation, the AHGM is composed of the following parameters

$$\text{AHGM}_1 = \{D_{s1}, \mu_{s1}, \sigma_{s1}\} \tag{32}$$

where $AHGM_1$ means an artificial human-gait model of the first feature vector, $D_{s1}$ means the distance, $\mu_{s1}$ means the mean and $\sigma_{s1}$ means the standard deviation based on step_length. Let $w_{norm}$ and $w_{abnorm}$ be the two target classes representing normal foot and abnormal foot respectively. The clusters of features have been estimated by taking the probability distribution of these features. This has been achieved by employing Bayes decision theory. Let $P(w_i)$ be the probabilities of the classes, such that, $i = 1,2,....M$ also let $p(\beta/w_i)$ be the conditional probability density. Assume an unknown gait image represented by the features, $\beta$. So, the conditional probability $p(w_j/\beta)$, which belongs to $j^{th}$ class, is given by Bayes rule as,

$$P\left(w_j/\beta\right) = \frac{p(\beta/w_j)P(w_j)}{p(\beta)} \quad (33)$$

So, for the class $j = 1$ to 2, the probability density function $p(\beta)$, yields,

$$P\left(\beta\right) = \sum_{j=1}^{2} p(\beta / w_j)P(w_j) \quad (34)$$

Equation (33) gives a posteriori probability in terms of a priori probability $P(w_j)$. Hence it is quite logical to classify the signal, $\beta$, as follows,

If $P(w_{norm}/\ \beta) > P(w_{abnorm}/\ \beta)$, then the decision yields $\beta \in w_{norm}$ means 'normal behaviour' else the decision yields $\beta \in w_{abnorm}$ means 'abnormal behaviour'. If $P(w_{norm}/\ \beta) = P(w_{abnorm}/\ \beta)$, then it remains undecided or there may be 50% chance of being right decision making. The solution methodology with developed algorithm has been given below for the complete analysis through human-gait, made so far in the present chapter of the book.

Step 1. Read an unknown human-gait image of size 'n'
Step 2. Set the frame counter, fcount = 1
Step 3. Do while fcount <= n
Step 4. Read the human-gait image[fcount]
Step 5. Convert into grayscale
Step 6. Remove noises from the image and hence normalize it
Step 7. Apply DCT for loss-less compression of the normalized output
Step 8. Compute the connected components for the segmentation of image
Step 9. Crop the image for locating the Region of Interest and Object of Interest
Step 10. Compute the step-length, knee-to-ankle-distance, foot-length, shank-width, foot-angle and walking-speed
Step 11. Compute the genetic parameters using the relation as,
UB=(((mmax–mmean)/2)*A)+mmean
LB=(((mmean–mmin)/2)*A)+mmin
where 'A' is the pre-emphasis coefficient, mmax is the maximum value and mmean is the mean value and mmin is the minimum value, UB is the upper-bound value and LB is the lower-bound value. Store the feature vectors in a look-up table as a template.
Step 12. Perform the best-fit matching with the data set of AHGM (stored in a master file) using genetic algorithm.
Step 13. Employ Bayes classification for a two-class problem and then make decision
Step 14. Enddo
Step 15. Display result with 'NORMAL BEHAVIOUR' and 'ABNORMAL BEHAVIOUR'

**Algorithm 1.** NGBBCR {Neuri-Genetic Based Behavioral Characteristics Recognition}

Next for the formation of an artificial human-face model (AHFM) the illustration has been thoroughly done in the next subsequent section of this chapter of the book.

### 2.2. Illustration of an Artificial Human-Face Model (AHFM)

In the recent times, frontal portion of the human-face images have been used for the biometrical authentication. The present section of the chapter incorporates the frontal-human-face images only for the formation of corpus. But for the recognition of physiological and behavioural traits of the subject (human-being), side-view of the human-face has to be analysed using hybrid approach, which means the combination of artificial neural network (ANN) and genetic algorithm (GA). The work has to be carried out in two stages. In the first stage, formation of the AHFM, as a corpus using frontal-human-face images of the different subjects have to be done. In the second stage, the model or the corpus has to be utilized at the back-end for the recognition of physiological and behavioural traits of the subject. An algorithm has to be developed that performs the above specified objective using neuro-genetic approach. The algorithm will be also helpful for the biometrical authentication. The algorithm has been called as HABBCR (Hybrid Approach Based Behavioural Characteristics Recognition). The recognition process has to be carried out with the help of test image of human-face captured at an angle of ninety-degree, such that the human-face is parallel to the surface of the image. Hence relevant geometrical features with reducing orientation in image from ninety-degree to lower degree with five-degree change have to be matched with the features stored in a database. The classification process of acceptance and rejection has to be done after best-fit matching process. The developed algorithm has to be tested with 100 subjects of varying age groups. The result has been found very satisfactory with the data sets and will be helpful in bridging the gap between computer and authorized subject for more system security. More illustrations through human-face are explained in the next subsection of this chapter of the book.

#### *2.2.1. Mathematical formulation for extraction of physiological traits from human-face*

The relevant physiological traits have to be extracted from the frontal-human-face images and the template matching has to be employed for the recognition of behavioural traits of the subject. Little work has been done in the area of human-face recognition by extracting features from the side-view of the human-face. When frontal images are tested for its recognition with minimum orientation in the face or the image boundaries, the performance of the recognition system degrades. In the present chapter, side-view of the face has to be considered with 90-degree orientation. After enhancement and segmentation of the image relevant physiological features have to be extracted. These features have to be matched using an evolutionary algorithm called genetic algorithm. Many researchers like Zhao and Chellappa, in the year 2000, proposed a shape from shading (SFS) method for pre-processing of 2D images. In the same year, that is, 2000, Hu et al. have modified the same work by proposing 3D model approach and creating synthetic images under different poses. In the same year, Lee et al. also has proposed a similar idea and given a method where edge model and colour region are combined for face recognition after synthetic image were created by a deformable

3D model. In the year 2004, Xu et al. proposed a surface based approach that uses Gaussian moments. A new strategy has been proposed (Chua et al. 1997 and Chua et al. 2000), with two zones of the frontal-face. They are forehead portion, nose and eyes portion. In the present work, the training of the system has to be carried out using frontal portion of the face, considering four zones of human-face for the recognition of physiological characteristics or traits or features. They are:

First head portion, second fore-head portion, third eyes and nose portion and fourth mouth and chin portion. From the literature survey it has been observed that still there is a scope in face recognition using ANN and GA (Hybrid approach). For the above discussion the mathematical formulation is same as done for the human-gait analysis.

### 2.2.2. *Mathematical formulation for extraction of behavioral traits from human-face*

A path between pixels 'pix$_1$' and 'pix$_n$' is a sequence of pixels pix$_1$, pix$_2$, pix$_3$,.....,pix$_{n-1}$,pix$_n$, such that pix$_k$ is adjacent to $p_{k+1}$, for $1 \leq k < n$. Thus connected component is defined, which has to be obtained from the path defined from a set of pixels and which in return depends upon the adjacency position of the pixel in that path. In order to compute the orientation using reducing strategy, phase-angle must be calculated first for an original image. Hence considering equation (12), it yields, to considerable mathematical modelling.

Let $I_k$ be the side-view of an image with orientation 'k'. If k = 90, then $I_{90}$ is the image with actual side-view.If the real and imaginary component of this oriented image is $R_k$ and $A_k$. For k = 90 degree orientation,

$$\Rightarrow |I_k| = [R_k^2 + A_k^2]^{1/2} \tag{35}$$

For k = 90$^0$, orientation,

$$\Rightarrow |I_{90}| = [R_{90}^2 + A_{90}^2]^{1/52} \tag{36}$$

Thus phase angle of image with k = 90 orientations is

$$\phi_k = \tan^{-1}\left[\frac{A_k}{R_k}\right] \tag{37}$$

If k = k-5, (applying reducing strategy), equation (37) yields,

$$\varphi_{k-5} = \tan^{-1}\left[\frac{A_{k-5}}{R_{k-5}}\right]_{k-5} \tag{38}$$

From equation (37) and (38) there will be lot of variation in the output. Hence it has to be normalized, by imposing logarithmic to both equations (37) and (38)

$$\varphi_{normalize} = \log\left(1+\left(\varphi_k - \varphi_{k-5}\right)\right) \tag{39}$$

Taking the covariance of (39), it yields to perfect orientation between two side-view of the images, that is, $I_{90}$ and I85

$$I_{perfect-orientation} = \text{Cov}\left(\varphi_{normalize}\right) \tag{40}$$

The distances between the connected-components have to be computed using Euclidean distance method. A perfect matching has to be done with the corpus with best-fit measures using genetic algorithm. If the matching fails, then the orientation is to be reduced further by $5^0$, that is k = k-5 and the process is repeated till k = $45^0$.

The developed algorithm for the recognition of behavioural traits through human-face has been postulated below.

```
Step1. Read the unknown 90-degree oriented human-face image.
Step2. Set the frame counter, fcount = 90
Step3. Set the flag for best fit as fbest = 1
Step4. Do
        Read the human-face image[fcount]
        Enhance the image
        Apply loss-less compression using DCT
        Perform the segmentation using connected components method
        Crop the image for locating the ROI and OOI
        Compute the relevant physiological features
        Compute the genetic parameters (same as in algorithm-1)
        Perform the best-fit matching with the data set of AHFM (stored in a master file)
        Compute maximum matching of parameters
        If true then set the flag fbest = 0
        Employ Bayes classification for a two-class problem and then make decision
    End do
Step5. Display the result with 'NORMAL BEHAVIOUR' and 'ABNORMAL BEHAVIOUR'
```

**Algorithm 2.** HABBCR {Hybrid Approach Based Bihevioral Characteristics Recognition}

The understanding of the two formed models with mathematical analysis has been illustrated in the subsequent sections of this chapter of the book.

## 2.3. Understanding of AHGM and AHFM with mathematical analysis

The recognition of physiological and behavioral traits of the subject (human-being), a test image has to be fed as input. This has been shown in figure 3 below.

From figure 3, first the test image has to be captured and hence to be filtered using DCT after proper conversion of original image to grayscale image. Later on it has to be segmented for further processing and hence to be normalized. Relevant physiological and behavioral features have to be extracted and proper matching has to be done using the developed algorithms named as NGBBCR and HABBCR. In the present chapter two environments: *open-air* space and *under-water* space have been considered.

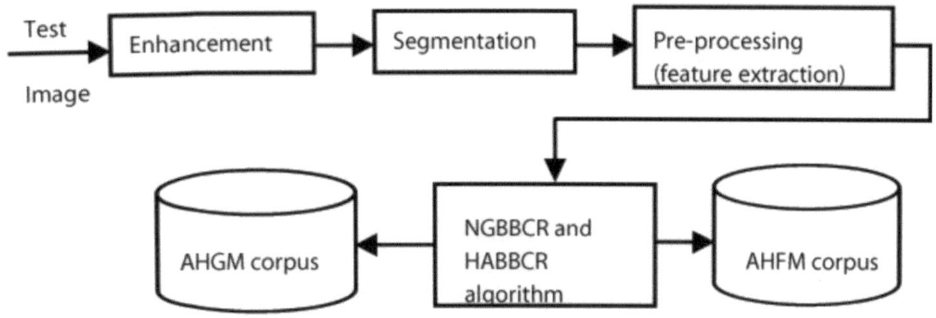


**Figure 3.** General outline for the understanding of AHGM and AHFM models

*2.3.1. How open-air space environment has been considered for recognition?*

Simply a test image in an open-air space (either a human-gait or human-face) has to be captured. It has to be converted into a grayscale image. Later on it has to be filtered using DCT. Hence normalized and then localized for the region of interests (ROI) with object of interests (OOI). Hence a segmentation process has to be completed. Sufficient number of physiological and behavioral traits or features or characteristics has to be extracted from the test image and a template (say OATEMPLATE has to be formed. Using Euclidean distance measures, the differences have to be calculated from that stored in the corpus (AHGM and AHFM). This has to be carried out using lifting-scheme of wavelet transform (LSWT). The details can be explained through the figure 4, as shown below.

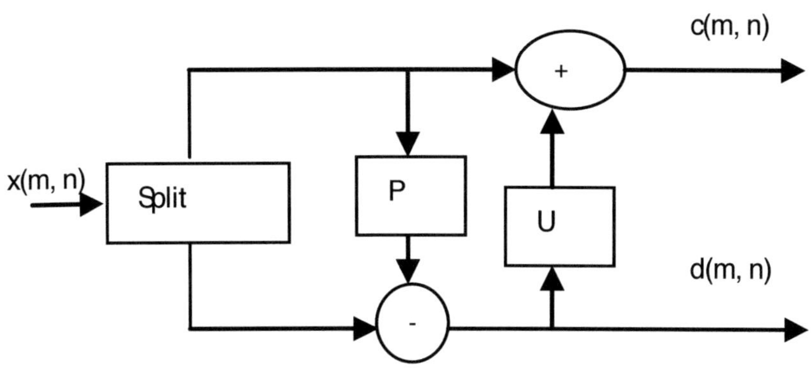


**Figure 4.** Lifting-scheme of wavelet transforms

Figure 4, shows that the enhanced and segmented part of the test image, x(m, n) has to be split into two components: detail component and coarser component. Considering both the obtained components, additional parameters have to be computed using mathematical approximations. These parameters (referred as prediction (P) and updation(U) coefficients) have to be used for an optimal and robust recognition process.

With reference to figure 4, first the enhanced and segmented part of the test image x(m, n), has to be separated into disjoint subsets f sample, say xe(m, n) and xo(m, n). From these the detail value, d(m, n), has to be generated along with a prediction operator, P. Similarly, the coarser value, c(m, n), has also to be generated along with an updation operator, U, which has to be multiplied with the detail signal and added with the even components of the enhanced and segmented part of the test image. These lifting-scheme parameters have to be computed using Polar method or Box-Muller method.

Let us assume X(m, n) be the digitized speech signal after enhancement. Split this speech signal into two disjoint subsets of samples. Thus dividing the signal into even and odd component: $X_e(m, n)$ and $X_o(m, n)$ respectively. It simplifies to $X_e(m, n) = X(2m, 2n)$ and $X_o(m, n) = X(2m+1, 2n+1)$. From this simplification two new values have to be generated called detail value d(m, n) and coarser value c(m, n).

The detail value d(m, n) has to be generated using the prediction operator P, as depicted in figure 4. Thus it yields,

$$d(m,n) = X_o(m,n) - P\left(X_e(m,n)\right) \tag{41}$$

Similarly, the coarser value c(m, n) has to be generated using the updation operator U and hence applied to d(m, n) and adding the result to $X_e(m, n)$, it yields,

$$c(m,n) = X_e(m,n) + U\left(d(m,n)\right) \tag{42}$$

After substituting equation (41) in equation (42), it yields,

$$c(m,n) = X_e(m,n) + U\,X_o(m,n) - UP\left(X_e(m,n)\right) \tag{43}$$

The lifting – scheme parameters, P and U, has to be computed initially using simple iterative method of numerical computation, but it took lot of time to display the result. Hence to overcome such difficulty polar method or Box-Muller method has to be applied. The algorithm 3 has been depicted below for such computations.

http://dx.doi.org/10.5772/52565

1. Generate two random numbers for U and P.
2. Calculate U′ and P′ (by rescaling U and P from –N to +N) and also compute S (scaling factor) using the formulae:
   $U' = ((2 * U) - 1)$
   $P' = ((2 * P) - 1)$
   $S = (U')^2 + (P')^2$
3. If the value calculated is not within the N circle then repeat step 2 else do step 4.
4. Compute standardized normally distributed random variables:
   $U = U' * (-2 \log(S)/S)$
   $P = P' * (-2 \log(S)/S)$

**Algorithm 3.** Computation of U and P values

As per the polar or Box-Muller method, rescaling of the un-standardized random variables can be standardized using the mean and variance of the test image. This can be more clearly expressed as follows: let Q be an un-standardized variable or parameter and Q′ be its standardized form. Thus $Q' = (Q - \mu)/\sigma$ relation rescales the un-standardized parameters to standardized form $Q = \sigma Q' + \mu$, where $\mu$ is the mean and $\sigma$ is the standard deviation.

Further the computed values of U and P has to be utilized for the application of inverse mechanism of lifting scheme of wavelet transform. Further for crosschecking the computed values of the lifting scheme parameters, inverse mechanism of lifting-scheme of wavelet transform (IALS-WT) has to be employed, that has been depicted in figure 5.

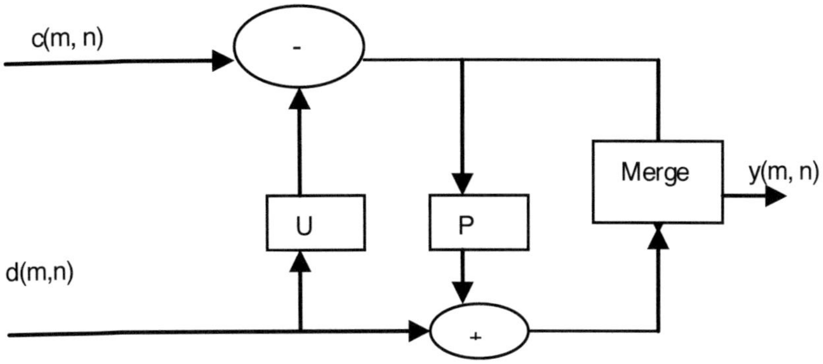


**Figure 5.** Inverse-lifting-scheme of wavelet transforms

With reference to figure 5, the coarser and detail values have to be utilized along with the values of lifting scheme parameters. Later the resultant form has to be merged and the output, y(m, n) has to be obtained. Further a comparison has to be made with the output y(m, n) and the enhanced and segmented part of the image x(m, n). If this gets unmatched then using feedback mechanism the lifting – scheme parameters have to be calibrated and again the whole scenario has to be repeated till the values of x(m, n) and y(m, n) are matched or close-to-matching scores are generated.

From figure 5, further analysis has to be carried out by merging or adding the two signals c″ (m, n) and d″(m, n) for the output signal Y(m, n). Thus it yields,

$$Y(m,n) = c''(m,n) + d''(m,n) \tag{44}$$

where c″(m, n) is the inverse of the coarser value c(m, n), and d″(m, n) is the inverse of the detail value d(m, n).From figure 5, it yields:

$$c''(m,n) = c(m,n) - U\,d(m,n) \tag{45}$$

and

$$d''(m,n) = d(m,n) + P\,c''(m,n) \tag{46}$$

On substituting equation (45) in equation (46), it gives:

$$d''(m,n) = (1 - UP)d(m,n) + P\,c(m,n) \tag{47}$$

On adding equations (46) and (47), it yields,

$$Y(m,n) = (1 + P)\,c(m,n) + (1 - U - UP)\,d(m,n) \tag{48}$$

To form a robust pattern matching model, assume the inputs to the node are the values $x_1$, $x_2,\ldots,x_n$, which typically takes the values of –1, 0, 1 or real values within the range (-1, 1). The weights $w_1$, $w_2,\ldots,w_n$, correspond to the synaptic strengths of the neuron. They serve to increase or decrease the effects of the corresponding '$x_i$' input values. The sum of the products $x_i * w_i$, i = 1 to n, serve as the total combined input to the node. So to perform the computation of the weights, assume the training input vector be '$G_i$' and the testing vector be '$H_i$' for i = 1 to n. The weights of the network have to be re-calculated iteratively comparing both the training and testing data sets so that the error is minimized.

If there results to zero errors a robust pattern matching model is formed. The process for the formation of this model is given in algorithm-4.

1. Read the test image, say X(m, n).
2. Form an array of data of n dimension after removing any background noise using spectral subtraction method.
3. Separate the array of data into two classes of dimension N1 and N2 using dispersion method of FLDA. Say array A1 and array A2.
4. Compress both the array of data using DCT method.
5. Compute the lifting scheme parameters P and U using both the array of data.
6. Use these parameters by employing inverse mechanism and obtain the output say Y(m, n)
7. If X(m, n) = Y (m, n), then do step 8 else repeat step 3.
8. Extract the physiological and behavioral traits or features for matching with the master database
9. Match the parameters with the template and regenerate the image for further analysis

**Algorithm 4.** Robust pattern matching model

Depending upon the distances, the best test-matching scores are mapped using unidirectional-temporary associated memory of artificial neural network (UTAM). The term unidirectional has to be used because each input component is mapped with the output component forming one-to-one relationship. Each component has to be designated with a unique codeword. The set of codewords is called a codebook. The concept of UTAM has to be employed in the present work, as mapping-function for two different cases:

1. Distortion measure between unknown and known images
2. Locating codeword between unknown and known image feature

To illustrate these cases mathematically, Let $K_{in} = \{I_1, I_2, \ldots, I_n\}$ and $K_{out} = \{O_1, O_2, \ldots\ldots, O_m\}$ consisting of 'n' and 'm' input and output codeword respectively. The values of 'n' and 'm' are the maximum size of the corpus. In the recognition stage, a test image, represented by a sequence of feature vector, $U = \{U_1, U_2, \ldots, U_u\}$, has to be compared with a trained image stored in the form of model (AHGM and AHFM), represented by a sequence of feature vector, $K_{database} = \{K_1, K_2, \ldots, K_q\}$. Hence to satisfy the unidirectional associatively condition, that is, $K_{out} = K_{in}$, AHGM and AHFM has to be utilized for proper matching of features. The matching of features, have to be performed on computing the distortion measure. The value with lowest distortion has to be chosen. This yield to, the relation,

$$C_{found} = \underset{1<=q<=n}{\arg\min}\left\{S(U_u, K_q)\right\} \tag{49}$$

The distortion measure has to be computed by taking the average of the Euclidean distance

$$S(U, K_i) = \frac{1}{Q}\sum_{i=1}^{Q} d(u_i, C_{\min}^{i,q}) \tag{50}$$

where $C_{\min}^{i,q}$ denotes the nearest value in the template or AHGM or AHFM and d(.) is the Euclidean distance. Thus, each feature vector in the sequence 'U' has to be compared with the codeword in AHGM and AHFM, and the minimum average distance has to be chosen as the best-match codeword. If the unknown vector is far from the other vectors, then it is very difficult to find the codeword from the AHGM and AHFM, resulting to out-of-corpus (OOC) problem. Assigning weights to all the codeword's in the database (called weighting method) has eliminated the OOC problem. So instead of using a distortion measure a similarity measure that should be maximized are considered. Thus it yields,

$$S_w(U, K_i) = \frac{1}{Q}\sum_{i=1}^{Q} \frac{1}{d(u_i, C_{\min}^{i,q})} w(C_{\min}^{i,q}) \tag{51}$$

```
  for each C_I in S do
     for each C_J in C_I do
            sum = 0
            for each C_K and K != I, in S do
              d_min = distancetonearest(C_J,C_K);
                  sum = sum + 1 / d_min;
            endfor;
        w(C_IJ) = 1 / sum;
    endfor
endfor
return weights = w(C_IJ)
```

**Algorithm 5.** Procedure to compute weight (S)

Dividing equation (50) by equation (51), it yields,

$$\gamma = \text{recognition rate} = \frac{S(U,K_i)}{S_w(U,K_i)} = \frac{unweighted}{weighted} \quad (52)$$

The procedure for computing the weights, has been depicted in an algorithm – 5 below:

Next for locating the codeword, hybrid approach of soft computing has to be applied in the well-defined way in the present chapter.The hybrid approach of soft computing techniques utilizes some bit of concepts from forward-backward dynamic programming and some bit of neural-networks. From the literature it has been observed that, for an optimal solution, genetic algorithm is the best search algorithm based on the mechanics of natural selection, crossover, mutation and reproduction. It combines survival of the fittest among string structures with a structured yet randomized information exchange. In every generation, new sets of artificial strings are created and hence tried for a new measure. It efficiently exploits historical information to speculate on new search points with expected improved performance. In other words genetic algorithms are theoretically and computationally simple and thus provide robust and optimized search methods in complex spaces. The selection operation has to be performed by selecting the physiological and behavioral features of the human-gait and face images, as chromosomes from the population with respect to some probability distribution based on fitness values. The crossover operation has to be performed by combining the information of the selected chromosomes (human-gait and human-face image) and generates the offspring. The mutation operation has to be utilized by modifying the offspring values after selection and crossover for the optimal solution. Here in the present chapter, a robust pattern matching model signifies the population of genes or physiological and behavioral features. Using neuro-genetic approach a similar type of work has been done by TilendraShishir Sinha et al. (2010) for the recognition of anomalous in foot using a proposed algorithm NGBAFR (neuro-genetic based abnormal foot recognition). The methodology adopted was different in classification and recognition process and the work has been further modified by them and has been highlighted in the present part of the book using soft computing techniques of genetic and artificial neural network. Hence the classification and decision process are to be carried as per the algorithm discussed earlier in this chapter of the book.

*2.3.2. How an underwater space environment has to be considered for recognition?*

Simply a test image of a subject (either walking or swimming in water), has to be captured, keeping the camera in an open-air space at a ninety-degree angle to the surface of the water. It has to be converted into a grayscale image. Later on it has to be filtered using DCT. Hence normalized and then localized for the region of interests (ROI) with object of interests (OOI). Later on segmentation process has to be done using structural analysis method. Sufficient number of physiological and behavioral traits or features or characteristics has to be extracted from the test image and a template (say UWTEMPLATE) has to be formed. Using Euclidean distance measures, the differences between the test-data-set and the trained-data-set has to be calculated. Depending upon the distances obtained, the best test-matching scores are generated using genetic algorithm for an optimal classification process and finally the decision process are to be carried out.

## 2.4. Experimental results and discussions through case studies

In the present chapter, human-gait and human-face have been captured in an open-air space. The testing of the physiological and behavioural characteristics or features or traits of the subject is not only done in an open-air space but also in under-water space.

*2.4.1. Case study: In an open-air space*

In an open-air space, first a human-gait image has to be captured and fed as input. Next it has to be enhanced. Later on it is compressed for distortion removal with loss less information. Next it has to be segmented for contour detection and the relevant physiological features have to be extracted. All the features of the human-gait image are stored in a corpus called AHGM. Similarly, in an open-air space, human-face image has also to be captured and fed as input. Next it is enhanced, compressed, segmented and relevant physiological features are extracted. The extracted physiological features are stored in a corpus called AHFM. For the recognition of physiological and behavioural traits, test images of human-gait and human-face (from side-view) are fed as input. Both the images are enhanced and compressed for distortion removal. Then both are segmented for the extraction of relevant physiological and behavioural features. By using the computer algorithm's(depicted in algorithm-2 and algorithm-3) the extracted features have to be compared with that stored in the corpus (AHGM and AHFM). Depending upon the result of comparison the classification has to be made. Relevant testing with necessary test data considering 10 frames of 100 different subjects of varying ages proves the developed algorithm. The efficiency of recognizing the physiological and behavioural traits have been kept at a threshold range of 90% to 100% and verified from the trained-data-set. Using genetic algorithm the best-fit scores have been achieved. Figure 6, shows the original image of one subject along with the segmented portion of the human-gait in standing mode.

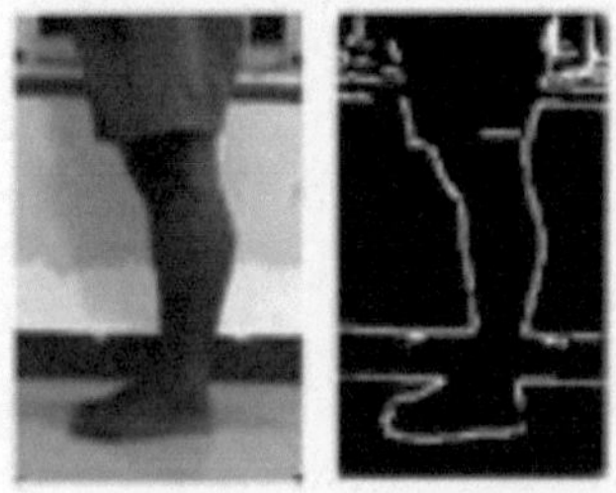

**Figure 6.** Segmented image in standing mode of human-gait

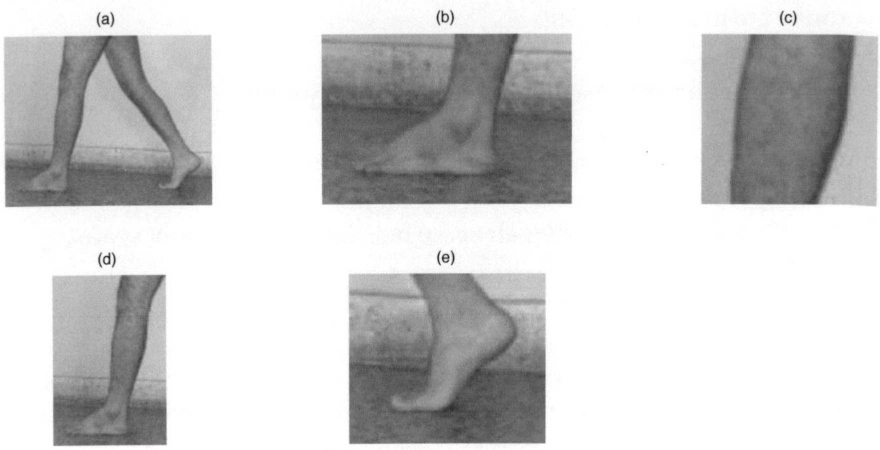


**Figure 7.** a) Original Gait Image (b) ROI Foot Image (c) ROI Shank Image (d) ROI Leg Image (e) ROI Swing Foot Image

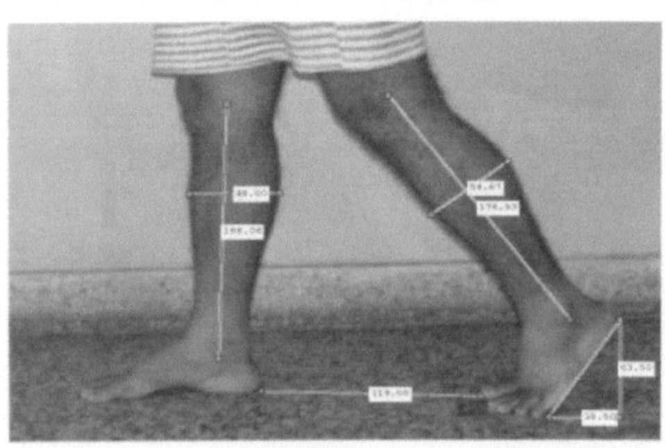

**Figure 8.** Physiological feature of human-gait in walking mode of subject #1 with right leg at the front

After segmentation of human-gait image in walking mode, extraction of physiological features using relevant mathematical analysis has to be done. Some of the distance measures of subject #1 with right leg at the front have been shown in figure 8. Similarly, distance measures of subject #1 with left leg at the front have been shown in figure 9.

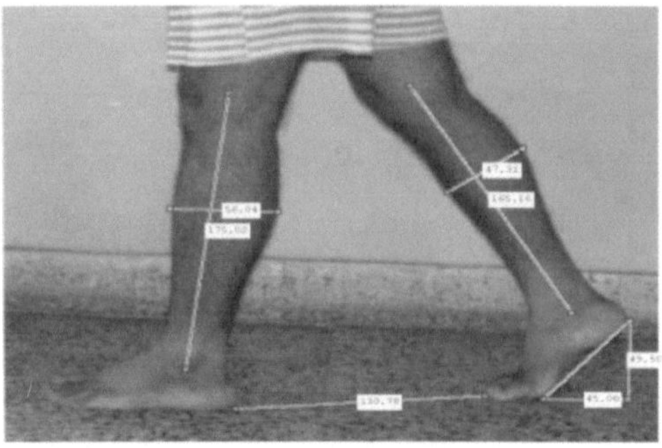

**Figure 9.** Physiological feature of human-gait in walking mode of subject #1 with left leg at the front

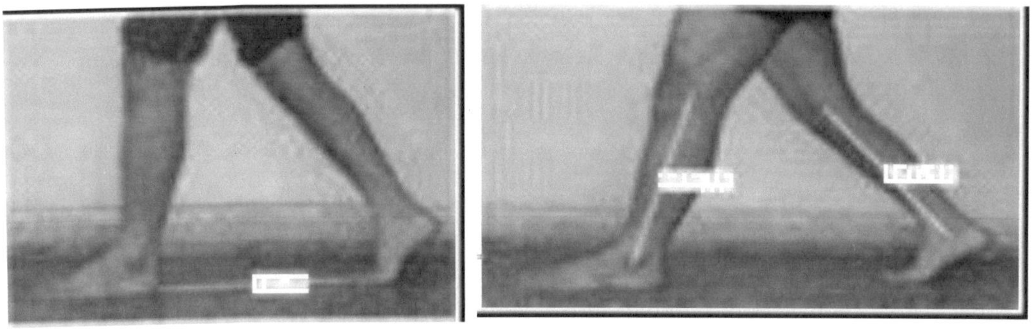

**Figure 10.** Step-length and Knee-to-ankle measure in walking mode of the subject

The relevant physiological feature, that is, step-length and knee-to-ankle distance has been also extracted that has been shown in figure 11.

As per the developed algorithm called NGBBCR, for most of the test cases, 'NORMAL BEHAVIOUR' has been achieved. Very few test cases for 'ABNORMAL BEHAVIOUR' have been achieved. Table 1, depicted below describes the physiological features extracted in standing and walking mode of subject #1.

| Image Files | Gait / Physical Characteristics | Foot Angle in Degrees | Step Length in Pixels | K_A Distance in Pixels (Left Leg) | K_A Distance in Pixels (Right Leg) | Foot Length in Pixels | Shank Width in Pixels (Left Leg) | Shank Width in Pixels (Right Leg) |
|---|---|---|---|---|---|---|---|---|
| IMG1 | Standing (Left Leg facing towards Camera) | 0 | 0 | 176.0 | 176.5 | 103 | 54.0 | 54.5 |
| IMG2 | Standing (Right Leg facing towards Camera) | 0 | 0 | 176.0 | 176.5 | 104 | 54.0 | 54.5 |
| IMG3 | Walking (Left Leg Movement) | 60.6 | 122.5 | 175.8 | 165.5 | 102 | 54.3 | 47.5 |
| IMG4 | Walking (Right Leg Movement) | 47.0 | 129.4 | 176.1 | 165.7 | 103 | 56.0 | 47.8 |
| IMG5 | Walking (Left Leg Movement) | 58.7 | 119.0 | 176.5 | 166.0 | 101 | 54.6 | 48.0 |
| IMG6 | Walking (Right Leg Movement) | 47.7 | 130.7 | 175.6 | 165.1 | 104 | 56.0 | 47.3 |

**Table 1.** Physiological features extracted in standing and walking mode of subject #1

From table 1, it has been observed that minimum variations have been found from one frame to other. This has been plotted in figure 11, below, for the graphical analysis. The extracted parameters with respect to physiological features that have been verified for best-fit scores using NGBBCR has been shown in table 2a and in table 2b. The graphical representation of table 2a and table 2b has been depicted in figure 12.

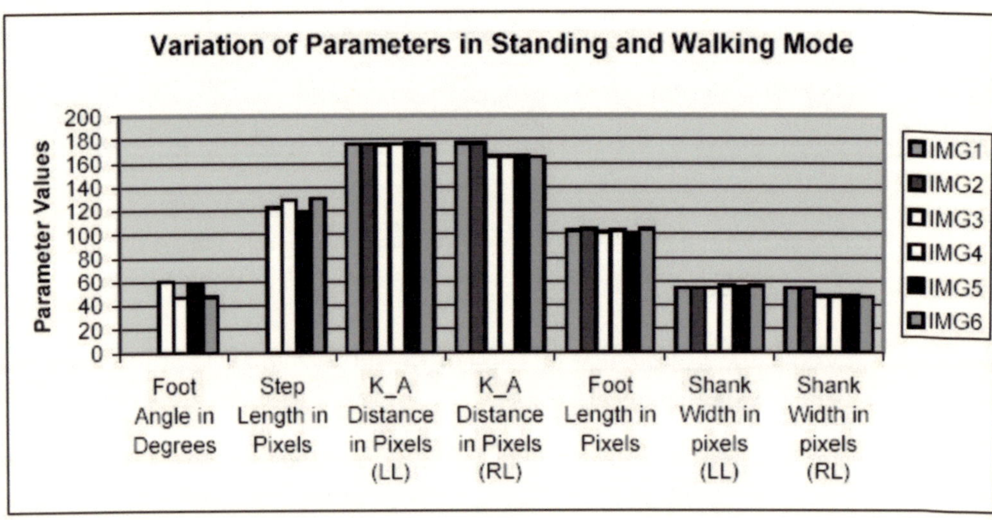


**Figure 11.** Graphical representation of physiological features extracted in standing and walking mode of subject #1

**2a**

| Image Files | Gait Characteristics | Mean | LB | UB | SD | Auto Corr. |
|---|---|---|---|---|---|---|
| IMG1 | Standing (Left Leg facing towards Camera) | 10.152 | -269.408 | 2620.94 | 156.513 | 30050 |
| IMG2 | Standing (Right Leg facing towards Camera) | 10.2679 | -242.651 | 2584.98 | 156.12 | 28665.2 |
| IMG3 | Walking (Left Leg Movement) | 9.10686 | -290.723 | 2637.0 | 151.059 | 36575.5 |
| IMG4 | Walking (Right Leg Movement) | 9.04764 | -430.713 | 2548.37 | 148.452 | 41360 |
| IMG5 | Walking (Left Leg Movement) | 9.2831 | -412.108 | 2658.3 | 152.113 | 43500.5 |
| IMG6 | Walking (Right Leg Movement) | 9.07875 | -365.896 | 2650.96 | 150.842 | 41360 |
| IMG7 | Walking (Left Leg Movement) | 9.67294 | -384.685 | 2544.82 | 149.573 | 36796.7 |
| IMG8 | Walking (Right Leg Movement) | 9.67004 | -376.443 | 2612.81 | 152.036 | 39045 |
| IMG9 | Walking (Left Leg Movement) | 9.83117 | -423.315 | 2702.1 | 155.715 | 41125.5 |
| IMG10 | Walking (Right Leg Movement) | 9.8643 | -349.463 | 2486.73 | 147.951 | 35262.5 |

**2b**

| Image Files | Gait Characteristics | Psd | Approx. Coeff. | Detail Coeff. | Eigen Vector | Eigen Value |
|---|---|---|---|---|---|---|
| IMG1 | Standing (Left Leg facing towards Camera) | 6.1983e+008 | 28.974 | -3.99699 | 0.000427322 | 130.005 |
| IMG2 | Standing (Right Leg facing towards Camera) | 6.1983e+008 | 15.9459 | 9.62817 | 0.00041897 | 127.639 |
| IMG3 | Walking (Left Leg Movement) | 6.1983e+008 | 14.5305 | 3.19103 | 0.000178086 | 69.244 |
| IMG4 | Walking (Right Leg Movement) | 6.1983e+008 | 25.63 | -8.18713 | 0.000171731 | 62.8614 |

| | | | | | | |
|---|---|---|---|---|---|---|
| IMG5 | Walking (Left Leg Movement) | 6.1983e+008 | 14.3655 | 3.43852 | 0.000154456 | 64.3655 |
| IMG6 | Walking (Right Leg Movement) | 6.1983e+008 | 24.8326 | -8.01451 | 0.000174672 | 64.7545 |
| IMG7 | Walking (Left Leg Movement) | 6.1983e+008 | 27.8642 | -9.02633 | 0.000184038 | 67.9991 |
| IMG8 | Walking (Right Leg Movement) | 6.1983e+008 | 26.4634 | -8.32745 | 0.000172107 | 67.8427 |
| IMG9 | Walking (Left Leg Movement) | 6.1983e+008 | 14.376 | 3.38278 | 0.000160546 | 69.2694 |
| IMG10 | Walking (Right Leg Movement) | 6.1983e+008 | 13.9372 | 3.50317 | 0.000197328 | 67.6806 |

**Table 2.** 2a. The extracted parameters with respect to gait features of subject # 1; 2b. The extracted parameters with respect to gait features of subject # 1

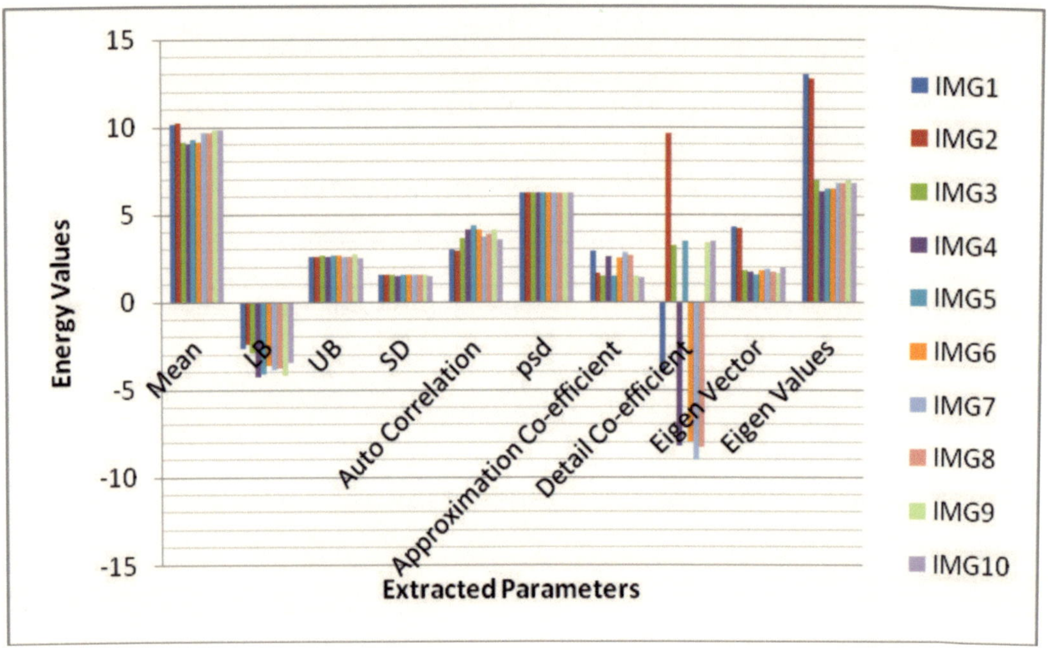


**Figure 12.** Graphical representation of physiological features of subject #1

From figure 12, it has been observed that the energy values (on Y-axis) are lying in between -10 to +15, for all the parameters. The parameters power spectral density (psd) and standard deviation (SD) have been found constant for any frame of the subject. The eigenvector and eigenvalues are also satisfying their mathematical properties. For the rest of the extracted parameters in the work, minimum variations have been observed.

Next the frontal part of human-face has been captured, with four zones that have been depicted in figure 13, below.

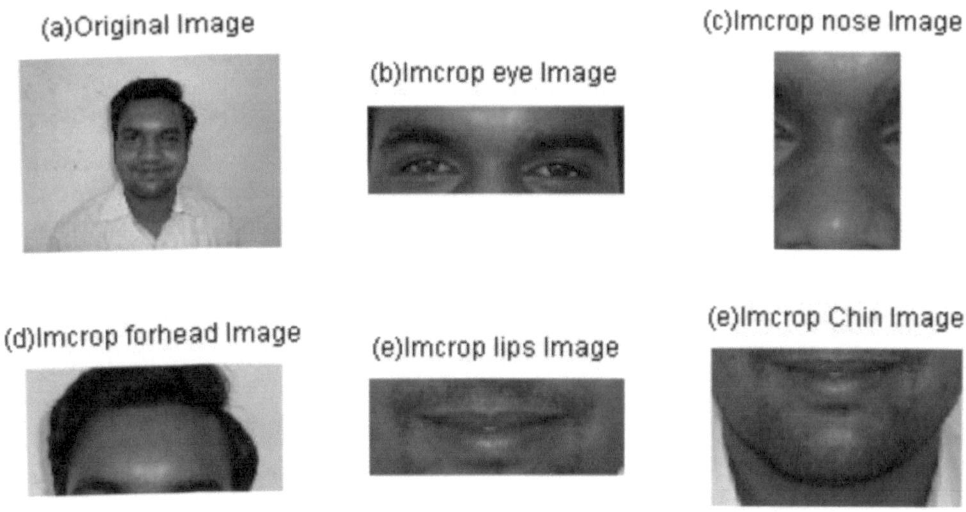


**Figure 13.** a) Original image (b) ROI Eye Image (c) ROI Nose Image(d) ROI Forehead Image (e) ROI Lips Image (f) ROI Chin Image

The relevant physiological features measured from side-view have been shown in table 3 below.

| Image Files | Angle Position from side | FHL | ENL | LN | NLL | LCL |
|---|---|---|---|---|---|---|
| IMG1 | 0 | 40.26 | 56.60 | 56.08 | 32.06 | 47.04 |
| IMG2 | 5 | 40.26 | 56.23 | 56.08 | 32.06 | 47.04 |
| IMG3 | 10 | 40.05 | 56.23 | 56.01 | 32.06 | 47.04 |
| IMG4 | 15 | 40.05 | 58.31 | 55.07 | 32.06 | 47.03 |
| IMG5 | 20 | 40.10 | 58.52 | 52.30 | 32.03 | 47.04 |
| IMG6 | 25 | 40.11 | 59.91 | 51.88 | 32.05 | 47.04 |
| IMG7 | 30 | 40.06 | 60.37 | 51.61 | 32.04 | 47.06 |
| IMG8 | 35 | 40.05 | 61.06 | 51.43 | 32.04 | 47.04 |
| IMG9 | 40 | 40.07 | 58.31 | 51.48 | 32.03 | 47.07 |
| IMG10 | 45 | 40.10 | 58.52 | 50.3 | 32.04 | 47.08 |

**Table 3.** Physiological features of human-face from side-view of subject #1

*2.4.2. Case study: In under-water space*

In under-water space, first a human-gait image has to be captured and fed as input. Next it has to be enhanced. Later on it is compressed for distortion removal with loss less information. Next it has to be segmented for contour detection and the relevant physiological features have to be extracted. All the features of the human-gait image are stored in a corpus called UWHGM (under water human-gait model). Similarly, in under-water space, human-face image has also to be captured and fed as input. Next it is enhanced, compressed, segmented and relevant physiological features are extracted. The extracted physiological features are stored in a corpus called UWHFM (under water human-face model). For the recognition of physiological and behavioural traits, test images of human-gait and human-face are fed as input. Both the images are enhanced and compressed for distortion removal. Then both are segmented for the extraction of relevant physiological and behavioural features. By using the computer algorithm's(depicted in algorithm-2 and algorithm-3) the extracted features have to be compared with that stored in the corpus (AHGM and AHFM). Depending upon the result of comparison the classification has to be made. Relevant testing with necessary test data considering 10 frames of 100 different subjects of varying ages proves the developed algorithm. The efficiency of recognizing the physiological and behavioural traits have been kept at a threshold range of 90% to 100% and verified from the trained-data-set. Using genetic algorithm the best-fit scores have been achieved. Figure 14, shows the original image of one subject along with the segmented portion of the human-gait in walking-mode in under-water space.

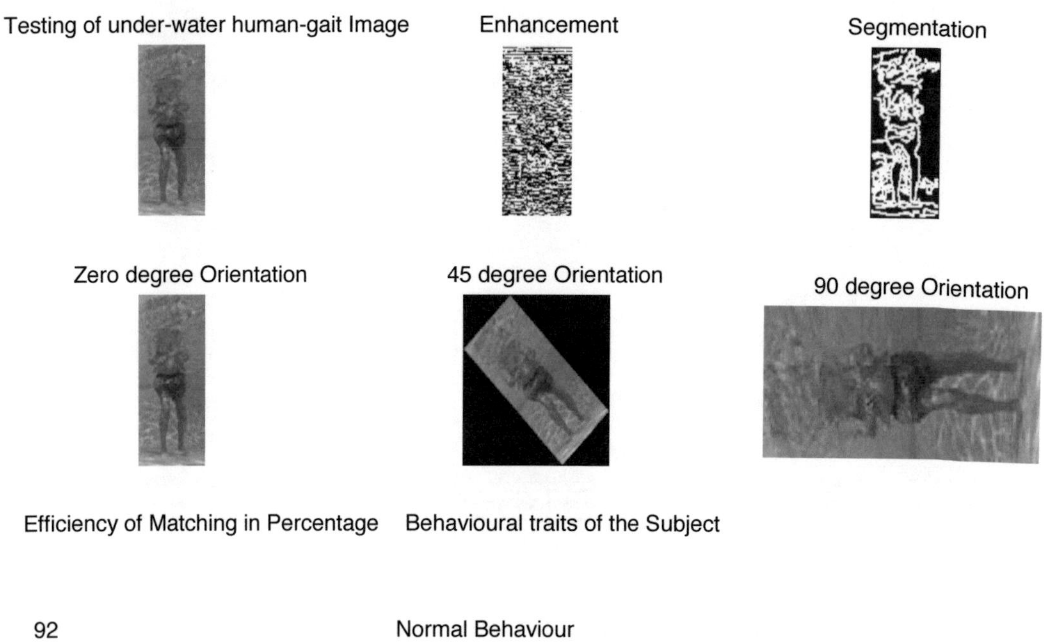


**Figure 14.** Testing of under-water human-gait image for subject #1

## 3. Conclusion and further scope

This chapter includes in-depth discussion of an algorithm developed for the formation of a noise-free AHGM and AHFM using relevant physiological and behavioural features or traits or characteristics of the subject using human-gait and human-face image. The algorithm has been named NGBBCR and HABBCR. It may be noted that the algorithms have been tested on a vast amount of data and have been found subject independent and environment independent. The algorithms have been tested not only in an open-air space but also in under-water space. A thorough case study has been also done. The trained-data set is matched with the test-data set for the best fit and this involves the application of artificial neural network, fuzzy set rules and genetic algorithm (GA). At every step in the chapter thorough mathematical formulations and derivations have been explained.

Human-gait analysis may be of immense use in medical field for recognition of anomalies and also to track the prosodic features like mood, age, gender of the subject. It may also be used to track the recovery of a patient from injury and operation. Further it will prove to be handy to spot and track individuals in a crowd and hence help investigation department.

Human-face analysis also will help in medical field to treat various diseases like squint, facial distortions and other problems which show their symptoms through facial anomalies. It will be of great help for plastic surgeons to rectify features and enhance the beauty of the subjects.

Underwater object recognition itself is a vast and challenging area and is proving to be of great help in fields of environmental-biology, geology, defence, oceanography and agriculture. Understanding the life and possible dangers of deep water animals, tracking submarines and destructive materials like explosives and harmful wastes are some areas of interest in this field.

## Author details

Tilendra Shishir Sinha[1], Devanshu Chakravarty[2], Rajkumar Patra[2] and Rohit Raja[2]

1 Principal (Engineering), ITM University, Raipur, Chhattisgarh State, India

2 Computer Science & Engineering Department, Dr. C.V. Raman University, Bilaspur, Chhattisgarh State, India

## References

[1] Cunado, D., Nixon, M. S., & Carter, J. N. (1997). Using gait as a biometric, via phase-weighted magnitude spectra. in the proceedings of First International Conference, AVBpA'97, Crans-Montana, Switzerland, , 95-102.

[2] Huang, P. S., Harris, C. J., & Nixon, M. M.S.,(1999). Recognizing humans by gait via parametric cannonical space, Artificial Intelligence in Engineering, , 13(4), 359-366.

[3] Huang, P. S., Harris, C. J., & Nixon, M. S. (1999). Human gait recognition in canonical space using temporal templates. IEEE Proceedings Vision Image and Signal Processing, , 146(2), 93-100.

[4] Scholhorn, W. I., Nigg, B. M., Stephanshyn, D. J., & Liu, W. (2002). Identification of individual walking patterns using time discrete and time continuous data sets, Gait and Posture, , 15, 180-186.

[5] Garrett, M., & Luckwill, E. G. (1983). Role of reflex responses of knee musculature during the swing phase of walking in man. European Journal Application Physical Occup Physiology, , 52(1), 36-41.

[6] Berger, W., Dietz, V., & Quintern, J. (1984). Corrective reactions to stumbling in man: neuronal co-ordination of bilateral leg muscle activity during gait,. *The Journal of Physiology*, 357, 109-125.

[7] Yang, J. F., Winter, D. A., & Wells, R. P. (1990). Postural dynamics of walking in humans., Biological Cybernetics, , 62(4), 321-330.

[8] Grabiner, M. D., & Davis, B. L. (1993). Footwear and balance in older men. *Journal of the American Geriatrics Society*, 41(9), 1011-1012.

[9] Eng, J. J., Winter, D. A., & Patla, A. E. (1994). Strategies for recovery from a trip in early and late swing during human walking. Experimentation Cerebrale, (2), 339-349.

[10] Schillings, A. M., Van Wezel, B. M., & Duysens, J. (1996). Mechanically induced stumbling during human treadmill walking. Journal of Neuro Science Methods, , 67(1), 11-17.

[11] Schillings, A. M., van Wezel, B. M., Mulder, T., & Duysens, J. (1999). Widespread short-latency stretch reflexes and their modulation during stumbling over obstacles. *Brain Research*, 816(2), 480-486.

[12] Smeesters, C., Hayes, W. C., & Mc Mahon, T. A. (2001). The threshold trip duration for which recovery is no longer possible is associated with strength and reaction time,. *Journal of Biomechanics*, 34(5), 589-595.

[13] Yang, X. D. (1989). An improved Algorithm for Labeling connected Components in a Binary Image. TR , 89-981.

[14] Lumia, R. (1983). A New Three-dimensional connected components Algorithm. Computer VisionGraphics, and Image Processing, , 23, 207-217.

[15] Harris, R. I., & Beath, T. (1948). Etiology of Personal Spatic Flat Foot, The Journal of Bone and Joint Surgery, , 30B(4), 624-634.

[16] Kover, T., Vigh, D., & Vamossy, Z. (2006). MYRA- Face Detection and Face Recognition system, in the proceedings of Fourth International Symposium on Applied Machine Intelligence, SAMI 2006, Herlany, Slovakia, , 255-265.

[17] Rein-Lien, Hsu., Mohammad-Mottaleb, Abdel., & Anil, K. Jain, (2002). Face detection in color images. in IEEE transactions of Pattern Analysis and Machine Intelligence, , 24(5), 696-706.

[18] Zhang, J., Yan, Y., Lades, M., & 199, . (1997). Face recognition: eigenface, elastic matching and neural nets, in the proceedings of IEEE, , 85(9), 1493-1435.

[19] Turk, M. A., & Pentland, A. P. (1991). , Face recognition using eigenfaces, in the proceedings of IEEE Computer society conference on computer vision and pattern recognition, ., 586-591.

[20] Zhao, W. Y., & Chellapa, R. (2000). SFS Based View Synthesis for Robust Face Recognition in the proceedings of IEEE international Automatic Face and Gesture recognition.

[21] Hu., Y., Jaing, D., Yan, S., Zhang, L., and Zhang, H., Automatic 3d reconstruction for face recognition, in the proceedings of IEEE International Conferences on Automatic Face and Gesture Recognition 2000.

[22] Lee, C. H., Park, S. W., Chang, W., & Park, J. W. Improving the performance of Multiclass SVMs in face recognition with nearest neighbours rule in the proceedings of IEEE International conference on tools with Artificial Intelligence (2000).

[23] Xu, C., Wang, Y., Tan, T., Quan, L., Automatic 3D Face recognition combining global geometric features with local shape variation information, in the proceedings of IEEE International Conference for Automatic Face and Gesture Recognition 2004.

[24] Chua, C.S., Jarvia, R., Point Signature : A new Representation for 3D Object Recognition, International Journal on Computer Vision vol 25, 1997.

[25] Chua, C.S., Han, F, Ho, Y.K., 3D Human face recognition using point signature, in the proceedings of IEEE International Conference on Automatic Face and Gesture Recognition 2000.

[26] Sinha, Tilendra., Shishir, Patra., Rajkumar, , & Raja, Rohit. (2011). A Comprehensive analysis for abnormal foot recognition of human-gait using neuro-genetic approach. *International Journal of Tomography and Statistics*, 16(W11), 56-73.

# Density Estimation and Wavelet Thresholding via Bayesian Methods: A Wavelet Probability Band and Related Metrics Approach to Assess Agitation and Sedation in ICU Patients

In Kang, Irene Hudson, Andrew Rudge and J. Geoffrey Chase

Additional information is available at the end of the chapter

http://dx.doi.org/10.5772/52434

## 1. Introduction

A wave is usually defined as an oscillating function that is localized in both time and frequency. A wavelet is a "small wave", which has its energy concentrated in time providing a tool for the analysis of transient, non-stationary, or time-varying phenomena [1, 2]. Wavelets have the ability to allow simultaneous time and frequency analysis via a flexible mathematical foundation. Wavelets are well suited to the analysis of transient signals in particular. The localizing property of wavelets allows a wavelet expansion of a transient component on an orthogonal basis to be modelled using a small number of wavelet coefficients using a low pass filter [3]. This wavelet paradigm has been applied in a wide range of fields, such as signal processing, data compression and image analysis [4 -10].

Typically agitation-sedation cycling in critically ill patients involves oscillations between states of agitation and over-sedation, which is detrimental to patient health, and increases hospital length of stay [11-14]. The goal of the research specifically in reference [14] was to develop a physiologically representative model that captures the fundamental dynamics of the agitation-sedation system. The resulting model can serve as a platform to develop and test semi-automated sedation management controllers that offer the potential of improved agitation management and reduce length of stay in the intensive care unit (ICU). A minimal differential equation model to predict or simulate each patient's agitation-sedation status over time was presented in [14] for 37 ICU patients, and was shown to capture patient A-S dynamics. Current agitation management methods rely on subjective agitation assessment and an appropriate sedation input response from recorded at bedside agitation scales [15, - 19]. The carers then select an appropriate infusion rate based upon their evaluation of these scales, their experience and intuition [20]. This process is depicted in Figure 1 (see [14]). Recently a more refined A-S model, which utilised kernel regression with an Epanechnikov kernel and better captured the fundamental agitation-sedation (A-S) dynamics was formulated [12, 13].

A secondary aim of this chapter is to test the feasibility of wavelet statistics to help distinguish between patients whose simulated A-S profiles were "close" to their mean profile versus those for whom this was not the case (i.e. their simulated profiles are not "close" to their actual recorded profiles). This chapter builds on a preliminary study [21] to assess wavelet signatures for modelling ICU agitation-sedation profiles, so as to, as in this chapter, evaluate "closeness" or "discrimination" of simulated versus actual A-S profiles with respect to wavelet scales - as recently analysed using DWT and wavelet correlation methods in [29] (see also [22]-[24]). The recent work of Kang et al. [29] investigated the use of DWT signatures and statistics on the simulated profiles derived in [12] and [13], to test for commonality across patients, in terms of wavelet (cross) correlations. Another earlier application of this approach was the study of historical Australian flowering time series [22], where it was established that wavelets add credibility to the use of phenological records to detect climate change. This study was also recently expanded and reported by Hudson et al. [23, 24] (see also references [25-28]).

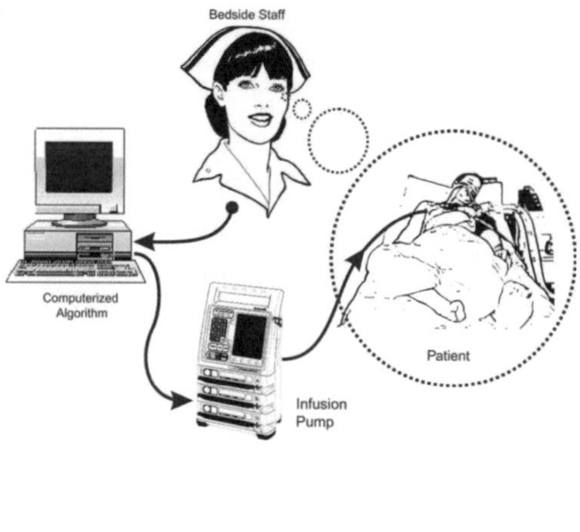


**Figure 1.** Diagram of the feedback loop employing nursing staff's feedback of subjectively assessed patient agitation through the infusion controller (diagram is sourced from [14]).

The density function is very important in statistics and data analysis. A variety of approaches to density estimation exist. Indeed the density estimation problem has a long history and many solutions [30, 31, 32]. A large body of existing literature on nonparametric statistics is devoted to the theory and practice of density estimation [32-36]. The local character of wavelet functions is the basis for their inherent advantage over projection estimators – specifically that wavelets are straightforward and well localized in both space and frequency. The relevant estimation methods belong to the class of so-called projection estimators, as introduced by [36] or their non-linear modifications. Section 3 traces, in brief, the development of some basic methods used in density estimation. We then link these and apply wavelet methods for (density) function estimation to the ICU data of [29].

In this chapter the density is estimated using wavelet shrinkage methods, as based on Bayesian methods. Specifically the minimax estimator is used to obtain a patient specific wavelet tracking coverage index (WTCI). All values of the WTCI are obtained using Bayesian wavelet thresholding, and are shown to differentiate between poor versus good tracking. A Bayesian approach is also suggested in this chapter by which to assess a parametric A-S model – this by constructing a wavelet probability band (WPB) for the proposed model and then checking how much the *nonparametric* regression curve lies within the band. The wavelet probability band (WPB) is shown to provide a useful tool to measure the comparability between the patient's simulated and recorded profiles. Moreover, the density profile is then successfully used to define and compute two numerical measures, namely the average normalized wavelet density (ANWD) and relative average normalized wavelet density (RANWD) – both measures of agreement between the recorded infusion rate and simulated infusion rate. Our WPB method is shown to be a good tool for detecting regions where the simulated infusion rate (model) performs poorly, thus providing ways to help improve and distil the deterministic A-S model. The so-called Wavelet Time Coverage Index (WTCI) developed is analogous to the metrics based on a kernel based probability band of [13, 14]. The research in [29] and that formulated in this chapter have successfully developed novel quantitative measures based on wavelets for the analysis of A-S dynamics.

## 2. Density estimation using wavelet smoothing

In order to apply wavelets to various function estimation problems, it is useful to examine some of the existing techniques in use. This provides a useful lead in to a discussion of wavelet methods for (density) function estimation, since typical techniques can be modified in a straightforward manner for use in a wavelets approach and for a subsequent wavelets based analysis.

In exploratory data analysis it is important to have an idea of the shape of the data distribution, whereby interesting features become evident. For example, in describing the shape of the data, by a histogram, we easily obtain an overall feel for the data. Specialised versions of histograms that can be constructed using the Haar wavelet basis are now discussed in brief. Important theoretical properties of this estimator are discussed further in [37]. The Haar wavelet approach and histogram leads naturally to density estimators with smoother wavelet bases and lend themselves to histogram estimators, as we require.

Given the Haar scaling function, as on the left hand side of Equation (1), and then applying the usual dilation and translation gives,

$$\phi(t)=\begin{Bmatrix}1, \text{ if } 0\le t<1\\ 0, \text{otherwise}\end{Bmatrix}\Rightarrow \phi_{j,k}(t)=\begin{Bmatrix}2^{j/2}, 2^{-j}k\le t<2^{-j}(k+1)\\ 0, \quad \text{otherwise}\end{Bmatrix}. \tag{1}$$

We can then count the number of data points that lie within a particular interval, say, $[2^{-j}k, 2^{-j}(k+1))$ using the quantity $2^{-j/2}\sum_{i=1}^{n}\phi_{j,k}(t_i)$.

Now for any $t\in R$ and $j\in Z$,

$$2^{-j}\left[2^{j}t\right]\le t<2^{-j}\left(2^{j}t+1\right), \tag{2}$$

where $[t]$ denotes the greatest integer function of $t$, the number of data points that lie in the same interval as any real number $t$ can be computed by

$$2^{-j}\sum_{i=1}^{n}\phi_{j,\left[2^{j}t\right]}(t_i)=\sum_{i=1}^{n}\phi\left(2^{j}t_i-2^{j}t\right). \tag{3}$$

The histogram density estimator with origin 0 and bins of width $2^{-J}$ is given by

$$\tilde{f}_J(t)=\frac{1}{n}2^{J/2}\sum_{i=1}^{n}\phi_{J,\left[2^{J}t\right]}(t_i). \tag{4}$$

This estimator can be regarded as being the best estimator of the density $f$ on the approximation space $V_{J,}$ where $V_J$ is defined as length $N/2^J$ vector scaling coefficients associated with averages on a scale of length $2^J=2\lambda_{J.}$ Construction of histograms using the Haar basis, then leads to more general wavelet density estimators. The decomposition algorithm can be applied to Equation (1) and the resultant histogram can be written in terms of the Haar wavelets as follows:

$$\tilde{f}_J(x)=\sum_{k}\tilde{c}_{j_0,k}\Phi_{j_0,k}(x)+\sum_{j=j_0+1}^{J-1}\sum_{k}\tilde{d}_{j,k}\Psi_{j,k}(x). \tag{5}$$

The Haar-based histograms are given in Figure 2 (for level 1, 2, 3, and 4) for Patient 12 and Patient 18, with the simulated infusion rate (light) and the recorded infusion rate (dark) shown. Figure 2 shows a similar distribution between each patient's recorded and simulated infusion rates - skewed right for both patients (P12 and P18). Correspondingly Figure 3 presents the simulated data and recorded A-S data of Patient 2 and Patient 27. Each patient's simulated and recorded series are clearly from a differing distribution type to each other for these poor trackers (P2 and P27) (Figure 3). Figures 2-3 are clearly more informative than the histogram

http://dx.doi.org/10.5772/52434

where the former density estimates are based on the Haar wavelet basis. These graphical comparisons allow us to visualize differences in the distribution between the poor and good tracking patients in ICU.

Estimating density functions using smooth wavelets can be performed in the same way for any orthogonal series. This estimation procedure, which is a natural application of wavelets, results from a straightforward extension of the Haar-based histogram approach [30]. The same approach used to estimate a density in terms of the Haar basis above can thus also be used with smooth wavelet bases, as we now illustrate.

Let $\phi$ and $\psi$ be an orthogonal scaling function and mother wavelet pair that generates a series of approximating spaces $\{V_j\}_{j \in \mathbb{Z}}$, then $f(x)$, which is a square integrable density function, is

$$f(x) = \sum_k c_{j_0,k}\phi_{j_0,k}(x) + \sum_{j>j_0}\sum_k d_{j,k}\psi_{j,k}(x), \tag{6}$$

where $j_0$ represents a coarse level of approximation. Haar coefficients are estimated using

$$\hat{c}_{j,k} = \langle f^{\sim}, \phi_{j,k} \rangle = \frac{1}{n}\sum_{i=1}^{n}\phi_{j,k}(X_i) \tag{7}$$

$$\hat{d}_{j,k} = \langle f^{\sim}, \psi_{j,k} \rangle = \frac{1}{n}\sum_{i=1}^{n}\psi_{j,k}(X_i). \tag{8}$$

From Equations (7) and (8) above, the wavelet estimator for $f$ at level $J \geq j_0$ is given by

$$\begin{aligned} \hat{f}_J(x) &= \sum_k \hat{c}_{j_0,k}\phi_{j_0,k}(x) + \sum_{j>j_0}\sum_k \hat{d}_{j,k}\psi_{j,k}(x) \\ &= \sum_k \hat{c}_{J,k}\phi_{J,k}(x). \end{aligned} \tag{9}$$

The smoothing parameter in Equation (9) is the index $J$ of the highest level considered. Smooth wavelet-based density estimates are plotted in Figure 4 for levels 4, 6, and 8, using Patient 4's simulated infusion and recorded infusion rate data (via Daub (4) which denotes the Daubechies wavelet filter of length 4). We sampled 2048 (=$2^{10}$) data points without loss of any generality from the original data of Patient 4.

Figure 5 shows Patient 29's smooth wavelet-based density estimates (using Daub (4)). Figures 4 and 5 indicate that Patent 4 (P4) is potentially a poor tracker and Patient 29 (P29) a good tracker, given that the original and wavelet smooth densities are similar in P29, but not for P4. Note that when level $J$ is increased, abrupt jumps disappear but can also lead to over-smoothing and loss of information.

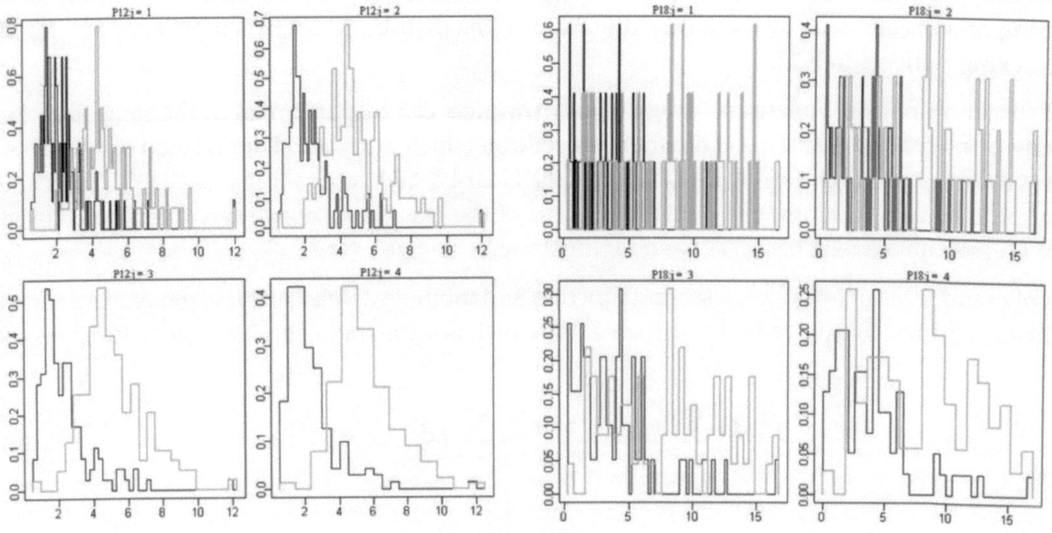


**Figure 2.** Haar-based histogram of the simulated series (light) and recorded empirical A-S series (dark) for varying resolution levels for two "good trackers": Patient 12 (left side, 4 plots) and Patient 18 (right side, 4 plots).

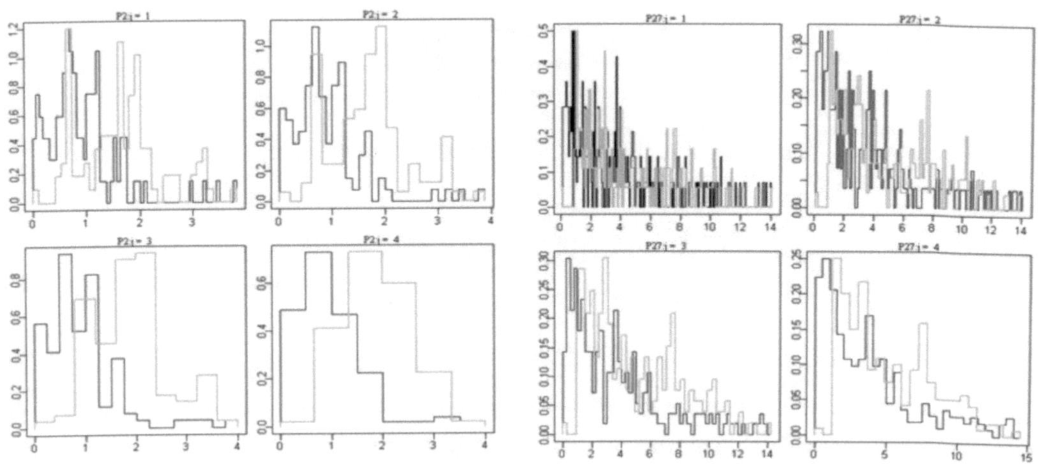


**Figure 3.** Haar-based histogram of the simulated series (light) and recorded series (dark) for varying resolution levels for two "poor trackers": Patients 27 (right side, 4 plots) and 2 (left side, 4 plots).

To quantify the relationship between the two variables $(x_i, y_i)$, we can employ the standard regression model as follows,

$$y_i = f(x_i) + \varepsilon_i,\ i = 1,\ldots,n, \tag{10}$$

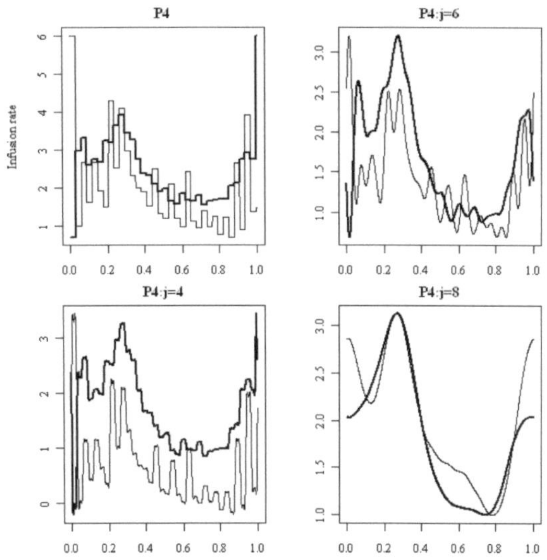


**Figure 4.** Smooth wavelet-based density estimates for P4's recorded data (light) and simulated data (dark) using the Daubechies wavelet (Daub4) with sub- sample N=2048 and for different choices of *J*.

where the $\varepsilon_i$'s are independent and identically distributed $N(0, \sigma^2)$ random variables. It will be assumed that the design points $(x_1, \ldots, x_n)$ are equally spaced, and, without further loss of generality, that they lie on the unit interval: $x_i = 1/n, \ i=1, \ldots, n$. Our approach constitutes projecting the raw estimator $f$ onto the approximating space $V_J$, for any choice of the smoothing parameter $J$, which represents a linear estimation approach. In contrast to this, the approach reference [38] offers a non-linear wavelet based approach to this problem of nonparametric regression. The approach in [38] begins with computing the DWT of the data $y_i$, by generating a new data set of empirical wavelet coefficients with which to represent the underlying regression function $f$.

The estimation procedure in [38] has three main steps as follows: First, transform the data $y_i$ to the wavelet domain by applying a DWT. If $d$ is the DWT of $f$, and $d' = [c'_{0,0}, d'_{0,0}, \ldots, d'_{J-1,2^J-1}]^T$ the vector of empirical coefficients, we then have a sequence of wavelet coefficients $d' = \mathrm{d} + \varepsilon'$, where $\varepsilon'$ is a vector of $n$ independent $N(0, \sigma^2)$. In the second step, the true coefficients $d$ are estimated by applying the thresholding rule to the empirical coefficients $d'$ to obtain estimates, $\tilde{d}$. Finally, the sampled function values $f$ are estimated by applying the inverse DWT (IDWT) to obtain $\tilde{f} = W^T \tilde{d}$, where $W^T$ is the transpose of an orthonormal $n \times n$ matrix. We can then represent the DWT as the sum

$$\tilde{f}(x) = \tilde{c}_{0,0}\phi(x) + \sum_{j=0}^{J} \sum_{k=0}^{2^j-1} \tilde{d}_{j,k}\psi_{j,k}(x) \tag{11}$$

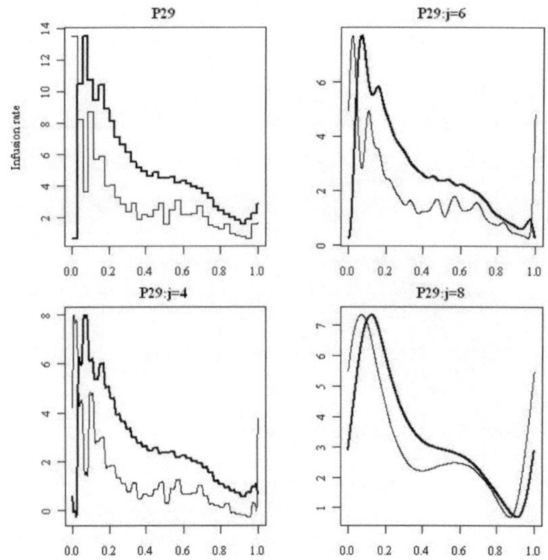


**Figure 5.** Smooth wavelet-based density estimates for P29's recorded (light) and simulated data (dark) using the Daubechies wavelet (Daub4) with N=2048 and for different choices of *J*.

This procedure, as formulated in [38], is schematised below:

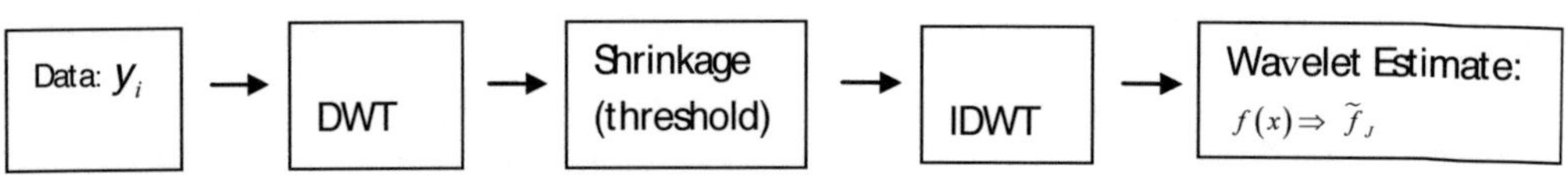


**Scheme 1.** Schema of DWT procedural steps.

A technique for selective wavelet reconstruction similar to this general approach was proposed in [39] in a study to remove random noise from magnetic resonance images. The technique is further developed from a statistical point of view in [38] by framing selective wavelet reconstruction as a problem in multivariate normal decision theory. From [38] estimating an unknown function involves including only coefficients larger than some specific threshold value. A large coefficient is taken to mean that it is large in absolute value. Choosing an excessively large threshold will make it difficult for a coefficient to be judged significant and be included in the reconstruction, resulting in over smoothing. On the other hand, a very small threshold allows many coefficients to be included in the reconstruction, resulting in undersmoothed estimates.

Two methods of global wavelet thresholding were proposed in [38], namely the universal threshold and the minimax threshold method. The wavelet assumption of a dyadic length of the time series is not always true. A natural approach would then be to pre-condition the original data set, so as to obtain a set of values of length $2^J$ for some positive integer $J$. The resulting pre-conditioned data is then plugged directly into any standard DWT. We observed that most of the 37 ICU patient data is not to the power of two. One obvious remedy was to pad the series with values and increase its length to the next power of two. There are several choices for the value of these padded coefficients. The approach adopted in this chapter was to pad with zeros so as to increase the size of the data set to the next larger power of two, or some other higher composite number, and then apply the DWT. The minimax estimator approach with soft thresholding, as applied to the simulated infusion profile of Patient 2, for example, yielded the profile in Figure 6.

## 3. New non Bayesian wavelet based metrics for tracking (WTCI, ANWD, RANWD)

Based on the development of density estimation via wavelet smoothing discussed in section 2, specifically equations (9) to (11), we now derive three new wavelet based, but non Bayesian metrics for tracking, namely the Wavelet Time Coverage Index (WTCI) (section 3.1), the Average Normalized Wavelet Density (ANWD) and the Relative Average Normalized Wavelet Density (RANWD) (section 3.2).

### 3.1. Numerical approach 1: Wavelet Time Coverage Index (WTCI)

The most commonly used criterion to obtain a successful wavelet estimator of the signal $\tilde{y}$ in estimating $y$ is the mean square error (MSE) [40]. In this chapter we devise a variant based on the development of the smoothed recorded infusion. This then lays the foundation for the development of our Wavelet Time Coverage Index (WTCI). The WTCI is a quantitative parameter indicating how well the patient's simulated infusion represents their average recorded infusion profile over the entire time series. Our approach uses wavelet coefficients on a scale by scale basis.

The WTCI is defined as follows:

$$\mathrm{WTCI} = \left\{ 1 - \frac{\sum_{j,k} \left| \tilde{d}_{j,k} - d_{j,k} \right|}{\sum_{j,k} \tilde{d}_{j,k}} \right\} \times 100 \tag{12}$$

where $\tilde{d}_{j,k}$ is given in Equation (11) and $d_{j,k}$ is the DWT of $f$ in Equation (10). A WTCI of 100% represents perfect tracking, which arises when the DE simulated infusion profile is identical to that of the wavelet smoothed infusion profile.

Figure 7 presents the box and whisker plot for values of the WTCI from bootstrap [56] realizations (per patient). Each box and whisker [57] in Figure 7 displays two main components of information. First, the median represents a measure of how well the agitation-sedation simulation models the recorded infusion profile on average. Second, the spread of the box and whisper provides an indication of how reliable that particular WTCI median is per patient. Further details regarding interpretation of the WTCI are given in section 5.1.

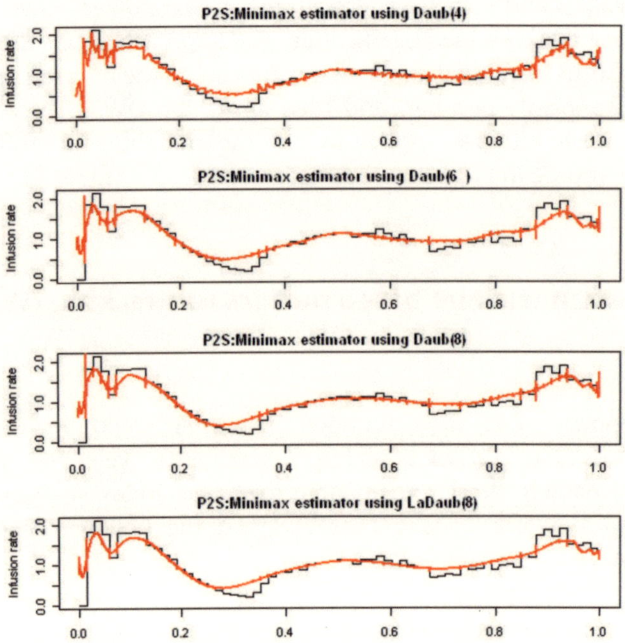


**Figure 6.** Minimax estimator applied to Patient 2's simulated profile. The thick line represents the wavelet threshold estimator of the simulated infusion rate and the thin line that of the recorded infusion data. A soft thresholding rule was used to obtain all estimates.

## 3.2. Numerical approach 2: Average Normalized Wavelet Density (ANWD) and the Relative Average Normalized Wavelet Density (RANWD)

We now propose wavelet analogues of the AND and RAND diagnostics developed in [12] and [13]. The density profile is used to compute the numerical measures of ANWD and RANWD, so that objective comparisons of model performance can be made across different patients. The ANWD value for the simulated infusion rates is the average of these normalized density values over all time points for a given patient. Similarly, the RANWD value for the smoothed infusion rate is obtained by superimposing the smoothed values by using the first cumulant from a normal posterior distribution onto the same density profile, after which RANWD can be readily computed.

Let $y_t = \{y_1, y_2, \ldots, y_n\}$ be the output data produced by a proposed model. These are often called the simulated data. Define the average normalized wavelet density (ANWD) of $y_t$ as

$$\mathrm{ANWD}\left(y_t\right) = \frac{1}{n}\sum_{t=1}^{n}\frac{\tilde{f}_t\left(y_t\right)}{\max\left(\tilde{f}_t\right)} \tag{13}$$

where $\max(\tilde{f}_t)$denotes the maximum value of the wavelet density function $\tilde{f}_t$, which is estimated by wavelet smoothing via Equation (9) at time $t$. Thus, ANWD is an average of

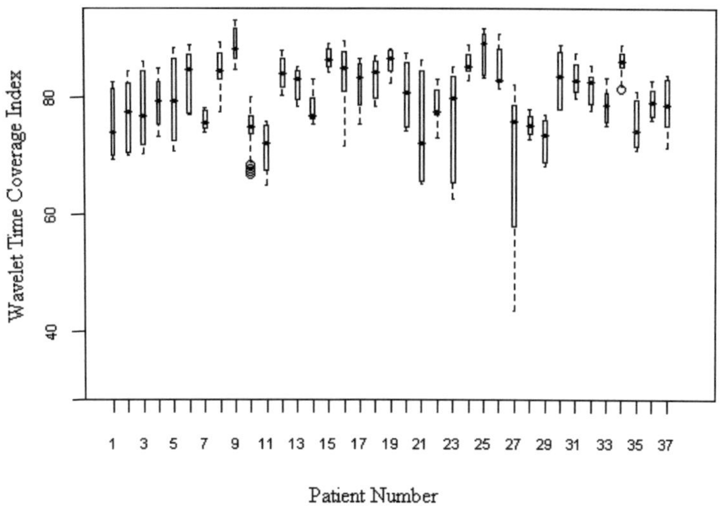


**Figure 7.** Box and whisker plot of the WTCI index for each of the 37 patients.

normalized densities, where each component in the sum is the value of $\tilde{f}_t$ at $y_t$ normalized by $\max(\tilde{f}_t)$. At time $t$ the normalized wavelet density equals 1 when $X_t$ coincides with the point where $\tilde{f}_t$ is maximum. An infusion profile that coincides with the maximum wavelet density at every time point would therefore have ANWD equal to 1. Whereas the value of ANWD for an infusion profile distant from the high-density regions would approach 0. Finally, ANWD $(y)$ is calibrated using the ANWD from the wavelet smoothed recorded infusion data, denoted by $\tilde{y}$ giving the relative average normalized wavelet density (RANWD):

$$\mathrm{RANWD} = \frac{\mathrm{ANWD}(y)}{\mathrm{ANWD}(\tilde{y})} \tag{14}$$

RANWD indicates the value of ANWD $(y)$ relative to a typical realisation in the form of $\tilde{y}$ from the density profile. Therefore, the RANWD statistic estimates how *probabilistically* alike the model outputs are to the smoothed data, and hence the degree of comparability between the model (simulated) and the actual (recorded) data. A RANWD of 0.6 implies that the model outputs are 60% similar, on average, to the wavelet smoothed data. Greater similarity means higher values of RANWD for the given patient under investigation.

## 4. Wavelet thresholding via Bayesian methods

Bayesian wavelet shrinkage methods are discussed in section 4.1, and are subsequently used to develop a novel 90% wavelet probability band (WPB 90%) per patient (section 4.2). A 90% wavelet probability band is constructed for each of the 37 patient profiles, and the time and duration of any deviations from the wavelet probability band is recorded. A WPB 90% value of 70% implies that for at least 70% (time under ICU observation), the estimated mean value of the recorded infusion rate, for a given patient, lies within the 90% confidence interval of its wavelet probability band. For illustration, we refer the reader to Figure 8 which shows the WPB 90% curves for 4 patients: two good trackers (Patients 8 and 25) and two poor trackers (Patients 9 and 34).

### 4.1. Brief mathematical background

Recall the regression equation (Equation (10)) for an observed data vector $y_1, y_{2,...,}y_n$ satisfying

$$y_i = f(x_i) + \varepsilon_i, \qquad i = 1, ..., n,$$

where the $\varepsilon_i$'s are independent and identically distributed $N(0, \sigma^2)$ random variables, assuming that $(x_1, ..., x_n)$ are fixed points.

We now consider a method to approximate the posterior distribution of each $f(x_i)$, using the same prior utilised by the BayesThresh method of [41] and [42]. Posterior probability intervals of any nominal coverage probability can be calculated accordingly. For Haar wavelets, the scaling function and mother wavelet are $\phi(t) = I(0 \le t < 1)$ and $\psi(t) = I(0 \le t < 1/2) - I(1/2 \le t < 1)$, respectively, where $I(\cdot)$ is the indicator function. Clearly the square of the Haar wavelet is just the Haar scaling function, $\psi_{j,k}^2(t) = 2^{j/2}\phi_{j,k}(t)$, $\psi_{j,k}^3(t) = 2^j\psi_{j,k}(t)$; $\psi^3(t) = \psi(t)$ and $\psi^2(t) = \psi^4(t) = \phi(t)$ and $\psi_{j,k}^4(t) = 2^{3j/2}\phi_{j,k}(t)$. All these terms can be included in a modified version of the IDWT algorithm which incorporates scaling function coefficients. By the development in [43] we approximate a general wavelet $\psi_{j_0,0}^r$, $(0 \le j_0 \le J - m)$, by

$$\psi_{j_0,0}^r \sim \sum_t e_{j_0-m,l}\phi_{j_0-m,l}(t) \tag{15}$$

for $r = 2, 3, 4$, where $m$ is a positive integer. The choice of $m$ follows below, since scaling functions (instead of wavelets), as the span of the set of scaling functions at a given level $j$, are the same as that of the sum of $\phi(t)$ and the wavelets at levels 0, 1,..., $j$-1. Moreover, if scaling functions $\phi_{j,k}(t)$are used to approximate some function $h(t)$, and both $\phi$ and $h$ have at least ν derivatives, then the mean squared error in the approximation is bounded by $C2^{-\nu j}$, where $C$ is some positive constant, (see, for example reference [44]).

To approximate $\psi_{j_0,k}^r(t)$ for some fixed $j_0$, we simply compute $y_{j_0,0}^r(t)$ using the pyramid algorithm [45], then take the DWT and set the coefficients $e_{m_0,l}$ to be equal to the scaling function coefficients $e_{m_0,k}$ at level $m_0$, where $m_0 = j_0 + m$. Recall that the wavelets at level $j$ are simply shifts of each other $y_{j,k}(t) = y_{j,0}(t - 2^{-j}k)$, hence

$$y^r_{j_0,k}(t)\ y^r_{j_0,0} \approx \sum_t e_{m_0,l-2^m k} \phi_{m_0,l}(t) \tag{16}$$

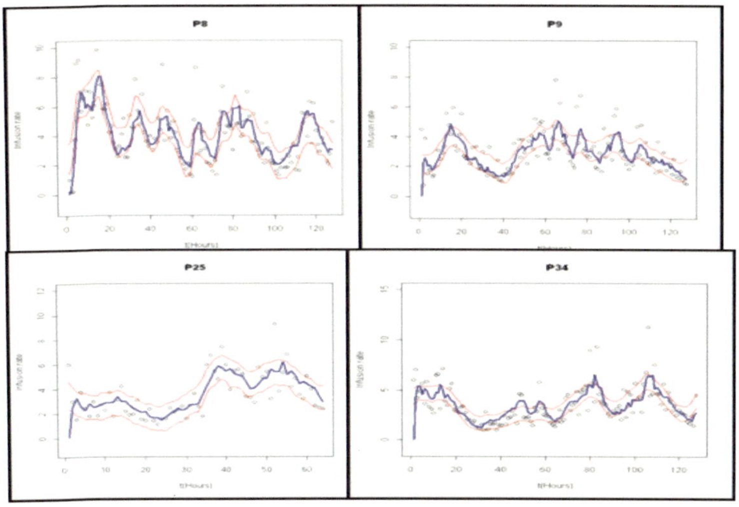

**Figure 8.** Wavelet Probability Bands (WPB 90%'s) (thin lines) with simulated infusion profile (thick line) for Patients 8, 25 (P8, P25: good trackers, LHS) and Patients 9, 34 (P9, P34: poor trackers, RHS).

As we are assuming periodic boundary conditions, the $e_{m_0,l}$ can be cycled periodically. Given the localised nature of wavelets, the coefficients $e_{m_0+1,l}$ employed to approximate $\psi^r_{j_0-1,0}(t)$ can be found by inserting $2^{m_0}$ zeros into the vector of $e_{m_0,l}$

$$e_{m+1,l} = \begin{cases} \sqrt{2}e_{m_0,l} & l = 0,...2^{m_0-1}-1 \\ 0 & l = 2^{m_0-1},...,2^{m_0+1}-2^{m_0-1}-1 \\ \sqrt{2}e_{m_0,l-2^{m_0}} & l = 2^{m_0+1}-2^{m_0-1},...,2^{m_0-1}-1 \end{cases} \tag{17}$$

The approximation in Equation (15) cannot be employed for wavelets at the $m$ finest levels $J-m$, ..., $J-1$. These wavelets are however, written in terms of both scaling functions and wavelets at the finest level of detail, level $J$-1, via the block-shifting method as delineated above.

From Equation (11) we have that $[f_i \mid y]$ is the convolution of the posteriors of the wavelet coefficients and the scaling coefficient given by,

$$[f \mid y] = \left[c_{0,0} \mid c''_{0,0}\right]\phi(t_i) + \sum_j \sum_k \left[d_{j,k} \mid d''_{j,k}\right] \psi_{j,k}(t_i). \tag{18}$$

If $X$ and $Y$ are independent random variables and $a$ and $b$ are real constants, then

$$\kappa_r(aX+b)=\begin{cases} a\kappa_1(X)+b, & r=1 \\ a^r\kappa_r(X), & r=2,3,\cdots \end{cases} \tag{19}$$

and we have by the additivity property

$$\kappa_r(X+Y)=\kappa_r(X)+\kappa_r(Y),\ r\in\mathbb{Z} \tag{20}$$

for all $r$. Applying Equations (19) and (20) to Equation (17) shows $[f_i \mid y]$ (where $f_i=f(x_i)$) can be estimated from its cumulants as

$$\kappa_r(f_i \mid y)=\kappa_r\left(c_{0,0} \mid c''_{0,0}\right)\phi^r_{j,k}(t_i)+\sum_j\sum_k\kappa_r\left(d_{j,k} \mid d''_{j,k}\right)\psi^r_{j,k}(t_i). \tag{21}$$

The first cumulant $\kappa_1(y)$, is the mean of $y$, the second cumulant, $\kappa_2(y)$, is the variance of $y$, $\kappa_3(y)/\kappa_2^{3/2}(y)$ is the skewness, and $\kappa_4(y)/\kappa_2^2(y)+3$ is the kurtosis. Note that the third cumulant $\kappa_3(y)$ and the fourth cumulant $\kappa_4(y)$ are zero if $y$ is Gaussian. From Equations (16) and (21), we can now re-write the fourth cumulant as follows,

$$\begin{aligned}\kappa_r(f_i \mid y)&=\kappa_r\left(c_{0,0} \mid c^*_{0,0}\right)\phi^r_{j,k}(t_i)+\sum_j\sum_k\kappa_r\left(d_{j,k} \mid d^*_{j,k}\right)\psi^r_{j,k}(t_i)\\ &=\kappa_r\left(c_{0,0} \mid c^*_{0,0}\right)\phi^r_{j,k}(t_i)+\sum_{j,k}\left\{\kappa_r\left(d_{j,k} \mid d^*_{j,k}\right)\sum_l e_{j-3,l}\phi_{j-3,l}(t_i)\right\},\\ &=\sum_{j,k}\rho_{j,k}\phi_{j,k}(t_i)\end{aligned} \tag{22}$$

for $\kappa_r(y)$ the $r^{th}$ cumulant of $y$, and for suitable coefficients, $\rho_{j,k}$ acquired via the IDWT algorithm which incorporates scaling function coefficients to assess this sum [41, 42, 46]. Bayesian wavelet regression estimates have thus been developed including priors on the wavelet coefficients $d_{j,k}$, which are updated by the observed coefficients $d''_{j,k}$ to obtain posterior distributions $[d_{j,k} \mid {}_{j,k}]$ (refer to Equation (18)). The $\tilde{d}_{j,k}$ (point estimates) can then be computed from such posterior distributions and the Inverse Discrete Wavelet Transform (IDWT) used to estimate $f(x_i)$.

The Bayesian wavelet shrinkage rules discussed in this section have used mixture distributions as priors on the coefficients to model a small proportion of the coefficients which contain substantial signal [41]. Indeed the BayesThresh method of [41] assumes independent priors on the coefficients,

$$d_{j,k} \sim \gamma_j N\left(0, \tau_j^2\right) + \left(1 - \gamma_j\right)\delta\left(0\right),\ j = 0, \ldots, J - 1;\ k = 0, \ldots, 2^j - 1, \tag{23}$$

where $0 \le \gamma_j \le 1.0$, $\delta(0)$ is a point mass at zero and $d_{j,k}$ are independent. The hyper-parameters are assumed to be of the form $\tau_j^2 = C_1 2^{-\alpha j}$, $\gamma_j = \min\left(1, C_2 2^{-\beta j}\right)$ for non-negative constants $C_1$ and $C_2$ chosen empirically from the data and the $\alpha$ and $\beta$'s are selected by the user. The choice of $\alpha$ and $\beta$ corresponds to choosing priors in certain Besov spaces [41] and incorporating prior knowledge about the smoothness of $f(x_i)$ into the prior. See reference [55].

### 4.2. New Bayesian 90% wavelet probability band metric for tracking (WPB 90%)

Bayesian wavelet shrinkage methods as discussed in section 4.1 can be used to create a wavelet probability band (WPB). A 90% wavelet probability band (WPB 90%) is constructed for each of the 37 patient profiles, and the time and duration of any significant deviations from the wavelet probability band is recorded. A WPB 90% value of 70% implies that for at least 70% of the time (of the time in ICU observation), the estimated mean value of the recorded infusion rate for a given patient lies within its 90% confidence interval of its wavelet probability band. Figure 8 shows the WPB for 4 patients: two good trackers (Patients 8 and 25) and two poor trackers (Patients 9 and 34). The circle symbol represents the hourly recorded infusion rate, the thin line represents the 90% WPB curve and the solid thick line represents the simulated profile (Figure 8). Brief spikes which may occur in the WPB bands are typical of wavelet regression methods. These spikes can be smoothed out by using different values for $\alpha$ and $\beta$, but this risks over-smoothing the data due to loss of information. According to [41], setting $\alpha$=0.5 and $\beta$=1 is the best practical approach for Bayesian smoothing. Therefore we set $\alpha$=0.5 and $\beta$=1 and employ Daubeches' least asymmetric wavelet with eight vanishing moments, namely LaDaub (8), as this is a widely used wavelet and is applicable to a broad variety of data types.

While our WPB approach is graphically very useful (Figure 8), it is however useful to marry this with an objective numerical measure of *how close* the simulated infusion profile is to the empirical, recorded data. The percentage WPB cannot serve this purpose of objective quantification, because it quantifies visual proximity, by means of artificial hard boundaries, and ignores the fact that the in-band region does not have the same probabilistic significance everywhere. Thus wavelet density numerical metrics, namely ANWD and RANWD, comparing the model outputs to the recorded data were also developed using the posterior densities determined from the smoothed recorded data. The density profile is considered to be informative as unlike the wavelet probability band (WPB) it does discriminate between regions of high or low probability within a band.

## 5. WTCI based results

### 5.1. Choice of Wavelet filter and Bootstrap: WTCI

In order to judge the reliability of the wavelet time coverage index (WTCI) for a given patient's infusion profile, the moving blocks bootstrap was utilized [56]. A total of 1000 bootstrap realizations were generated for each patient's recorded infusion profiles. A wavelet time coverage index (WTCI), as defined in Equation (12), can then be evaluated for each bootstrap realization, providing a collection of 1000 values of the WTCI. The median WTCI and its standard error, SE, can then be reported for each patient using [57] (see Table 1, where a bold Patient no. indicates a poor tracker by the DWT, WCORR and WCCORR diagnostics in [29]). When the DWT is implemented via the pyramid algorithm [58], an important feature when analysing a given time, is the need to choose the appropriate wavelet filter (basis). The choice of a wavelet basis function is crucial for two reasons. First, the length of a DWT determines how well it approximates an ideal band-pass filter, which in turn dictates how well the filter is able to isolate features to specific frequency intervals. Secondly, as illustrated in the MODWT MRAs shown in [29], the wavelet basis function is being used to represent information contained in the time series of interest and should thus imitate its underlying features. A reasonable overall strategy is to use the shortest width of wavelet filters $L$= 4, 8 and longer wavelet filters $L$ = 10, 12, as both choices give reasonable results in this ICU A-S application.

| Patient no. | Data size (Min) | Median WTCI | SE |
|---|---|---|---|
| 1 | 3601 | 78.55 | 0.538 |
| **2** | **6421** | **87.14** | **0.294** |
| 3 | 6541 | 87.85 | 0.106 |
| **4** | **4921** | **87.94** | **0.076** |
| 5 | 2941 | 88.89 | 0.103 |
| 6 | 5701 | 88.73 | 0.104 |
| **7** | **3901** | **84.78** | **0.324** |
| 8 | 10561 | 93.61 | 0.037 |
| **9** | **8581** | **93.28** | **0.046** |
| **10** | **20701** | **88.46** | **0.053** |
| **11** | **6721** | **92.46** | **0.085** |
| 12 | 8521 | 91.15 | 0.323 |
| 13 | 5161 | 91.37 | 0.091 |
| 14 | 3001 | 82.09 | 0.449 |
| 15 | 4981 | 92.09 | 0.072 |
| 16 | 13621 | 94.57 | 0.073 |
| 17 | 5941 | 90.27 | 0.086 |
| 18 | 4681 | 93.83 | 0.036 |
| 19 | 7921 | 96.34 | 0.012 |

| Patient no. | Data size (Min) | Median WTCI | SE |
|---|---|---|---|
| 20 | 9661 | 90.49 | 0.088 |
| **21** | **3721** | **83.07** | **0.685** |
| **22** | **9661** | **91.85** | **0.056** |
| 23 | 3481 | 85.07 | 0.300 |
| 24 | 8461 | 92.41 | 0.058 |
| 25 | 3841 | 93.44 | 0.082 |
| 26 | 3901 | 85.49 | 0.275 |
| **27** | **13441** | **93.66** | **0.039** |
| **28** | **12241** | **89.47** | **0.051** |
| **29** | **3241** | **89.3** | **0.262** |
| 30 | 3661 | 85.81 | 0.092 |
| 31 | 18301 | 94.34 | 0.022 |
| **32** | **15181** | **95.82** | **0.020** |
| **33** | **25261** | **95.63** | **0.036** |
| **34** | **8101** | **93.77** | **0.070** |
| **35** | **12721** | **87.64** | **0.018** |
| 36 | 3481 | 92.17 | 0.059 |
| 37 | 7501 | 90.79 | 0.079 |
| **Median** | | **90.790** | **0.079** |
| 95%CI | | (88.75, 92.39) | (0.058, 0.092) |

**Table 1.** Wavelet Time Coverage Index (WTCI) per patient. Data size (column 2) indicates the length of the patient's A-S series. A bolded /shaded Patient indicates a poor tracker by the criteria in [29].

Table 1 presents the data size (time series length) and median bootstrapped WTCI and its standard error (SE) for each of the 37 patients studied. The poor trackers, as classified by the criteria in [29], are bolded in the first column. From Table 1, we note that some poor trackers (Patients 9, 11, 22, 27, 32, 34) have relatively high values of median WTCI and some good trackers (Patients 1, 14) have a low WTCI. The reason for this is padding, used as a reasonable solution to produce data of the size power of two, but this dilutes the signal near the end of the original data set, since the filters are not applied evenly. Hence multiplying by a signal element, constrained to have magnitude zero, is equivalent to omitting the filter coefficient, and then the orthogonality of the transform is not strictly maintained. To overcome this problem we change the current *minutes driven length* of the A-S data set to an hourly meta-meter, and then apply Bayesian wavelet shrinkage using a universal threshold as developed in section 5.2.

## 5.2. Alternative WTCI measure via Bayesian Wavelet Thresholding

In Section 5.1 the minimax estimator [59] was used to obtain patient specific WTCI measures (see also section 4.1). In this section we calculate an alternative WTCI using Bayesian wavelet thresholding [53, 44, 50, 41, 42]. Table 2 reports the WTCI measures, which are obtained by employing a Bayesian wavelet thresholding as computed by the WaveThresh software package in R [42] (adopting a LaDaub (8) filter).

The relative total dose, defined as the total drug dose delivered by the simulation (as a percentage of the total recorded drug dose) is also presented for each patient in Table 2. From Table 2 high values of median WTCI clearly indicate the validity of the A-S simulation for a given patient. The median WTCI value (across all patients) is 79.8% with a 95% interpolated confidence interval (CI) of (77.57%, 83.23%) and a range [71.9% to 88.9%]. This indicates some significant merit of the mathematical model of [14] and its physiological validity (Table 2).

Furthermore, the overall patient median relative total dose is 89.1% with a range [77.0% to 95.0%] indicating that the simulated and recorded total drug doses are similar, with the simulator consistently administering slightly less than 100% of the recorded actual sedative dose (Table 2). Slightly decreased levels as such are linked with the sudden-response nature of the recorded infusion profiles, in contrast to the consistent, smooth quality of the simulated infusion. These features are chiefly the result of the consistency of the computer implemented simulation in contrast to the inherent variation between different nurses' assessment of patient agitation and appropriate feedback of sedation [14, 11, 12, 13].

Overall from Table 2 the values of the WTCI from the bootstrap realizations (per patient) have high median WTCI and a low spread per patient, indicating high reliability of the median WTCI and in turn of the A-S simulation. Larger spread indicates poor reliability, which may be caused by insufficient data, and also by the choice of wavelet filters, the chosen thresholding method, or by the model simulation method itself.

| Patient no. | Median WTCI | SE | Relative total Dose (%) |
|---|---|---|---|
| 1 | 74.0 | 0.378 | 87.8 |
| **2** | **77.4** | **0.461** | **85.9** |
| 3 | 76.6 | 0.264 | 86.1 |
| **4** | **79.2** | **0.650** | **86.6** |
| 5 | 79.3 | 0.324 | 90.3 |
| 6 | 84.6 | 0.697 | 87.5 |
| **7** | **75.5** | **0.083** | **81.0** |
| 8 | 84.3 | 0.381 | 92.1 |
| **9** | **88.1** | **0.359** | **89.1** |
| **10** | **74.9** | **0.175** | **90.2** |

http://dx.doi.org/10.5772/52434

| Patient no. | Median WTCI | SE | Relative total Dose (%) |
|---|---|---|---|
| **11** | **72.0** | **0.395** | **87.8** |
| 12 | 83.8 | 0.261 | 86.5 |
| 13 | 82.8 | 0.166 | 90.2 |
| 14 | 76.6 | 0.248 | 88.5 |
| 15 | 86.3 | 0.145 | 90.7 |
| 16 | 84.8 | 0.431 | 90.4 |
| 17 | 83.3 | 0.430 | 85.2 |
| 18 | 84.2 | 0.161 | 95.0 |
| 19 | 86.5 | 0.341 | 91.0 |
| 20 | 80.5 | 0.303 | 90.4 |
| **21** | **72.1** | **0.498** | **87.8** |
| **22** | **77.5** | **0.171** | **89.5** |
| 23 | 79.8 | 0.673 | 91.7 |
| 24 | 85.1 | 0.127 | 89.9 |
| 25 | 88.9 | 0.075 | 91.2 |
| 26 | 82.8 | 0.061 | 88.5 |
| **27** | **75.7** | **0.663** | **87.5** |
| **28** | **75.0** | **0.202** | **90.6** |
| **29** | **73.4** | **0.442** | **77.0** |
| 30 | 83.3 | 0.224 | 94.5 |
| 31 | 82.6 | 0.146 | 90.0 |
| **32** | **82.6** | **0.271** | **91.2** |
| **33** | **78.5** | **0.430** | **90.4** |
| **34** | **85.9** | **0.193** | **89.0** |
| **35** | **74.1** | **0.361** | **88.1** |
| 36 | 79.1 | 0.293 | 81.6 |
| 37 | 78.6 | 0.283 | 88.9 |
| $75^{th}$ percentile | 84.3 | 0.43 | 90.4 |
| **Median** | **79.8** | **0.293** | **89.1** |
| 95% CI: Median | (77.57, 83.23) | | |
| $25^{th}$ percentile | 76.14 | 0.173 | 87.5 |

**Table 2.** Alternative Wavelet Time Coverage Index (WTCI) summary for the 37 patients. A bolded/shaded patient indicates a poor tracker by the DWT WCORR and WCCORR threshold criteria in [29].

## 6. Bayesian WPB results

### 6.1. Wavelet probability band metric for tracking (WPB 90%)

Table 3 presents the time per patient that the simulated infusion rate lies within the 90% wavelet probability band (WPB 90%). Generally high values of WPB 90% are evident across most of the 37 patients (second column of Table 3). With the exception of thirteen (13) patients (Patients 2, 4, 7, 9, 10, 11, 21, 22, 27, 28, 32, 33, 34), all simulated infusion profiles lie within the wavelet probability band at least 75% of the time. These 13 patients were also all deemed to be "poor trackers" according to the WCORR and WCCORR diagnostics developed in [29]. The main reason for the reduced total time within the WPB for these 13 poor trackers seems to be their poor performance throughout the total length of the patient's simulation. This feature is observed in Figure 8 for patient 9 and for patient 34, and indicates that the simulated infusion profile deviates from the recorded profile over some particular period, and takes some time before tending towards the recorded infusion rate again (see Patients 9 and 34 in Figure 8).

### 6.2. Comparison of WPB 90% with WTCI measures

Patients 25 and 34 will now be used to illustrate some of the concepts linking and differentiating the different wavelet measures in Table 2 and Table 3. Note that Patient 25 has the maximum WTCI of 88.9% with a high value of relative total dose of 91.2% (Table 2), and patient 25 exhibits low spread in the bootstrapped realization in Figure 7. Table 3 similarly shows that Patient 25's simulated infusion rate lies within the 90% WPB for 89.06% of the time, indicative of good performance (or tracking), as is evident in the WPB plot (Figure 8). By contrast, Patient 34 has a high WTCI of 85.9%, a relative total dose of 89.0% (Table 2), and exhibits low spread in the bootstrapped realizations, but by contrast Patient 34 has a very low WPB 90% value of 48.44% (Table 3 and Figure 8).

Recall from [29] that Patient 25 is deemed to be a good tracker and Patient 34 a poor tracker by earlier DWT WCORR criteria. Hence whilst the WTCI values of Patient 25 and Patient 34 are both high, 88.9% and 85.9%, respectively; it is only the WPB 90% measure, and not the WTCI measure, that distinguishes between the tracking performance of Patient 25 (WPB 90% = 89.06%) and Patient 34 (WPB 90% = 48.44%). Patient 34's simulation infusion rate is outside the WPB band for 51.56% of the time indicating that a large maximum departure time between the patient's recorded and simulated infusion rate occurs in the ICU observation period (see [29]).

### 6.3. Comparison of WPB 90% with ANWD and RANWD measures

The higher the percentage that the simulated infusion profile lies within the wavelet probability band, for a given patient, the better the simulation model captures the specific dynamics of the agitation-sedation system for that patient. Patient-specific WPB 90% values are reported in Table 3. Columns 3 and 4 in Table 3 present the two novel and alternative performance measures of ANWD and RANWD per patient. Recall that the posterior distribution of the regression curve is used as the density for all patients as described in reference [14]. RANWD thus measures how *probabilistically similar* the model outputs are to the smoothed observed data, and hence is a measure of the degree of comparability between the simulated and the empirical A-S data. The density profile is used to compute the numerical measures of ANWD and RANWD, so that objective comparisons of model performance can be made across different patients. The ANWD value for the simulated infusion rates is the average of these normalized density values over all time points for a given patient. Similarly, the RANWD value for the smoothed infusion rate is obtained by superimposing the smoothed values by using the first cumulant from a normal posterior distribution onto the same density profile, after which RANWD can be readily computed.

| Patient no. | WPB 90% | ANWD | RANWD |
|---|---|---|---|
| 1 | 95.31 | 0.537 | 0.553 |
| **2** | **64.06** | **0.431** | **0.499** |
| 3 | 96.88 | 0.632 | 0.737 |
| **4** | **59.38** | **0.338** | **0.475** |
| 5 | 93.75 | 0.495 | 0.504 |
| 6 | 95.31 | 0.659 | 0.980 |
| **7** | **67.19** | **0.417** | **0.455** |
| 8 | 87.50 | 0.567 | 0.688 |
| **9** | **57.81** | **0.343** | **0.412** |
| **10** | **66.80** | **0.300** | **0.388** |
| **11** | **74.34** | **0.423** | **0.434** |
| 12 | 84.38 | 0.622 | 0.662 |
| 13 | 73.44 | 0.442 | 0.504 |
| 14 | 96.88 | 0.449 | 0.476 |
| 15 | 89.06 | 0.702 | 0.761 |
| 16 | 82.81 | 0.596 | 0.770 |
| 17 | 85.94 | 0.506 | 0.566 |
| 18 | 93.75 | 0.548 | 0.558 |
| 19 | 74.22 | 0.759 | 0.780 |
| 20 | 96.88 | 0.487 | 0.581 |
| **21** | **65.62** | **0.407** | **0.413** |
| **22** | **65.62** | **0.422** | **0.455** |
| 23 | 92.19 | 0.288 | 0.341 |
| 24 | 71.00 | 0.655 | 0.635 |

| Patient no. | WPB 90% | ANWD | RANWD |
|---|---|---|---|
| 25 | 89.06 | 0.635 | 0.670 |
| 26 | 96.88 | 0.600 | 0.601 |
| **27** | **47.27** | **0.368** | **0.608** |
| **28** | **50.78** | **0.501** | **0.540** |
| 29 | 82.81 | 0.343 | 0.394 |
| 30 | 96.88 | 0.554 | 0.597 |
| 31 | 87.50 | 0.562 | 0.669 |
| **32** | **68.36** | **0.326** | **0.362** |
| **33** | **58.79** | **0.373** | **0.499** |
| **34** | **48.44** | **0.505** | **0.551** |
| 35 | 96.10 | 0.371 | 0.533 |
| 36 | 75.00 | 0.573 | 0.763 |
| 37 | 79.69 | 0.448 | 0.607 |
| Min | 47.27 | 0.288 | 0.341 |
| **Median** | **82.81** | **0.495** | **0.552** |
| Max | 96.88 | 0.759 | 0.981 |

**Table 3.** Wavelet probability band (WPB 90%), ANWD and RANWD measures per patient. A bold patient no. indicates a poor tracker by the RANWD and WPB criteria (developed in section 6.4). (The 13 poor trackers are P2, P4, P7, P9, P10, P11, P21, P22, P27, P28, P32, P33 and P34).

An overall median RANWD of 0.552 (Table 3) with range [0.341 to 0.981] is an objective measure that supports the WPB 90% measures and visual clue of closeness based on the WPB (see Figure 8). It should be noted that as the model is deterministic, its outputs do not belong to the same probabilistic mechanism that generated the data, hence RANWD is an extremely stringent measure.

### 6.4. WPB 90% and RANWD criteria for poor tracking

Given the conservative nature of the RANWD metric, consistently high RANWD values close to 1.00 are not expected, even for a good simulation model. A reasonable and practical threshold for adequate model performance is RANWD ≥ 0.5, which suggests that the model outputs are more alike than not to the smoothed data. Justification for our 0.5 threshold for RANWD is given in this section, as is a threshold for WPB 90%. Poor trackers according to the metrics developed in this chapter are assumed to satisfy the following:

RANWD≤0.5 and/or a WPB 90% ≤70%.

Thirteen (13) patients have a low RANWD (deemed below the threshold, RANWD ≤ 0.50), namely Patients 2, 4, 7, 9, 10, 11, 14, 21, 22, 23, 29, 32 and 33 (Table 4). Specifically 9 of these patients have RANWD values from 0.412 to 0.499, and 4 have RANWD values between 0.341 and 0.394. Furthermore 11 patients have a WPB 90% value less or equal to 70% (Patients 2, 4, 7, 9, 10, 11, 27, 28, 32, 33, 34). Whilst Patients 14 and 23 have low RANWD values they exhibit very high WPB 90% (> 92%) values (like P29) (Table 3). Note that these 3 patients (P14, P23, P29) were also classified as good trackers according to the criteria developed earlier in [13], [14] and [29]; and as such, given their high WPB 90%, values, will be classified as good trackers in this chapter. Clearly the WBP 90% measure can help find patients (good trackers, say) who have elevated percentage time in the WPB ( (range 83% - 97%) for these 3 patients (P14, P23, P29) even though they exhibit relatively low RANWD values (range 0.34-0.47) (see column 3 Table 6).

Thirteen patients which satisfy our criterion for poor tracking (RANWD ≤ 0.5, and/or a WPB 90% ≤ 70%) are P2, P4, P7, P9, P10, P11, P21, P22, P27, P28, P32, P33 and P34 - all of whom, were also identified as poor trackers by the WCORR and WCCORR DWT diagnostics of [29]. Of these 13 poor trackers 8 have both lower than threshold WPB 90% and low RANWD, 3 exhibit low WPB 90% but above threshold RANWD > 0.5, and 2 exhibit low RANWD but above threshold WPB 90% (see Table 6). This indicates a significant and high agreement between the WPB and the RANWD (dichotomized) criteria (*kappa* = 0.6679); P (estimated *kappa* ≤ 0.40) = 0.025).

The resultant, RANWD and WPB 90% thresholds also provide very strong support for the DWT wavelet diagnostics derived in reference [29], in that of the 15 DWT based poor trackers identified in [29] (see Table 6), 13 of these also exhibit a low WPB (WPB 90% < 70%) and/or a low wavelet density based RANWD (RANWD ≤ 0.5). Statistically speaking the wavelet probability band and density diagnostics developed in this chapter mirror the DWT based poor versus good classification of [29] (*kappa* = 0.87, *p* = 0.0001).

Our 13 poor trackers have WPB and density profiles (not all reported here) which have specific regions where the patient's DE model did not appear to capture the observed A-S dynamics. In some scenarios, this may occur in the absence of a stimulus or when low drug concentrations coincide with an agitation level that is decreasing (but not close to zero), thus causing the patient's agitation to remain at a constant non-zero level, despite their recorded infusion rate dropping to near zero.

### 6.5. Comparison of WPB 90% with Rudge's physiological model [13] (AND, RAND measures)

The non-wavelets based and earlier performance metrics of AND and of RAND per patient are also given in Table 4. Table 4 thus provides a comparison between the WPB 90%, ANWD and RANWD and TIB, AND and RAND measures from Rudge's Physiological Model [12, 13]. A highlighted patient is a poor tracker by the WCORR/WCCORR criteria in [29]. Table 4 along with Table 3, allows comparison between Rudge's [13] values of AND and RAND, with our WPB model diagnostics (WPB) and our wavelet-based estimates of ANWD and RANWD. An underlined patient indicates a poor tracker by our RANWD and WPB criteria (see also Table 6).

| Patient no. | WPB model | | | Rudge's Physiological Model | | |
|---|---|---|---|---|---|---|
| | WPB 90% | ANWD | RANWD | TIB 90% | AND | RAND |
| 1 | 95.31 | 0.537 | 0.553 | 96 | 0.51 | 0.62 |
| **2** | **64.06** | **0.431** | **0.499** | **90** | **0.53** | **0.66** |
| 3 | 96.88 | 0.632 | 0.737 | 97 | 0.70 | 0.83 |
| **4** | **59.38** | **0.338** | **0.475** | **93** | **0.56** | **0.62** |
| 5 | 93.75 | 0.495 | 0.504 | 97 | 0.60 | 0.80 |
| 6 | 95.31 | 0.659 | 0.980 | 95 | 0.70 | 0.84 |
| 7 | 67.19 | 0.417 | 0.455 | 67 | 0.33 | 0.43 |
| 8 | 87.50 | 0.567 | 0.688 | 90 | 0.45 | 0.59 |
| **9** | **57.81** | **0.343** | **0.412** | **89** | **0.49** | **0.62** |
| **10** | **66.80** | **0.300** | **0.388** | **53** | **0.27** | **0.34** |
| **11** | **77.34** | **0.423** | **0.434** | **59** | **0.31** | **0.38** |
| 12 | 84.38 | 0.622 | 0.662 | 96 | 0.61 | 0.77 |
| 13 | 73.44 | 0.442 | 0.504 | 85 | 0.37 | 0.45 |
| 14 | 96.88 | 0.449 | 0.476 | 95 | 0.48 | 0.56 |
| 15 | 89.06 | 0.702 | 0.761 | 95 | 0.45 | 0.60 |
| 16 | 82.81 | 0.596 | 0.770 | 91 | 0.44 | 0.57 |
| 17 | 85.94 | 0.506 | 0.566 | 91 | 0.61 | 0.72 |
| 18 | 93.75 | 0.548 | 0.558 | 92 | 0.55 | 0.68 |
| 19 | 74.22 | 0.759 | 0.780 | 90 | 0.50 | 0.66 |
| 20 | 96.88 | 0.487 | 0.581 | 91 | 0.53 | 0.65 |
| **21** | **65.62** | **0.407** | **0.413** | **95** | **0.53** | **0.72** |
| **22** | **65.62** | **0.422** | **0.455** | **83** | **0.35** | **0.45** |
| 23 | 92.19 | 0.288 | 0.341 | 95 | 0.72 | 0.85 |
| 24 | 71.10 | 0.655 | 0.635 | 91 | 0.43 | 0.54 |
| 25 | 89.06 | 0.635 | 0.670 | 86 | 0.50 | 0.66 |
| 26 | 96.88 | 0.600 | 0.601 | 92 | 0.68 | 0.88 |
| **27** | **47.27** | **0.368** | **0.608** | **84** | **0.39** | **0.49** |
| **28** | **50.78** | **0.501** | **0.540** | **76** | **0.34** | **0.44** |
| 29 | 82.81 | 0.343 | 0.394 | 90 | 0.38 | 0.45 |
| 30 | 96.88 | 0.554 | 0.597 | 97 | 0.63 | 0.82 |
| 31 | 87.50 | 0.562 | 0.669 | 74 | 0.40 | 0.51 |
| **32** | **68.36** | **0.326** | **0.362** | **74** | **0.38** | **0.50** |

| Patient no. | WPB model | | | Rudge's Physiological Model | | |
|---|---|---|---|---|---|---|
| | WPB 90% | ANWD | RANWD | TIB 90% | AND | RAND |
| 33 | 58.79 | 0.373 | 0.499 | 67 | 0.28 | 0.36 |
| **34** | **48.44** | **0.505** | **0.551** | **84** | **0.43** | **0.55** |
| 35 | 96.10 | 0.371 | 0.533 | 70 | 0.38 | 0.46 |
| 36 | 75.00 | 0.573 | 0.763 | 83 | 0.52 | 0.64 |
| 37 | 79.69 | 0.448 | 0.607 | 92 | 0.53 | 0.59 |
| Min | 47.27 | 0.288 | 0.341 | 53 | 0.27 | 0.34 |
| **Median** | **82.81** | **0.495** | **0.552** | **90** | **0.49** | **0.60** |

**Table 4.** Comparison between the WPB, ANWD and RANWD and TIB, AND and RAND from Rudge's Physiological Model [12, 13]. A boxed patient is a poor tracker by the WCORR /WCCORR criteria in [29]. A shaded patient indicates a poor tracker by our RANWD and WPB criteria (13 patients: P2, P4, P7, P9, P10, P11, P21, P22, P27, P28, P32, P33 and P34).

## 6.6. Comparison of WPB, WTCI, ANWD and RANWD across poor versus good tracking groups

Table 5 gives summary statistics of the wavelet density based metrics (WPB, WTCI, ANWD and RANWD) for the poor versus good trackers (classified using the threshold criterion for WPB 90% $\leq$ 70% and RANWD$\leq$ 0.50). The poor trackers have significantly lower median values of WPB 90% (64.84% versus 87.50%) ($p \leq 0.001$); a significantly lower median value of WTCI (76.56% versus 82.79%) ($p \leq 0.041$); a significantly lower median value of ANWD (0.41 versus 0.55) ($p \leq 0.001$) and a significantly lower median value for RANWD (0.46 versus 0.59) ($p \leq 0.001$) compared to the good tracking group.

| | WPB 90% | WTCI | ANWD | RANWD |
|---|---|---|---|---|
| **Poor trackers** | | | | |
| Min | 47.27 | 71.95 | 0.03 | 0.36 |
| Max | 77.34 | 88.05 | 0.50 | 0.61 |
| Range | 30.07 | 16.01 | 0.21 | 0.25 |
| Mean | 61.56 | 77.97 | 0.39 | 0.47 |
| 95% CI of Mean | (65.79, 67.32) | (74.72, 81.22) | (0.36, 0.44) | (0.42, 0.51) |
| **Median** | **64.84** | **76.56** | **0.41** | **0.46** |
| 95% CI of Median | (52.63, 67.09) | (74.89, 81.69) | (0.34, 0.43) | (0.41, 0.53) |
| **Good trackers** | | | | |
| Min | 58.79 | 73.37 | 0.29 | 0.34 |
| Max | 96.88 | 88.94 | 0.76 | 0.98 |

| | WPB 90% | WTCI | ANWD | RANWD |
|---|---|---|---|---|
| Range | 38.09 | 15.57 | 0.47 | 0.64 |
| Mean | 85.31 | 81.36 | 0.53 | 0.60 |
| 95% CI of Mean | (80.85, 89.77) | (76.62, 83.09) | (0.48, 0.57) | (0.55, 0.66) |
| **Median** | **87.50** | **82.79** | **0.55** | **0.59** |
| 95% CI of Median | (82.72, 93.79) | (79.13, 84.09) | (0.45, 0.60) | (0.53, 0.67) |
| Kruskal-Wallis test P value | 0.001 | 0.041 | 0.001 | 0.001 |

**Table 5.** Summary of the wavelet based performance metrics: poor versus good trackers.

## 6.7. Poor trackers compared across 3 studies (references [29], [14] and [13])

Table 6 summarises the patient numbers of the poor trackers according to the criteria of four studies, including the research described in this chapter (i.e. Kang's WPB diagnostics, see column 1). The four studies reported across columns 1, 4-6 in Table 6 are Kang's WPB, WCORR diagnostics [29], Chase diagnostics [14] and the earlier Rudge diagnostics [13].

| Kang WPB diagnostics (this chapter) | WPB ≤ 70% | RANWD≤ 0.50 | Kang WCORR diagnostics [29] | Chase et al. [14] diagnostics | Rudge el al. [13] diagnostics |
|---|---|---|---|---|---|
| - | | | - | - | - |
| 2 | 2 | 2 | 2 | - | - |
| - | - | - | - | - | - |
| 4 | 4 | 4 | 4 | - | - |
| - | - | - | - | - | - |
| - | - | - | - | 6 | - |
| 7 | 7 | 7 | 7 | 7 | 7 |
| - | - | - | - | - | - |
| 9 | 9 | 9 | 9 | 9 | - |
| 10 | 10 | 10 | 10 | - | 10 |
| 11 | 11 | 11 | 11 | - | 11 |
| - | - | - | - | 12 | - |
| - | - | - | - | - | 13 |

http://dx.doi.org/10.5772/52434

| Kang WPB diagnostics (this chapter) | WPB ≤ 70% | RANWD≤ 0.50 | Kang WCORR diagnostics [29] | Chase et al. [14] diagnostics | Rudge el al. [13] diagnostics |
|---|---|---|---|---|---|
| | | 14Φ | - | - | - |
| - | - | - | - | - | - |
| - | - | - | - | - | - |
| - | - | - | - | 17 | - |
| - | - | - | - | - | - |
| - | - | - | - | - | - |
| - | - | - | - | - | - |
| 21 | | 21 | 21 | 21 | - |
| 22 | - | 22 | 22 | - | 22 |
| | | 23Φ | - | - | - |
| - | - | - | - | - | - |
| - | - | - | - | - | - |
| - | - | - | - | - | - |
| 27 | 27 | | 27 | 27 | 27 |
| 28 | 28 | | 28 | - | 28 |
| - | - | 29Φ | 29 | - | 29 |
| - | - | - | - | - | - |
| - | - | - | - | - | - |
| 32 | 32 | 32 | 32 | - | - |
| 33 | 33 | 33 | 33 | - | 33 |
| 34 | 34 | - | 34 | 34 | - |
| - | - | - | 35 | - | 35 |
| - | - | - | - | - | - |
| - | - | - | - | - | - |
| **Total: $N_1$= 13** | | | **Total: $N_2$=15** | **Total: $N_3$=8** | **Total: $N_4$=10** |

**Table 6.** Patient numbers of the poor trackers according to the criteria of 4 studies. Φ P14 and P23 have low RANWD values but high WPB 90% (> 92%) (like P29). P14, P23, P29 were classified as good trackers according to the criteria developed earlier in [13], [14] and [29], and as such, and given their high WPB 90%, are classified as good trackers by our Kang WPB diagnostics.

The resultant ANWD, RANWD, WTCI and WPB 90% thresholds also provide very strong support for the DWT wavelet diagnostics derived in reference [29], in that of the 15 DWT based poor trackers identified in [29], 13 also exhibit a low WPB (WPB 90% < 70%) and/or a low wavelet density based RANWD measure (RANWD ≤ 0.5), and are likewise deemed to be poor trackers (Table 6). Statistically speaking the wavelet probability band and density diagnostics developed in this chapter mirror the DWT based criterion of [29] (*kappa* = 0.87, *p* = 0.0001). Indeed of the 13 patients assessed by our WPB and RANWD criteria to be poor trackers, all were likewise judged to be poor trackers by the earlier DWT WCORR and WCCORR criteria developed in reference [29] (see Table 6 and also see Tables 4-5 of [29]). This indicates perfect agreement between the RANWD threshold developed in this chapter and the earlier DWT WCORR and WCCORR based criteria for poor tracking in [29] (*kappa* = 1.00, *p* = 0.0000).

The performance metrics of AND and RAND and their patient specific values are given in Table 4, which along with Table 3 also allows comparison between Rudge's [13] (AND and RAND) values with our WPB model diagnostics (WPB, ANWD, RANWD). Rudge's Physiological Model [12, 13] found 10 of the 37 patients (27%) have values of RAND ≤ 0.5, with 5 patients with 0.43< RAND<0.49, and 3 with 0.34 < RAND <0.38 (Tables 4 - 5). The model in [63] likewise found that 27 patients (73%) have RAND values greater than 0.57, with 10 poor trackers, with 6 RAND values ranging from 0.43 to 0.49, and with 3 patients exhibiting RAND values between 0.34 and 0.38. The main reason for the reduced total time within the WPB (and the non-significant WCORRs) for this minority group of 10 - 13 poor trackers (of the total 37 patients), is the consistently poor performance of the DE model throughout their *total* length of the A-S simulation. Of the 13 patients assessed by our RANWD and WPB criteria to be poor trackers, 7 patients (P7, P10, P11, P22, P27, P28, P33) were likewise judged to be poor trackers by the earlier Physiological Model of Rudge [13] (*kappa* = 0.30, *p* = 0.03). This shows significant agreement between the physiological Model [13] based criteria for poor tracking and the RANWD and WPB 90% thresholds formulated in this chapter (Table 6).

## 7. Discussion and conclusions

Agitation management via effective sedation management is an important and fundamental activity in the ICU. However, in clinical practice a lack of understanding of the underlying dynamics, combined with a lack of subjective assessment tools, makes effective and consistent clinical agitation management difficult [14, 12, 13]. The main goal of ICU sedation is to control agitation, while preventing over-sedation and over-use of drugs. Current clinical practice employs subjective agitation and sedation assessment scales, combined with medical staff experience and intuition, to deliver appropriate sedation. This approach usually leads to the administration of largely continuous infusions which lack a bolus-focused approach, and commonly results in either over sedation, or insufficient sedation [12, 13]. Several recent studies have emphasised the cost and health-care advantages of drug delivery protocols based on assessment scales of agitation and sedation. Table 7 gives an overview of recent ICU agitation studies, and provides a brief overview of the equations used for simulations of a patient's A-S status and also of the methods derived in this chapter (and by other studies) with the aim of establishing the validity of the models in reflecting a patient's true A-S status.

In this chapter, we successfully developed a density estimation approach via wavelet smoothing to assess the validity of deterministic dynamic A-S models. This wavelet density approach provided graphical assessment and numerical metrics (WTCI and WPB 90%, ANWD and RANWD) to assess the comparability between the modelled and the recorded A-S data per patient. Our new wavelet regression diagnostics identified 13 ICU patients (patients 2, 4, 7, 9, 10, 11, 21, 22, 27, 28, 32, 33 and 34) (out of 37 analysed) [29], whose simulated A-S profiles were poor indicators of their true A-S status, the remaining patients tracked exceptionally well.

All of these 13 poor trackers were also identified as poor trackers by the DWT measures derived in [29]. The WTCI and WPB 90% metrics derived in this chapter thus give strong support for the datawork in [29] and vice versa. Our wavelet regression diagnostics (WTCI, ANWD, RANWD, and WPB 90%) are thus valid for assessing control, as were the wavelet DWT, wavelet correlation (WCORR) and cross-correlation (WCCORR) measures derived in [29]. We have thus successfully assessed the patients A-S by the RANWD cut-point and also distinguished poor trackers, likewise identified by the DWT criteria of [29]. Ten of our 13 so-called poor trackers were also identified as poor trackers by either the kernel smoothing, tracking index and probability band approach of [14] and [13], respectively. Overall the various diagnostics strongly agree and confirm the value of A-S modelling in ICU. Our WPB method is also shown to be an excellent tool for detecting regions where the simulated infusion rate performs poorly, thus providing ways to help improve and distil the deterministic A-S model. The main reason for the reduced total time within the WPB for a minority group, of 13 (of 37) i.e. the poor trackers, is the consistently poor performance of the DE model throughout the *total* length of the simulation.

Wavelet modelling in this chapter and the earlier work of Kang [29] thereby demonstrate that the models of the recent A-S studies of [14, 11, 12, 13, 63] and of [64], are suitable for developing more advanced optimal infusion controllers. These offer significant clinical potential of improved agitation management and reduced length of stay in critical care. Further details are available in the recent PhD dissertation of Kang (circa 2012) [67]. The A-S time series profiles studied in this chapter are of disparate lengths (with a wide range [3,001 - 25,261] time points in minutes). Our approach is thus generalisable to any study which investigates the similarity or closeness of *bivariate* time series of, say, a large number of units (patients, households) and of time series of varying lengths and of possibly long length. This chapter demonstrates the value of wavelets for assessing ICU agitation-sedation deterministic models, and suggests new wavelet probability band and coverage diagnostics by which to mathematically assess A-S models. Future work will involve creation of singular spectrum analysis (SSA) based similarity indices following the development of Hudson and Keatley in [68]; and comparing results with the wavelet density-based indices developed in this chapter with the DWT metrics in [29] and in references [69] - [70].

| Authors | Equations and Model used | Methods | Aims of the study and the performance indicators derived |
|---|---|---|---|
| Kang et al.<br>(this chapter) | See the schema of the approach developed in this chapter below:<br>**Wavelet shrinkage (threshold) procedure**<br>Data $X_t$ → DWT → Threshold (minimax) → IDWT → $f(x) \Rightarrow \hat{f}_J$ (wavelet estimate)<br>$f(x)=\sum_k c_{j_0,k}\phi_{j_0,k}(x)+\sum_{j>j_0}\sum_k d_{j,k}\psi_{j,k}(x)$: a square intergrable density function<br>$\phi$: orthogonal scaling function, $\psi$: mother wavelet<br>$\hat{f}_J(x)=\sum_k \hat{c}_{j_0,k}\phi_{j_0,k}(x)+\sum_{j>j_0}\sum_k \hat{d}_{j,k}\psi_{j,k}(x)$: wavelet estimator for $f(x)$ at $J$ level<br>$\hat{c}_{j,k}=\frac{1}{n}\sum_{t=1}^{n}\phi_{j,k}(X_t),\ \hat{d}_{j,k}=\frac{1}{n}\sum_{t=t}^{n}\psi_{j,k}(X_t)$ | Density estimation<br>([30], [42])<br>Wavelet thresholding via BayesThresh methods<br>([41], [42])<br>Wavelet shrinkage (threshold)<br>( [60], [30], [42]) | Dvelop a density estimation approach via wavelet smoothing for assessing the validity of the deterministic dynamic models (simulated profiles) against the empirical / recorded data.<br>Construct a wavelet probability band (WPB).<br>Provide graphical assessment and numerical metrics of the compatibility between the model and the recorded agitation-sedation data.<br>Develop performance measures as follows:<br>1. Average normalized wavelet density (ANWD).<br>2. Relative average normalized wavelet density (RANWD).<br>3. Median of the Wavelet Time Coverage Index (WTCI). |
| Kang et al. [29] | See equations in the Chase et al. [14] and the row below, and schema in Kang et al. [29]<br>**DWT analysis and synthesis equations**<br>**X**= [$X_1, X_2,\ldots, X_N$], $N=2^J$, DWT analysis equation $\boldsymbol{W}=\mathcal{W}\boldsymbol{X}$, $\boldsymbol{W}$= discrete wavelet coefficients, $\mathcal{W}$= N x N orthonormal matrix<br>$\boldsymbol{W}=\mathcal{W}\boldsymbol{X}, \boldsymbol{W}=[\boldsymbol{W}_1,\boldsymbol{W}_2,\cdots,\boldsymbol{W}_J,\boldsymbol{V}_J]^T, \mathcal{W}=[\mathcal{W}_1,\mathcal{W}_2,\ldots,\mathcal{W}_J,\mathcal{V}_J]$<br>$\boldsymbol{X}=\mathcal{W}^T\boldsymbol{W}=[\mathcal{W}_1,\mathcal{W}_2,\ldots,\mathcal{W}_J,\mathcal{V}_J]^T[\boldsymbol{W}_1,\boldsymbol{W}_2,\ldots,\boldsymbol{W}_J,\boldsymbol{V}_J]^T$<br>$=\sum_{j=1}^{J}\mathcal{W}_j^T\boldsymbol{W}_j+\mathcal{V}_J^T\boldsymbol{V}_J \quad \Rightarrow$ DWT synthesis equation<br>**DWT-MRA**<br>$\boldsymbol{X}=\sum_{j=1}^{J}\mathcal{W}_j^T\boldsymbol{W}_j+\mathcal{V}_J^T\boldsymbol{V}_J=\sum_{j=1}^{J}D_j+S_J \Rightarrow$ Additive decomposition(=MRA)<br>$D_j=\mathcal{W}_j^T\boldsymbol{W}_j$ : Portion of synthesis due to scale $\lambda_j$, $j$th 'detail'<br>$S_J=\mathcal{V}_J^T\boldsymbol{V}$ : 'smooth' of $J$th order | Maximal Overlap Discrete Wavelet (MODWT) [62]<br>Multiresolution analysis (MRA) [62]<br>DWT-MRA,<br>MODWT-MRA<br>Wavelet shrinkage<br>([60], [30]) | Develop a wavelet correlation (WCORR) and wavelet cross-correlation (WCCORR) approach for assessing the validity of the deterministic dynamic models against the empirical agitation-sedation data per patient.<br>Provide graphical assessment tools and wavelet based numerical metrics of the compatibility between the simulated model and the recorded data via the discrete wavelet transform (DWT), partial DWT (PDWT), maximal overlap DWT (MODWT) and via Multiresolution analysis (MRA).<br>Investigate the lag/lead relationship between the simulated and recorded infusion series on a scale by scale basis via wavelet cross-correlation (WCCORR).<br>Develop performance measures as follows:<br>1. Modulus of the wavelet correlation at wavelet scale 1, $\lambda_1$.<br>2. Count the number (out of 8) of non-significant wavelet correlations at scales $\lambda_j$ (j = 1,2,…,8).<br>3. Median and 95% CI of the first 5 wavelet correlations at scales $\lambda_j$ (j = 1,2,…,5).<br>Test poor versus good tracker groups via the Kruskal Wallis test on 1, 2 and 3 above. |
| Rudge et al. [13] | I. Pharmocokinetics of morphine<br>$V_c^o\frac{dC_c^o}{dt}=-(K_{CL}^o+K_{ce}^o+K_{cp}^o)C_c^o+P^oU+K_{ce}^oC_e^o+K_{pc}^oC_p^o$<br>$V_p^o\frac{dC_p^o}{dt}=-K_{pc}^oC_p^o+K_{cp}^oC_c^o,\ V_e^o\frac{dC_e^o}{dt}=-K_{ec}^oC_e^o+K_{ce}^oC_c^o$<br>II.Pharmocokinetics of midazolam<br>$V_c^s\frac{dC_c^s}{dt}=-(K_{CL}^s+K_{ce}^s)C_c^s+P^sU+K_{ec}^sC_e^s,\ V_e^s\frac{dC_e^s}{dt}=-K_{ec}^sC_e^s+K_{ce}^sC_c^s$<br>III.Pharmacodynamics of morphine and midazolam<br>$\frac{dA}{dt}=w_1S-w_2K_T\int_0^t E_{comb}(\zeta)e^{-K_T(t-\zeta)}d\zeta,\ E_{Comb}=E_0+[E_{max}(\theta)-E_0]\frac{\left(\frac{C_o+C_S}{C_{50}(\theta)}\right)^{\gamma(\theta)}}{1+\left(\frac{C_o+C_S}{C_{50}(\theta)}\right)^{\gamma(\theta)}}$ | Kernel smoothing:<br>Chebychev's inequality for the probability band [14]<br>Relative average normalised density (RAND)<br>Average normalised density (AND) | Develop a physiologically representative model that incorporates endogenous agitation reduction (EAR).<br>Use performance measures as follows:<br>1. RTD: relative total dose (RTD) expresses the total dose administered in the simulation as a percentage of the actual total recorded dose.<br>2. Relative average normalised density (RAND) measures how probabilistically similar the model outputs are to the smoothed data, and hence the degree of comparability between the model and the empirical data.<br>3. Percentage time in band (TIB). |
| Rudge et al. [11] | The agitation-sedation system model:<br>Phamarcokinetic model adding patient agitation as a third state variable<br>$\frac{dC_c}{dt}=-K_1C_c+\frac{U}{V_d}$<br>$\frac{dC_p}{dt}=-K_2C_p+K_3C_c$<br>$\frac{dA}{dt}=w_1S-w_2\int_0^t C_p(\tau)e^{-K_4(t-\tau)}d\tau$ | Infinite Impulse Response (IIR) filter<br>Proportional Derivative (PD) control with respect to agitation for infusion rate (U)<br>Moving blocks bootstrap [56]<br>Tracking Index (TI) | Develop a control model to capture the essential dynamics of the agitation-sedation system.<br>Use performance measures as follows:<br>1. $U=K_pA+K_d\dot{A}$ for the infusion rate.<br>2. Tracking Index (TI): Quantitative parameter to indicate how well the simulated infusion rate profile represents the average recorded infusion profile over the entire time series. |
| Lee et al. [64] | I. Pharmocokinetics of morphine<br>$V_c^o\frac{dC_c^o}{dt}=-(K_{CL}^o+K_{ce}^o+K_{cp}^o)C_c^o+P^oU+K_{ce}^oC_e^o+K_{pc}^oC_p^o$<br>$V_p^o\frac{dC_p^o}{dt}=-K_{pc}^oC_p^o+K_{cp}^oC_c^o,\ V_e^o\frac{dC_e^o}{dt}=-K_{ec}^oC_e^o+K_{ce}^oC_c^o$<br>II.Pharmocokinetics of midazolam<br>$V_c^s\frac{dC_c^s}{dt}=-(K_{CL}^s+K_{ce}^s)C_c^s+P^sU+K_{ec}^sC_e^s,\ V_e^s\frac{dC_e^s}{dt}=-K_{ec}^sC_e^s+K_{ce}^sC_c^s$<br>III.Pharmacodynamics of morphine and midazolam<br>$\frac{dA}{dt}=w_1S-w_2K_T\int_0^t E_{comb}(\zeta)e^{-K_T(t-\zeta)}d\zeta,\ E_{Comb}=E_0+[E_{max}(\theta)-E_0]\frac{\left(\frac{C_o+C_S}{C_{50}(\theta)}\right)^{\gamma(\theta)}}{1+\left(\frac{C_o+C_S}{C_{50}(\theta)}\right)^{\gamma(\theta)}}$ | Kernel regression [65]<br>Kernel density estimation:<br>marginal density function of the regression function estimate<br>**Nonparametric regression:**<br>Chebychev's inequality for the probability band [14] | Develop a nonparametric approach for assessing the validity of deterministic dynamics models against empirical data.<br>Use performance measures as follows:<br>1. Kernel regression and density estimation to yield visual graphical display of data.<br>2. Construct a probability band for the nonparametric regression curve and check whether the proposed model lies within the band.<br>3. Average normalised density (AND) to measure how well the simulated values coincide with the maximum density at every time point and relative average normalised density (RAND). |

| | | | |
|---|---|---|---|
| Chase et al [14] | The agitation-sedation Phamarcokinetic model adding patient agitation as a third state variable<br>$\frac{dC_c}{dt} = -K_1 C_c + \frac{U}{V_d}$<br>$\frac{dC_p}{dt} = -K_2 C_p + K_3 C_c$<br>$\frac{dA}{dt} = w_1 S - w_2 \int_0^t C_p(\tau) e^{-K_4(t-\tau)} d\tau$<br>Uniform kernel with bandwidth $h$ [65]<br>$K_h = \begin{cases} 0 & \text{if } t < -\frac{h}{2} \\ 1 & \text{if } t\ -\frac{h}{2} < t \le \frac{h}{2} \\ 0 & \text{if } t > \frac{h}{2} \end{cases}$ | Infinite Impluse Response (IIR) filter Proportional-Derivative (PD) control with agitation for infusion rate (U) Tracking Index (TI) Chebychev's inequality for probability band [14] | Develop a mathematical model to capture the essential dynamics of the agitation-sedation system and test for statistical validity using the recorded infusion data for the 37 ICU patients.<br>Use performance measures as follows:<br>1. Kernel smoothing using the uniform kernel.<br>2. Tracking Index (TI).<br>3. Moving blocks bootstrap to gain an understanding of the reliability of the TI for a given patient's infusion profile<br>4. 90% Probability Band - by definition the range within at least 90% of the time, the estimated mean value of the recorded infusion rate lies within the band. |

$C_c$, $C_p$ and $C_e$ are, respectively, the drug concentrations (mg $L^{-1}$) in the central, peripheral and effect compartments;, $U$ is the intravenous infusion rate; $V_d$, $V_c$, $V_p$ and $V_e$, respectively, the volume of distribution, the distribution volumes (L) of the central, peripheral and effect compartments; $A$ is an agitation index, $S$ is the stimulus invoking agitation; $K_1$–$K_3$ are parameters relating to drug elimination and transport and $K_{ij}$ the transfer rate (L $min^{-1}$) from compartment $i$ to compartment $j$; $K_{CL}$ the drug clearance (L $min^{-1}$); $K_T$ the effect, and $w_1$ and $w_2$ are relative weighting coefficients of the stimulus and drug effect, respectively. Time is represented by $t$, and $\tau$ is the variable of integration in the convolution integral $V_c$, $V_p$ and $V_e$, respectively, the distribution volumes (L) of the central, peripheral and effect compartments; $U$ the intravenous infusion rate (mL $min^{-1}$); $A$ an agitation index; $S$ the stimulus invoking agitation; $K_{ij}$ the transfer rate (L min $^{-1}$) from compartment $i$ to compartment $j$; $K_{CL}$ the drug clearance (L $min^{-1}$); $K_T$ the effect time constant ($min^{-1}$); $P^o$ and $P^s$ are the concentrations of morphine and midazolam, respectively (mgm$L^{-1}$), where terms with superscript 'o' relate to the opioid morphine, and terms with superscript 's' relate to the sedative midazolam. Time is represented by $t$ (min), the variable of integration, and the terms $w_1$ and $w_2$ are the relative weights of stimulus and cumulative effect, representing the patient sensitivity. Finally, $E$comb is the combined pharmacodynamic effect of the individual effect site drug concentrations of morphine and midazolam determined using response surface modeling as defined in [66].

**Table 7.** Overview of Studies on ICU

## Author details

In Kang[1], Irene Hudson[2], Andrew Rudge[3] and J. Geoffrey Chase[4]

1 Department of Mathematics and Statistics, University of Canterbury, Christchurch, New Zealand

2 School of Mathematical and Physical Sciences, University of Newcastle, NSW, Australia

3 Faculty of Health, Engineering and Science, Victoria University, Melbourne, Australia

4 Department of Mechanical Engineering, University of Canterbury, Christchurch, New Zealand

## References

[1] Goupillaud, P, Grossmann, A, & Morlet, J. (1984). Cycle-octave and related transforms in seismic signal analysis. *Geoexploration, 23*(1), 85-102.

[2] Morlet, J. (1983). Sampling theory and wave propagation. *Issues in Acoustic Signal/ Image Processing and Recognition, 1233261*

[3] Barber, S, Nason, G. P, & Silverman, B. W. (2002). Posterior probability intervals for wavelet thresholding. *Journal of the Royal Statistical Society. Series B (Statistical Methodology), 64*(2), 189-205.

[4] Mallat, S. (1989). A theory for multiresolution signal decomposition: the wavelet representation. *IEEE Transactions on Pattern analysis and Machine Intelligence, 11674693*

[5] Meyer, F. G. (2003). Wavelet-based estimation of a semiparametric generalized linear model of fMRI time- series. *IEEE Transactions on Medical Imaging, 22*(3), 315-322.

[6] Kumar, P, & Foufoula-georgiou, E. (1993). A multicomponent decomposition of spatial rainfall fields. 1. Segregation of large- and small-scale features using wavelet transforms. *Water Resources Research, 29*(8), 2515-2532.

[7] Kumar, P. (1994). Role of coherent structures in the stochastic-dynamic variability of precipitation. *Journal of Geophysical Research-Atmospheres, 101(D21)*(26), 393-404.

[8] Donoho, D. L. (1995). De-noising by soft-thresholding. *IEEE Transactions on Information Theory, 41*(3), 613-627.

[9] Chang, S. G, Yu, B, & Vetterli, M. (2000a). Spatially adaptive wavelet thresholding based on context modeling for image denoising. *IEEE Transactions on Image Processing, 9*(9), 1522- 1531.

[10] Chang, S. G, Yu, B, & Vetterli, M. (2000b). Adaptive wavelet thresholding for image denoising and compression. *IEEE Transactions on Image Processing, 9*(9), 1532-1546.

[11] Rudge, A. D, Chase, J. G, Shaw, G. M, Lee, D, Wake, G. C, Hudson, I. L, et al. (2005). Impact of control on agitation-sedation dynamics. *Control Engineering Practice, 13*(9), 1139-1149.

[12] Rudge, A. D, Chase, J. G, Shaw, G. M, & Lee, D. (2006b). Physiological modelling of agitation-sedation dynamics. *Medical Engineering and Physics, 28*(1), 49-59.

[13] Rudge, A. D, Chase, J. G, Shaw, G. M, & Lee, D. (2006a). Physiological modelling of agitation-sedation dynamics including endogenous agitation reduction. *Medical Engineering Physics, 28*(7), 629-638.

[14] Chase, J. G, Rudge, A. D, Shaw, G. M, Wake, G. C, Lee, D, Hudson, I. L, et al. (2004). Modeling and control of the agitation-sedation cycle for critical care patients. *Medical Engineering and Physics, 26*(6), 459-471.

[15] Fraser, G. L, & Riker, R. R. (2001b). Monitoring sedation, agitation, analgesia, and delirium in critically ill adult patients. *Crit Care Clin, 17*(4), 967-987.

[16] Jaarsma, A. S, Knoester, H, Van Rooyen, F, & Bos, A. P. (2001). Biphasic positive airway pressure ventilation (pev+) in children. *Crit Care Clin, 5*(3), 174-177.

[17] Ramsay, M. A, Savege, T. M, Simpson, B. R, & Goodwin, R. (1974). Controlled sedation with alphaxalone-alphadolone. *Br Med J, 2*(920), 656-659.

[18] Riker, R. R, Picard, J. T, & Fraser, G. L. (1999). Prospective evaluation of the Sedation-Agitation Scale for adult critically ill patients. *Critical Care Medicine, 27*(7), 1325-1329.

[19] Sessler, C. N, Gosnell, M. S, Grap, M. J, Brophy, G. M, Neal, O, Keane, P. V, et al. (2002). The Richmond agitation-sedation scale: validity and reliability in adult intensive care unit patients. *Am J Respir Crit Care Med, 166*(10), 1338-1344.

[20] Kress, J. P, Pohlman, A. S, & Hall, J. B. (2002). Sedation and analgesia in the intensive care unit. *Am J Respir Crit Care Med, 166*(8), 1024-1028.

[21] Kang, I, Hudson, I. L, Rudge, A. D, & Chase, J. G. (2005). *Wavelet signature of Agitation-Sedation profiles of ICU patients.* In: Francis AR, Matawie KM, Oshlack A, Smyth GK (eds) Statistical Solutions to Modern Problems. 20th International Workshop on Statistical Modelling, Sydney, July 10-15, University of Western Sydney (Penrith), 1-74108-101-7, 293-296.

[22] Kang, I, Hudson, I. L, & Keatley, M. R. (2004). *Wavelet analysis in phenological research-the study of four flowering eucalypt species in relation to climate.* International Biometrics Conference (IBC 04), July, Cairns, Australia.

[23] Hudson, I. L. (2010). Interdisciplinary approaches: towards new statistical methods for phenological studies, *Climatic Change,* 100(1), 143-171.

[24] Hudson, I. L, & Keatley, M. R. (2010). *Phenological Research: Methods for Environmental and Climate Change Analysis*: Springer Dordrecht. 523p.

[25] Hudson, I. L, Kang, I, Rudge, A. D, Chase, J. G, & Shaw, G. M. (2004). *Wavelet signatures of agitation and sedation profiles: a preliminary study.* New Zealand Physics Engineering in Medicine (NZPEM) Christchurch New Zealand, Nov , 22-23.

[26] Hudson, I. L, Keatley, M. R, & Roberts, A. M. I. (2005). Statistical Methods in Phenological Research. Proceedings of the Statistical Solutions to Modern Problems. Proceedings of the 20th International Workshop on Statistical Modelling, eds. AR Francis, KM Matawie, A Oshlack GK Smyth, Sydney, Australia, 10-15 July, 1-74108-101-7, 259-270.

[27] Hudson, I. L, Kang, I, & Keatley, M. R. (2010b). Wavelet Analysis of Flowering and Climatic Niche Identification. In I. L. Hudson IL, Keatley MR, editors. *Phenological Research: Methods for Environmental and Climate Change Analysis.* Springer Dordrecht. , 361-391.

[28] Hudson, I. L, Keatley, M. R, & Kang, I. (2011). Wavelet characterisation of eucalypt flowering and the influence of climate. *Environmental & Ecological Statistics. 18*(3), 513-533.

[29] Kang, I, Hudson, I. L, Rudge, A, & Chase, J. G. (2011). Wavelet signatures and diagnostics for the assessment of ICU Agitation-Sedation protocols, In: Olkkonen H (editor) *Discrete Wavelet Transforms,* InTech. 978-9-53307-654-6, 321-348.

[30] Ogden, R. T. (1997). *Essential Wavelets for Statistical Applications and Data Analysis.* Boston: Birkhäuser.

[31] Silverman, B. W. (1986). Density Estimation for Statistics and Data Analysis, New York: Chapman Hall, , 45-47.

[32] Walnut, D. F. (2004). *An Introduction to Wavelet Analysis*: Birkhauser.

[33] Cline, D. B. H, Eubank, R. L, & Speckman, P. L. (1995). Nonparametric estimation of regression curves with discontinuous derivatives. *Journal of Statistical Research, 291730*

[34] Delouille, V, Franke, J, & Von Sachs, R. (2001). Nonparametric stochastic regression with design-adapted wavelets. *Sankhy : The Indian Journal of Statistics, Series A, 63*(3), 328-366.

[35] Vidakovic, B. (1999). *Statistical modelling by wavelets.* New York: John Wiley Sons.

[36] Cencov, N. N. (1962). Evaluation of an unknown distribution density from observations. *Soviet Mathematics, 315991562*

[37] Engel, J. (1990). Density estimation with Haar series. *Statistics Probability Letters, 9*(2), 111-117.

[38] Donoho, D. L, & Johnstone, I. M. (1994). Ideal spatial adaptation via wavelet shrinkage. *Biometrika, 81425455*

[39] Weaver, J. B, Yansun, X, Healy, D. M. J, & Cromwell, L. D. (1991). Filterring noise from images with wavelet transforms. *Magnetic Resonance in Medicine, 24288295*

[40] Donoho, D. L. (1995). De-noising by soft-thresholding. *IEEE Transactions on Information Theory, 41*(3), 613-627.

[41] Abramovich, F, Sapatinas, T, & Silverman, B. W. (1998). Wavelet thresholding via a Bayesian approach. *Journal of the Royal Statistical Society. Series B, Statistical Methodology,* , 725-749.

[42] Nason, G. P. (2008). *Wavelet Methods in Statistics with R*: Springer Verlag.

[43] Herrick, D. R. M. (2000). *Wavelet Methods for Curve and Surface Estimation.* Thesis. University of Bristol, Bristol, U.K.

[44] Vidakovic, B. (1998). Nonlinear Wavelet Shrinkage with Bayes Rules and Bayes Factors. *Journal of the American Statistical Association, 93*(441), 173-179.

[45] Daubechies, I. (1992). *Ten lectures on wavelets.* Philadelphia: Society for Industrial and Applied Mathematics.

[46] Barber, S, Nason, G. P, & Silverman, B. W. (2002). Posterior probability intervals for wavelet thresholding. *Journal of the Royal Statistical Society. Series B (Statistical Methodology), 64*(2), 189-205.

[47] Hill, I. D, Hill, R, & Holder, R. L. Fitting Johnson curves by moments. *Appl. Statist, 25180189*

[48] Hill, I. D. Normal-Johnson and Johnson-Normal transformationns. *Appl. Statist, 25190192*

[49] Johnson, N. L. (1949). Systems of frequency curves generated by methods of translation. *Biometrika, 36149176*

[50] Chipman, H. A, Kolaczyk, E. D, & Mcculloch, R. E. (1997). Adaptive Bayesian wavelet shrinkage. *Journal of the American Statistical Association, 92*(440).

[51] Chipman, H. A, & Wolfson, L. J. (1999). Prior elicitation in the wavelet domain. *Lecture Notes in Statistics, 1418394*

[52] Clyde, M, Parmigiani, G, & Vidakovic, B. (1998). Multiple shrinkage and subset selection in wavelets. *Biometrika, 85*(2), 391-402.

[53] Clyde, M, & George, E. I. (2000). Flexible empirical Bayes estimation for wavelets. *Journal of the Royal Statistical Society. Series B (Statistical Methodology), 62*(4), 681-698.

[54] Crouse, M. S, Nowak, R. D, & Baraniuk, R. G. (1998). Wavelet-based statistical signal processing using Hidden Markov models. *IEEE Transactions on Signal Processing, 46*(4), 886-902.

[55] Clyde, M, & George, E. I. (2000). Flexible empirical Bayes estimation for wavelets. *Journal of the Royal Statistical Society. Series B (Statistical Methodology), 62*(4), 681-698.

[56] Chipman, H. A, & Wolfson, L. J. (1999). Prior elicitation in the wavelet domain. *Lecture Notes in Statistics,* , 141, 83-94.

[57] Efron, B, & Tibshirani, R. J. (1993). *An introduction to the Bootstrap, (57of Monographs on Statistics and Applied Probability).*

[58] Hettmansperger, T. P, & Mckean, J. W. (1998). *Robust Nonparametric Statistical Methods*. London: Arnold.

[59] Mallat, S. (1989). A theory for multiresolution signal decomposition: the wavelet representation. *IEEE Transactions on Pattern analysis and Machine Intelligence, 11674693*

[60] Donoho, D. L, & Johnson, N. L. (1998). Minimax estimation via wavelet shrinkage. *Annals of Statistics, 26879921*

[61] Gencay, R, Selcuk, F, & Whitcher, B. (2002). *An introduction to wavelets and other filtering methods in finance and economics*: Academic Press.

[62] Kang, I, Hudson, I. L, Rudge, A. D, & Chase, J. G. Wavelet signatures and diagnostics for the assessment of ICU Agitation-Sedation protocols, for book entitled *Discrete*

*Wavelet Transforms-Biomedical Applications,* InTech Publishers, http://www.intech-web.org,Vienna, Austria, 978953307654

[63] Percival, D. B, & Walden, A. T. (2000). *Wavelet Methods for Time Series Analysis*. Cambridge, England: Cambridge University Press.

[64] Rudge, A. D, Chase, J. G, Shaw, G. M, & Wake, G. C. (2003). *Improved agitation management in critically ill patients via feedback control of sedation administration.* In: Proc World Congress on Medical Physics and Biomed Eng, August, Sydney, Australia.

[65] Lee, D. S, Rudge, A. D, Chase, J. G, & Shaw, G. M. (2005). A new model validation tool using kernel regression and density estimation. *Computer Methods and Programs in Biomedicine, 807587*

[66] Wand, M. P, & Jones, M. C. (1995). *Kernel smoothing*: Chapman Hall/CRC.

[67] Minto, C. F, Schnider, T. W, Short, T. G, Gregg, K. M, Gentilini, A, & Shafer, S. L. (2000). Response surface model for anesthetic drug interactions. *Anesthesiology, 92*(6), 1603-1616.

[68] Kang, I. (2012). *Wavelets, ICA and Statistical Parametric Mapping: with application to agitation-sedation modelling, detecting change points and to neuroinformatics*. PhD thesis University of Canterbury, Christchurch, New Zealand. 338 p.

[69] Hudson, I. L, & Keatley, M. R. (2010). Singular Spectrum Analysis: Climatic Niche Identification. In: Hudson IL, Keatley MR (eds) *Phenological Research: Methods for Environmental and Climate Change Analysis,* Springer, Dordrecht, , 393-424.

[70] Hudson, I. L, Keatley, M. R, & Kang, I. (2011). Wavelets and clustering: methods to assess synchronization. In: del Valle M, Muñoz R, Gutiérrez JM (eds) *Wavelets: Classification, Theory and Applications*. Nova Science Publishers. Chapter 5. 978-1-62100-252-9, 97-124.

[71] Hudson, I. L, Keatley, M. R, & Kang, I. (2011). Wavelet Signatures of Climate and Flowering: Identification of Species Groupings In: Olkkonen H (ed) *Discrete Wavelet Transforms Biomedical Applications,* InTech, publishers. Vienna. 978-9-53307-654-6, 267-296.

Chapter 7

# Wavelet–Neural–Network Control for Maximization of Energy Capture in Grid Connected Variable Speed Wind Driven Self-Excited Induction Generator System

Fayez F. M. El-Sousy and Awad Kh. Al-Asmari

Additional information is available at the end of the chapter

http://dx.doi.org/10.5772/51253

## 1. Introduction

Recently, the wind generation systems are attracting attention as a clean and safe renewable energy source. Induction machines have many advantageous characteristics such as high robustness, reliability and low cost. Therefore, induction machines are used in high-performance applications, which require independent torque and flux control. The induction machines may be used as a motor or a generator. Self-excited induction generators (SEIG) are good candidates for wind-power electricity generation especially in remote areas, because they do not need an external power supplies to produce the excitation magnetic fields in [1–3]. The excitation can be provided by a capacitor bank connected to the stator windings of the induction generator. Magnetizing inductance is the main factor for voltage build-up of the IG. The minimum and maximum values of capacitance required for self-excitation have been analyzed previously in [4–7].

The three phase current regulated pulse-width modulation (CRPWM) AC/DC/AC converters have been increasingly used for wind energy system applications. Their attractive features include: regulated DC-link voltage, low harmonic distortion of the induction generator currents and controllable power factor and efficiency in [8–9]. The current regulation of a SEIG in the synchronous frame has the advantages of fast dynamic current response, good accuracy, constant switching frequency and less sensitivity to parameter variations. In wind generation systems, a variable speed generation system is more attractive than a fixed speed one because of the improvement in the wind energy production. In a variable speed system, wind turbine can be operated to produce its maximum power at every wind speed by adjusting the shaft speed optimally. In order to achieve the maximum power point tracking

(MPPT) control, some control schemes have been studied. For example, a search-based or perturbation-based strategy in [10–11], a fuzzy- logic based control in [12], a wind speed-estimation-based algorithm has been applied. Since the squirrel-cage IGs have robust construction, lower initial, run-time and maintenance cost, squirrel-cage IGs are suitable for grid-connected as well as isolated power sources in small hydroelectric and wind-energy applications. Therefore an IG system using radial basis function network (RBFN) was proposed to yield maximum power output through the DC-link power control in [13-14].

In the past several years, much research has been carried out in neural network control. It has proven that an artificial neural network can approximate a wide range of nonlinear functions to any desired degree of accuracy under certain conditions. In the conventional gradient descent method of weight adaptation, the sensitivity of the controlled system is required in the on-line training process. However, it is difficult to acquire sensitivity information for unknown or highly non-linear dynamics. Wavelets have been combined with the neural network to create wavelet–neural–networks (WNNs). It combine the capability of artificial neural networks for learning from process and the capability of wavelet decomposition for identification and control of dynamic systems. The training algorithms for WNN typically converge in a smaller number of iterations than the conventional neural networks. Unlike the sigmoid functions used in the conventional neural networks, the second layer of WNN is a wavelet form, in which the translation and dilation parameters are included. Thus, WNN has been proved to be better than the other neural networks in that the structure can provide more potential to enrich the mapping relationship between inputs and outputs in [15-23].

Particle swarm optimization (PSO), first introduced by Kennedy and Eberhart in [24], is one of the modern heuristic algorithm. It was developed through simulation of a simplified social system and has been found to be robust in solving continuous nonlinear optimization problem in [25-29]. The PSO technique can generate a high quality solution within shorter calculation time and stable convergence characteristics than other stochastic methods in [30-34]. Much research is still in progress for proving the potential of the PSO in solving complex dynamical systems.

The recent evolution of power-electronics technologies has aided the advancement of variable-speed wind-turbine generation systems in [35–39]. In spite of the additional cost of power electronics and control circuits, the total energy captured in a variable-speed wind-turbine system is more than the conventional one. Thus, the variable-speed wind-turbine system has lower life-cycle cost. Moreover, the PWM converters not only can be used as a variable capacitor but also can supply the needed reactive power to load and to minimize the harmonic current and imbalance in the generator current. On the other hand, the variable speed wind turbine driven SEIG systems display highly resonant, nonlinear, and time-varying dynamics subject to wind turbulence and operating temperature of the SEIG. Furthermore, there is an appreciable amount of fluctuation in the magnitude and frequency of the generator terminal voltage owing to a varying rotor speed governed by the wind velocity and the pulsating input torque from the wind turbine. The phenomena of fluctuation are objectionable to some sensitive loads. Therefore, the employment of PWM converters with advanced control methodologies to control the wind turbine driven SEIG systems is necessary in [36–38]. In addition, for the research of wind energy conversion systems, the developments of wind turbine emulators are also necessary in [43, 44]. However, the fuzzy logic controller, the sliding-mode controller, and the PI controller adopted in [40–48] may not guarantee the robustness when parameter variations or external disturbance occurred in the control system in practical applications due to the lack of online learning ability.

This Chapter is organized as follows. Section 2 presents the variable speed wind generation system description. In this section the analysis of the wind turbine is carried out and the maximum power point tracking analysis is also introduced. In Section 3, the dynamic model of the self-excited induction generator is introduced to analyze all its characteristics. Section 4 provides the indirect field-orientation control (IFOC) dynamics for the IG (torque, slip angular frequency and voltage commands) which are derived from the dynamic model of SEIG. The d-q axes current control according to the IG rotor speed gives the maximum mechanical power from the wind turbine and the losses of the IG are minimized. In Section 5, the dynamic equations of the CRPWM converter in the synchronous reference frame are carried out based on the IFOC dynamics of the IG. The dynamic equations of the grid-side CRPWM voltage source inverter connected to the grid are given in Section 6. By using vector control technique, the currents of the CRPWM inverter are controlled with very high bandwidth. The vector control approach is used, with a reference frame oriented along the grid voltage vector position. This allows independent control of the active and reactive power. Section 7 considers the design procedures for the PID voltage controller of the IG-side CRPWM voltage source converter, the PID active power and reactive power controllers for the grid-side CRPWM inverter. In Section 8, an intelligent maximization hybrid control system based on the WNN with IPSO is proposed in order to control the DC-link voltage of the IG-side CRPWM voltage source converter, active power and reactive power of the grid-side CRPWM voltage source inverter effectively based on the MPPT from the wind driven SEIG system. Finally, to testify the design of the proposed hybrid control system and MPPT control scheme, the variable speed wind generation system is simulated in Section 9. The dynamic performance of the system has been studied under different wind velocities. The simulation results are provided to demonstrate the effectiveness of the proposed hybrid control for variable speed wind generation system.

## 2. Variable Speed Wind Generation System Description

The proposed wind generation system is shown in Figure 1. The wind turbine is coupled to the shaft of a SEIG. The output of the SEIG is connected to a double-sided CRPWM voltage source converter connected to a utility grid.

### 2.1. Double-Sided Converter System

The voltage-fed double-sided converter scheme used in the proposed wind energy conversion system is shown in Figure 1. The variable frequency variable voltage power genertated is rectified by a PWM converter. The PWM inverter topology is identical to that of the PWM converter and it supplies the generated power to the utility grid. The converter consists of six switches with their anti-parallel diodes that are switched using space vector pulse width modulation (SVPWM) pattern. The switching functions of the top and bottom devices are defined $S_a$, $S_b$ and $S_c$; and $S_a'$, $S_b'$ and $S_c'$ respectively. The switching function has a value of one when the switch is turned on and it is zero when it is turned off. The voltage equations for the converter in the stationary reference frame can be expressed in terms of the switching functions as given by (1-3).

$$V_a=\frac{1}{3}V_{dc}[2S_a-S_b-S_c] \tag{1}$$

$$V_b=\frac{1}{3}V_{dc}[-S_a+2S_b-S_c] \tag{2}$$

$$V_c=\frac{1}{3}V_{dc}[-S_a-S_b+2S_c] \tag{3}$$

### 2.2. Analysis of Wind Turbine

The wind turbine driven SEIG system has the following parameters. The Wind turbine parameters are $P_m$=1.5 kW at $V_\omega$=16m/s, turbine radius $R_T$=0.7m and $\lambda_{opt}$=6.5 while the IG parameters are $P_e$=1.5 kW, $V$=380 V, $I_s$=4 A, number of poles $P$=4, $f$=50 Hz, $R_s$ =6.29Ω, $R_r$ = 3.59Ω, $L_s$ =$L_r$ =480 mH, $L_m$ =464 mH and the total moment of inertia of the wind turbine and the IG $J$=2 kg. m$^2$.

The wind turbine is characterized by the non-dimensional curve of coefficient of performance as a function of tip-speed ratio $\lambda$. The mechanical input power $P_m$ of a fixed-pitch wind turbine as a function of the effective wind velocity $V_\omega$ through the blades, the air density, $\rho$, the blades radius $R_T$ and the power coefficient $C_P$ is given in [9, 12]:

$$P_{mT}=\frac{1}{2}\rho\pi R_T^2 V_\omega^3 C_P(\lambda) \tag{4}$$

Considering the rotational speed of the wind turbine $\omega_t$ and the torque coefficient $C_T(\lambda)$, the wind turbine mechanical torque is given by:

$$T_{mT}=\frac{1}{2}\rho\pi R_T^3 V_\omega^2 C_T(\lambda) \tag{5}$$

$$C_P(\lambda)=\lambda C_T(\lambda) \tag{6}$$

where $C_P(\lambda)$ is the turbine power coefficient, $C_T(\lambda)$ is the turbine torque coefficient, $V_\omega$ is the wind velocity (in m/s), $\rho$ is the air density (typically 1.25 kg/m$^3$), $R_T$ is the blades radius (in m) and $\lambda$ is tip-speed ratio and is defined as:

$$\lambda = \omega_T R_T / V_\omega \tag{7}$$

where $\omega_T$ is the wind turbine rotational speed (rad/s).

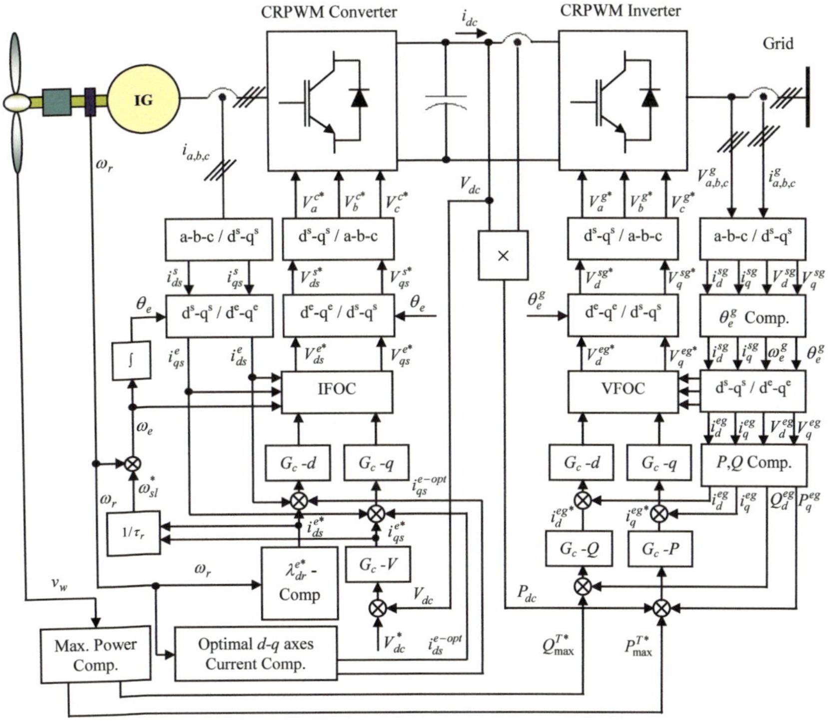


**Figure 1.** Intelligent maximization control of a variable speed wind driven self-excited induction generator system connected to a utility grid.

The turbine power coefficient $C_P(\lambda)$ and the turbine torque coefficient $C_T(\lambda)$ are functions of the tip-speed ratio of the blades if the pitch angle of the blade is constant. The turbine power coefficient is represented by various approximation expressions. In this Chapter, $C_P(\lambda)$ and $C_T(\lambda)$ are approximated by a fifth-order polynomial curve fit given by (8-9) and are shown in Figures (2 and 3). The power and torque versus speed curves of wind turbine can be calculated by (4)-(7) at various wind velocities. The optimum point corresponds to the condition where the power coefficient $C_P(\lambda)$ becomes the maximum. The maximum $C_P$ is 0.37 when $\lambda$=6.7.

$$\begin{aligned} C_P(\lambda) &= 0.0084948 + 0.05186\lambda - 0.022818\lambda^2 \\ &+ 0.01191\lambda^3 - 0.0017641\lambda^4 + 7.484x10^{-5}\lambda^5 \end{aligned} \tag{8}$$

$$C_T(\lambda)=0.00066294+0.0091889\lambda-0.0026952\lambda^2 \\ +0.001688\lambda^3-0.00028374\lambda^4+1.3269x10^{-5}\lambda^5 \tag{9}$$

### 2.3. Maximum Power Point Tracking Analysis

When the tip speed ratio is controlled by the optimum value regardless of the wind speed, the maximum mechanical power is obtained from the wind turbine. The optimum speed of the IG for maximum power of the wind turbine is given by (10) and the maximum mechanical power and the optimal torque are given by (11) and (12).

$$\omega_{opt} = K_{\omega-opt}V_{\omega} \tag{10}$$

$$P_{Tm-\max} = K^V_{p-\max}V^3_{\omega} \tag{11}$$

$$T_{Tm-opt} = K^V_{T-opt}V^2_{\omega} \tag{12}$$

$$K^V_{p-\max} = \frac{1}{2}\rho\pi R_T^2 C_{p,\max} \tag{13}$$

$$K^V_{T-opt} = \frac{1}{2}\rho\pi R_T^3 C_{p,\max} \Big/ \lambda_{opt} \tag{14}$$

$$K_{\omega-opt} = \lambda_{opt} / R_T \tag{15}$$

$$K^{\omega}_{p-\max} = K^V_{p-\max} / (K_{\omega-opt})^3 \tag{16}$$

$$K^{\omega}_{T-opt} = K^V_{T-opt} / (K_{\omega-opt})^2 \tag{17}$$

$$P_{Tm-\max} = K^{\omega}_{p-\max}\omega^3_{opt} \tag{18}$$

$$T_{Tm-opt} = K^{\omega}_{T-opt}\omega^2_{opt} \tag{19}$$

When the IG speed is always controlled at the optimum speed given in (10), the tip-speed ratio remains the optimum value and the maximum power point can be achieved. At any wind speed, we can calculate the optimum rotational speed of the IG from (10), and then the maximum mechanical power is calculated from (11). The maximum power is used as the reference power to the CRPWM converter in order to get the maximum load current.

From (10)-(17), the maximum power and optimal torque as function of the optimum rotational IG speed are calculated and given by (18)-(19). From Figure 4, it is clear that the maximum power can be achieved when the IG torque is controlled on the optimal torque curve according to the IG rotor speed.

$$T_{IG-opt} = -K_{T-opt}^{\omega-IG}\omega_r^2 \tag{20}$$

$$K_{T-opt}^{\omega-IG} = K_{T-opt}^{V} / G.(K_{\omega-opt})^2 \tag{21}$$

## 3. Dynamic Model of the Self-Excited Induction Generator

The dynamic model of the IG is helpful to analyze all its characteristics. The *d-q* model in the arbitrary reference frame provides the complete solution for dynamic analysis and control in [2-4]. The dynamic model is given by (22-24, 25).

$$\begin{bmatrix}0\\0\\0\\0\end{bmatrix} = \begin{bmatrix} (R_s + L_s\sigma\frac{d}{dt}) & \omega L_s\sigma & \frac{L_m}{L_r}\frac{d}{dt} & \frac{L_m}{L_r}\omega \\ -\omega L_s\sigma & (R_s + L_s\sigma\frac{d}{dt}) & -\omega\frac{L_m}{L_r} & \frac{L_m}{L_r}\frac{d}{dt} \\ -\frac{L_m}{L_r}R_r & 0 & \left(R_r / L_r + \frac{d}{dt}\right) & (\omega-\omega_r) \\ 0 & -\frac{L_m}{L_r}R_r & -(\omega-\omega_r) & \left(R_r / L_r + \frac{d}{dt}\right) \end{bmatrix} \begin{bmatrix} i_{qs}\\ i_{ds}\\ \lambda_{qr}\\ \lambda_{dr}\end{bmatrix} + \begin{bmatrix} V_{qs}\\ V_{ds}\\ V_{qr}\\ V_{dr}\end{bmatrix} \tag{22}$$

$$V_{qs} = \frac{1}{C}\int i_{qs}dt + V_{cq}\mid_{t=0} \tag{23}$$

$$V_{ds} = \frac{1}{C}\int i_{ds}dt + V_{cd}\mid_{t=0} \tag{24}$$

$$T_e = -\frac{3}{2}\frac{P}{2}\frac{L_m}{L_r}(\lambda_{dr}i_{qs} - \lambda_{qr}i_{ds}) \tag{25}$$

where, $V_{qs}$, $V_{ds}$, $i_{qs}$, and $i_{ds}$ are the stator voltages and currents, respectively. $v_{qr}$ and $v_{dr}$ are the rotor voltages. $\lambda_{qr}$ and $\lambda_{dr}$ are the rotor fluxes. $R_s$, $L_s$, $R_r$ and $L_r$ are the resistance and the self inductance of the stator and the rotor, respectively. $L_m$ is the mutual inductance.

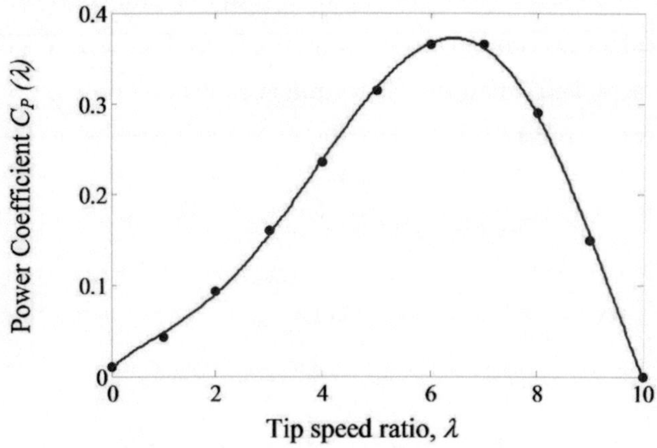


**Figure 2.** Power coefficient versus tip speed ratio.

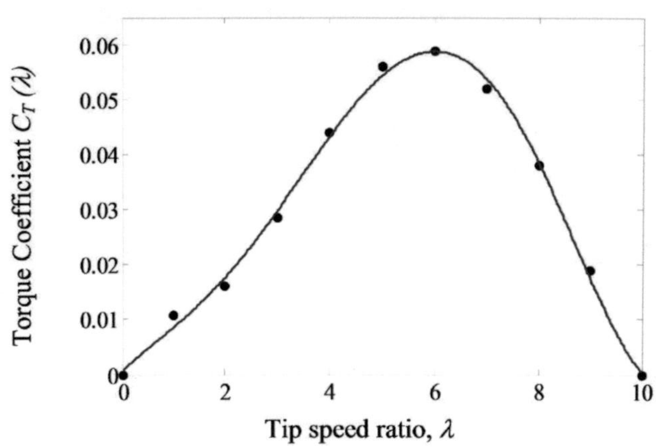


**Figure 3.** Torque coefficient versus tip speed ratio.

The relation between the wind turbine output torque and the electromagnetic torque of the IG is given by (26).

$$T_{Tm} = J\frac{d}{dt}\omega_m + \beta\omega_m + T_e \tag{26}$$

From (22-26), the state equations of the SEIG and wind turbine can be accomplished as in (27) and (28).

$$\frac{d}{dt}\omega_m = \frac{1}{J}T_{Tm} - \frac{\beta}{J}\omega_m - \frac{1}{J}T_e \tag{27}$$

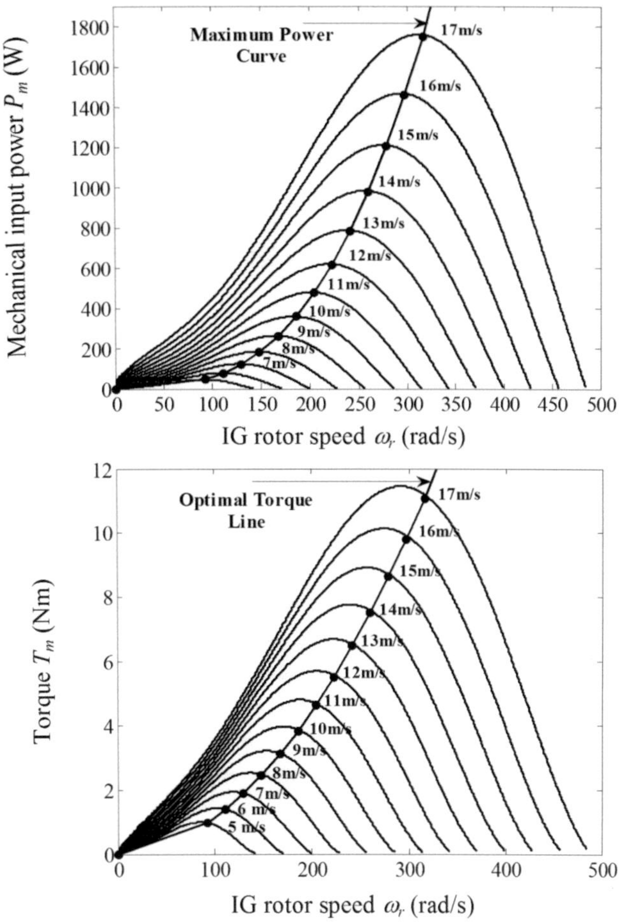


**Figure 4.** Characteristics of wind turbine at various wind speeds.

$$\frac{d}{dt}\begin{bmatrix} i_{qs} \\ i_{ds} \\ \lambda_{qr} \\ \lambda_{dr} \end{bmatrix} = \frac{1}{\sigma L_s L_r}\begin{bmatrix} -(R_s L_r + R_r L_m^2 / L_r) & -\omega\sigma L_s L_r & (L_m / L_r) R_r & -\omega_r L_m \\ \omega\sigma L_s L_r & -(R_s L_r + R_r L_m^2 / L_r) & \omega_r L_m & (L_m / L_r) R_r \\ \sigma L_s L_r L_m R_r / L_r & 0 & -\sigma L_s L_r R_r / L_r & -\sigma L_s L_r (\omega - \omega_r) \\ 0 & \sigma L_s L_r L_m R_r / L_r & \sigma L_s L_r (\omega - \omega_r) & -\sigma L_s L_r R_r / L_r \end{bmatrix} \begin{bmatrix} i_{qs} \\ i_{ds} \\ \lambda_{qr} \\ \lambda_{dr} \end{bmatrix} + \frac{1}{\sigma L_s L_r}\begin{bmatrix} L_m v_{qr} - L_r v_{qs} \\ L_m v_{dr} - L_r v_{ds} \\ -\sigma L_s L_r v_{qr} \\ -\sigma L_s L_r v_{dr} \end{bmatrix} \quad (28)$$

where $\omega_m$, $J$ and $\beta$ are the mechanical angular speeds of the wind turbine, the effective inertia of the wind turbine, the induction generator and the friction coefficient, respectively.

In order to model the induction machine when used for motoring application, it is important to determine the magnetizing inductance at rated voltage. In the SEIG, the variation of magnetizing inductance $L_m$ is the main factor in the dynamics of voltage buildup and stabilization. In this investigation, the magnetizing inductance is calculated by driving the induction machine at synchronous speed and taking measurements when the applied voltage was varied from zero to 100% of the rated voltage. The magnetizing inductance used in this experimental setup is given as shown in Figure 5. The test results are based on the rated frequency (50 Hz) of the IG while the dots are experimental results and the curve is a fifth-order curve fit given by

$$L_m = -1.023 \times 10^{-11} V_{ph}^5 + 6.162 \times 10^{-9} V_{ph}^4 - 1.25 \times 10^{-6} V_{ph}^3$$
$$+ 8.267 \times 10^{-5} V_{ph}^2 - 3.843 \times 10^{-5} V_{ph} + 0.1985$$

where $V_{ph}$ is the phase voltage.

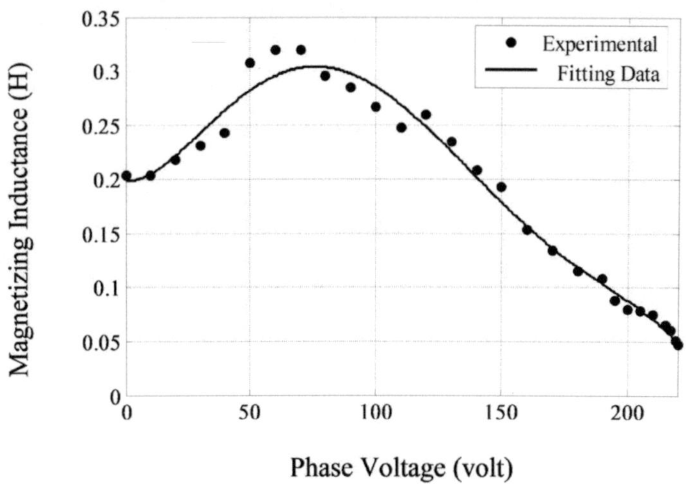


**Figure 5.** Magnetic curve of the SEIG.

## 4. Optimal IFOC of the Induction Generator

The IFOC dynamics for the IG can be derived from (22-25), respectively at $\lambda_{qr}=0$, $d\lambda_{qr}/dt=0$, $d\lambda_{dr}/dt=0$, and $\omega=\omega_e$. The torque and slip angular frequency for rotor field orientation are given in (26-27) while the voltage commands of the IFOC are given by (29-31) in [11, 12].

$$T_e = -K_t . i_{ds}^{e*} i_{qs}^{e*} = -K_{T-opt}^{\omega-IG} \omega_r^2 \quad (29)$$

$$\omega_{sl} = \frac{1}{\tau_r} \cdot \frac{i_{qs}^{e*}}{i_{ds}^{e*}} \tag{30}$$

$$\begin{bmatrix} V_{qs}^{e*} \\ V_{ds}^{e*} \end{bmatrix} = \begin{bmatrix} e_{qs}^{e} \\ e_{ds}^{e} \end{bmatrix} - \begin{bmatrix} R_s + \sigma L_s \frac{d}{dt} & \omega_e \sigma L_s \\ -\omega_e \sigma L_s & R_s + \sigma L_s \frac{d}{dt} \end{bmatrix} \begin{bmatrix} i_{qs}^{e} \\ i_{ds}^{e} \end{bmatrix} \tag{31}$$

where $K_t$=(3/2)(P/2)$(L_m)^2/L_r$ is the torque constant, $e^e_{qs}$ and $e^e_{ds}$ are the back EMFs of the IG. $T_e$, $\tau_r$, $\omega_{sl}$, and $\omega_e$ are the electromagnetic torque, the rotor time constant, the slip angular frequency, and the angular frequency of the synchronous reference frame, respectively.

$$\begin{bmatrix} e_{qs}^{e} \\ e_{ds}^{e} \end{bmatrix} = \begin{bmatrix} \omega_e \lambda_{dr}^{e} \frac{L_m}{L_r} \\ 0 \end{bmatrix} \tag{32}$$

In the previous analysis, the IG torque is given by (29) as a function of the rotor speed. Therefore, the d-axes current becomes a function only of the rotor speed. The optimal d-q axes currents $i_{ds}$ and $i_{qs}$ can be derived from (22) and (29) and are plotted as given in Figure 6. These plots show the relation of the optimal currents as function of the IG rotor speed and can be approximated by a third-order polynomials given by (34, 35).

$$i_{ds}^{e}(\omega_r) i_{qs}^{e}(\omega_r) = (K_{T-opt}^{\omega} / K_t)\omega_r^2 \tag{33}$$

$$i_{ds}^{e-opt}(\omega_r) = K_{d3}\omega_r^3 + K_{d2}\omega_r^2 + K_{d1}\omega_r + K_{d0} \tag{34}$$

$$i_{qs}^{e-opt}(\omega_r) = K_{q3}\omega_r^3 + K_{q2}\omega_r^2 + K_{q1}\omega_r + K_{q0} \tag{35}$$

By controlling the d-q axes currents utilizing (34)-(35) according to the IG rotor speed, the maximum mechanical power is obtained from the wind turbine and the losses of the IG are minimized. Also, from (29), it is clear that the IG torque is proportional to the q-axis current when the d-axis current is kept constant and thus he IG power is almost proportional to q-axis current. Therefore, the control of generated power becomes possible by adjusting the q-axis current according to the required generated power, where the d-axis current is given by (34).

## 5. Dynamic Model of the IG-Side CRPWM Voltage Source Converter

The block diagram of the CRPWM voltage source converter control system based on the IFOC-SEIG is shown in Figure 8. It is well known that the IFOC of induction machines allows for the independent control of two input variables, stator q-axis current $i^e_{qs}$ and stator d-axis current $i^{e}_{ds}$. This suggests that it is possible to control the output voltage and power factor and/or efficiency by controlling the two components of the stator currents. The dynamic equations of the CRPWM converter are based on the IFOC dynamics of the IG in [12-14] and are given by (36, 37).

$$e^{e}_{qs} - V^{ec}_{qs} = R_s i^{ec}_{qs} + \sigma L_s \frac{d}{dt} i^{ec}_{qs} + \omega_e \sigma L_s i^{ec}_{ds} \tag{36}$$

$$e^{e}_{ds} - V^{ec}_{ds} = R_s i^{ec}_{ds} + \sigma L_s \frac{d}{dt} i^{ec}_{ds} - \omega_e \sigma L_s i^{ec}_{qs} \tag{37}$$

By considering the converter as an ideal current regulated source, the energy is transferred between the IG and the DC-link. As a consequence, the instantaneous power of both the converter's AC-side and DC-side is the same.

$$V_{dc} i_{dc} = \frac{3}{2}\left(V^{e}_{qs} i^{e}_{qs} + V^{e}_{ds} i^{e}_{ds}\right) \tag{38}$$

From (38), the relation between the DC-link current $i_{dc}$ and the d-q axis currents $i^{e}_{qs}$ and $i^{e}_{ds}$ is as follows.

$$i_{dc} = \frac{3}{2}\left(\frac{V^{e}_{qs}}{V_{dc}} i^{e}_{qs} + \frac{V^{e}_{ds}}{V_{dc}} i^{e}_{ds}\right) \tag{39}$$

At FOC $V^{e}_{ds} \cong 0$, therefore, there is a direct relation between the DC-link current and the q-axis current of the IG.

$$i^{e}_{qs} = \frac{2}{3} \frac{V_{dc}}{V^{e}_{qs}} i_{dc} \tag{40}$$

The dynamics of the DC-link is given by (41-43).

$$C_{dc} \frac{d}{dt} V_{dc} + i_L = i_{dc} \tag{41}$$

$$C_{dc} \frac{d}{dt} V_{dc} + \frac{1}{R_L} V_{dc} = i_{dc} \tag{42}$$

$$i_{dc} = \frac{3}{2} \frac{V^{e}_{qs}}{V_{dc}} i^{e}_{qs} \tag{43}$$

where, $C_{dc}$ is the DC-link capacitor, $i_L$ is the load current and $i_{dc}$ is the DC-link current. The state equations of the CRPWM converter and DC-link are derived from (36-43) and are given in (44-45).

$$\frac{d}{dt}V_{dc}=\begin{bmatrix}\frac{1}{C_{dc}} & -\frac{1}{R_L\,C_{dc}}\end{bmatrix}\begin{bmatrix}i_{dc}\\ V_{dc}\end{bmatrix} \tag{44}$$

$$\frac{d}{dt}\begin{bmatrix}i_{qs}^{ec}\\ i_{ds}^{ec}\\ V_{dc}\end{bmatrix}=\frac{1}{\sigma L_s}\begin{bmatrix}-R_s & \omega_e\sigma L_s & 0\\ -\omega_e\sigma L_s & R_s & 0\\ \sigma L_s K_{dc}^{q} & \sigma L_s K_{dc}^{d} & 0\end{bmatrix}\begin{bmatrix}i_{qs}^{ec}\\ i_{ds}^{ec}\\ V_{dc}\end{bmatrix}+\frac{1}{\sigma L_s}\begin{bmatrix}\sigma L_s & 0 & 0\\ 0 & \sigma L_s & 0\\ 0 & 0 & -\sigma L_s\end{bmatrix}\begin{bmatrix}e_{qs}^{e}-V_{qs}^{ec}\\ e_{ds}^{e}-V_{ds}^{ec}\\ i_L\end{bmatrix} \tag{45}$$

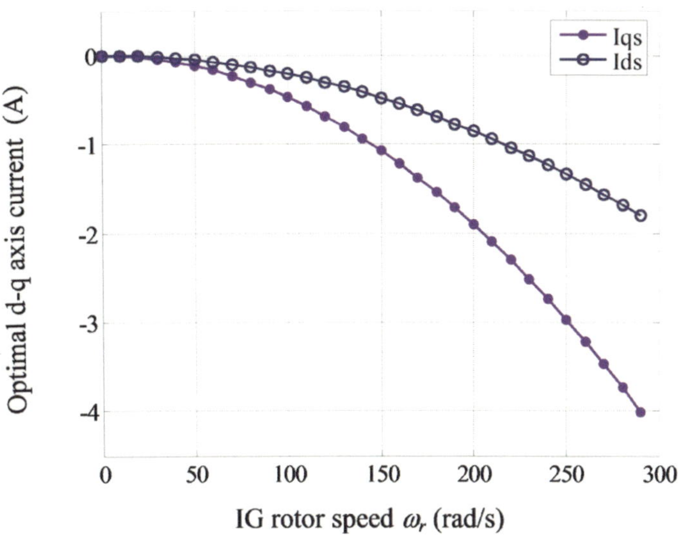


**Figure 6.** Optimal d-q axes currents as a function of IG rotor speed.

From (45), the current in q-axis $i_{qs}^{e}$ can be estimated as:

$$i_{qs}^{e}=A_n^{-1}[\dot{V}_{dc}-B_n i_L-C_n E_{qds}^{e}] \tag{46}$$

where, $A_n=[K_{dc}^{q}+K_{dc}^{d}/\tau_r.\omega_{sl}]$, $B_n=[-1/C_{dc}]$, $C_n=[1/C_{dc}]$ and $E_{qds}^{e}=[e_{qs}^{e*}-V_{qs}^{e*}\quad e_{ds}^{e*}-V_{ds}^{e*}]$.

At the steady state, the load current $i_L$ is approximately equals to the DC-link current $i_{dc}$. Therefore, the optimal load current can be approximated by (47). Figure 7 shows the optimal load current corresponding to the maximum mechanical power obtained from the wind turbine.

$$i_L^{opt}(\omega_r) = K_{L\ 3}\omega_r^3 + K_{L\ 2}\omega_r^2 + K_{L\ 1}\omega_r + K_{L\ 0} \tag{47}$$

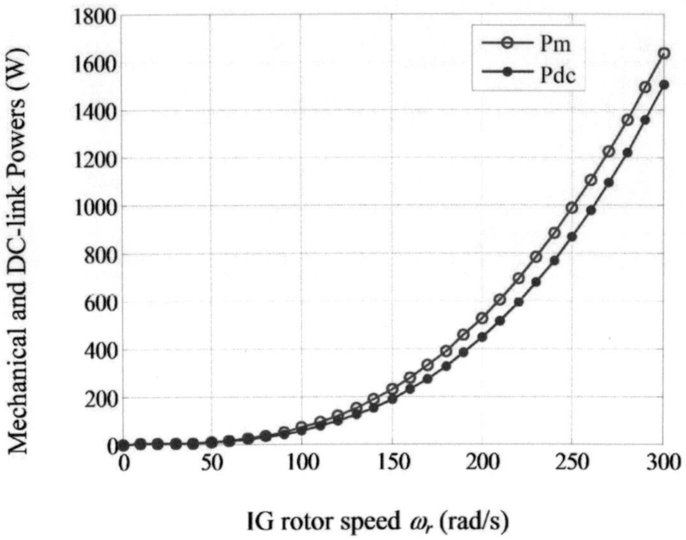


**Figure 7.** Optimal load current as a function of IG rotor speed.

## 6. Dynamic Model of the Grid-Side CRPWM Voltage Source Inverter

The grid-side CRPWM voltage source inverter is connected to the grid through three single-phase coils (control windings). With this configuration it is possible to operate using boost mode and have attractive features as constant DC–link voltage, low harmonic distortion of grid current, bidirectional power flow and adjustable power factor. The aim of the control of the grid-side CRPWM voltage source converter is to impose a current to the control winding and to control independently the active and reactive power to be injected to the grid. By using vector control technique, the currents of the CRPWM inverter are controlled with very high bandwidth. The vector control approach is used, with a reference frame oriented along the grid voltage vector position, such that $V_{qg} = V_{mg}$ and $V_{dg} = 0$. This allows independent control of the active and reactive power through currents $i_{qg}$ and $i_{dg}$ respectively. Usually, the reactive power component current is set to zero for unity power factor operation. The primary aim of this control scheme is to modulate the inverter to regulate the magnitude and the phase angle of the grid supply current, so that the active and reactive power entering the network can be controlled. The procedure for modeling the CRPWM inverter is based on the virtual-flux orientation control (VFOC) technique. The grid-side converter control, shown in Figure 9, is based on the d–q voltage equations of the grid-reactance-converter system according to following equations:

$$\begin{bmatrix} V_q^{eg*} \\ V_d^{eg*} \end{bmatrix} = \begin{bmatrix} e_q^{eg} \\ e_d^{eg} \end{bmatrix} + \begin{bmatrix} R_g + L_g p & \omega_{eg} L_g \\ -\omega_{eg} L_g & R_g + L_g p \end{bmatrix} \begin{bmatrix} i_q^{eg} \\ i_d^{eg} \end{bmatrix} \tag{48}$$

$$\begin{bmatrix} P \\ Q \end{bmatrix} = \frac{3}{2} \cdot \begin{bmatrix} V_q^{eg} & V_d^{eg} \\ V_d^{eg} & -V_q^{eg} \end{bmatrix} \begin{bmatrix} i_q^{eg} \\ i_d^{eg} \end{bmatrix} \tag{49}$$

The vector control of the grid-side CRPWM inverter is represented in the block diagram illustrated in Figure 9. The control of the reactive power is realized by acting over the control winding current, $i_{ds}$. The reference current is obtained by a PI current controller that adjusts the reactive power to a desired amount. Similarly, the control of the active power is realized by acting over the control winding current $i_{qs}$ and the reference current is given by a PI current controller. The possible situation for defining the current references is to track the maximum turbine power for each wind speed.

At VFOC, $V_{dg}=0$. Therefore, there are a direct relations between the active power, $P$ and q–axis current and the reactive power, $Q$ and d–axis current of the control windings. This allows independent control of the active and reactive power through currents $i_{qg}$ and $i_{dg}$ respectively according to following equations:

$$\begin{bmatrix} P \\ Q \end{bmatrix} = \frac{3}{2} \cdot \begin{bmatrix} +V_q^{eg} & 0 \\ 0 & -V_q^{eg} \end{bmatrix} \begin{bmatrix} i_q^{eg} \\ i_d^{eg} \end{bmatrix} \tag{50}$$

The d-q current commands of the inverter are expressed as:

$$\begin{bmatrix} i_q^{eg*} \\ i_d^{eg*} \end{bmatrix} = \frac{2}{3} \begin{bmatrix} +\dfrac{P^*}{V_q^{eg*}} \\ -\dfrac{Q^*}{V_q^{eg*}} \end{bmatrix} \tag{51}$$

where, $P^*$ and $Q^*$ denote the required maximum active and reactive power. To achieve the unity power factor operation, $Q^*$ must be zero. From (50), it is obvious that the current command of the d–axis must be zero for unity power factor operation and the current command of the q–axis can be evaluated from the required active power. It is seen from (47) that coupling terms exist in the d-q current control loops. The d–q voltage decouplers are designed to decouple the current control loops. Suitable feed-forward control components of grid voltages are also added to speed up current responses. The d-q current control loops of the CRPWM inverter in the proposed control system are shown in Figure 9.

## 7. Design of the PID Controllers for Double-Sided CRPWM AC/DC/AC Voltage Source Converters

This section considers the design procedures for the PID voltage controller of the IG-Side CRPWM voltage source converter, the PID active power and reactive power controllers for the grid-side CRPWM inverter. The design procedures are based on the integral time absolute error (ITAE) performance index response method to obtain the desired control performance in the nominal condition of command tracking.

### 7.1. PID Voltage Controller Design for IG-Side CRPWM Voltage Source Converter

A systematic design procedure for the PI current controllers capable of satisfying the desired specifications is given in [12]. The gains of the PI d-q axis current controllers have been determined using the ITAE performance index response method and are given by (51-52). From the block diagram shown in Figure 8, a back EMF estimator is adopted to q-axis current loop for voltage feed-forward control. The q-axis stator current of the IG is selected as the variable to be changed to regulate the DC-link voltage. The voltage control is carried out through a voltage control loop using a PID voltage controller and is designed to stabilize the voltage control loop. The gains of the PID controller have been determined using the ITAE performance index response method. By exercising the decoupling control, the dynamic model including the CRPWM converter and the IG can be simplified and the closed loop transfer function is given by (53) from Figure 7.

$$\begin{aligned} K_i^{cq} &= \omega_n^2 \sigma L_s \\ K_p^{cq} &= (1.4\omega_n \sigma L_s - R_s - T_q) \end{aligned} \tag{52}$$

$$\begin{aligned} K_i^{cd} &= \omega_n^2 \sigma L_s \\ K_p^{cd} &= (1.4\omega_n \sigma L_s - R_s - T_d) \end{aligned} \tag{53}$$

$$\begin{aligned} \left.\frac{V_{dc}(s)}{V_{dc}^*(s)}\right|_{i_L=0} &= \frac{a_3 s^3 + a_2 s^2 + a_1 s + a_0}{s^4 + b_3 s^3 + b_2 s^2 + b_1 s + b_0} \\ &\cong \frac{\omega_n^4}{s^4 + 2.1\omega_n s^3 + 3.4\omega_n^2 s^2 + 2.7\omega_n^3 s + \omega_n^4} \end{aligned} \tag{54}$$

The PID voltage controller parameters are given by (54-56).

$$K_P^v = \frac{1}{K_{dc}}.\frac{\sigma L_s}{K_i^{cq}}\left(2.7\omega_n^3 - \frac{K_p^{cq}}{K_i^{cq}}.\omega_n^4\right) \tag{55}$$

$$K_i^v = \frac{1}{K_{dc}}.\frac{\sigma L_s}{K_i^{cq}}.\omega_n^4 \tag{56}$$

$$K_d^v = \frac{1}{K_{dc}}.\frac{\sigma L_s}{K_i^{cq}}.\left(\omega_n^4.\frac{K_p^{cq}}{K_i^{cq}} - 2.7\omega_n^3.\frac{K_p^{cq}}{K_i^{cq}} + 3.4\omega_n^2 - \frac{K_i^{cq}}{\sigma L_s}\right) \tag{57}$$

## 7.2. PID Active Power Controller Design for Grid-Side CRPWM Voltage Source Inverter

A systematic design procedure for the PI current controllers is given in [12]. These controllers are designed based on the control windings dynamic model at VFOC. The gains of the PI d-q axis current controllers have been determined and are given by (57-58). The q-axis current of the control winding is selected as the variable to be changed to regulate the active power, *P*. The active power control is carried out through a power control loop using a PID controller and is designed to stabilize the active power control loop. The gains of the PID controller have been determined using the ITAE method. The block diagram of the active power control loop is shown in Figure 9. The closed loop transfer function of the active power control loop is given by (59).

$$\begin{aligned} K_i^{gq} &= \omega_n^2 L_g \\ K_p^{gq} &= (1.4\omega_n L_g - R_g) \end{aligned} \tag{58}$$

$$\begin{aligned} K_i^{gd} &= \omega_n^2 L_g \\ K_p^{gd} &= (1.4\omega_n L_g - R_g) \end{aligned} \tag{59}$$

$$\left.\frac{P_q^{eg}(s)}{P_{\max}^{T*}(s)}\right|_{VFOC} = \frac{c_3^P s^3 + c_2^P s^2 + c_1^P s + c_0^P}{s^3 + d_2^P s^2 + d_1^P s + d_0^P} \cong \frac{\omega_n^3}{s^3 + 1.75\omega_n s^2 + 2.15\omega_n^2 s + \omega_n^3} \tag{60}$$

The PID controller parameters are given by (60-62).

$$K_d^P = \frac{\left(1.75\omega_n L_g K_i^{qg} - R_g K_i^{qg} - 2.15\omega_n^2 L_g K_p^{qg}\right)}{\left(K_q^P K_i^{2qg} + 2.15\omega_n^2 K_q^P K_p^{2qg} - 1.75\omega_n K_q^P K_p^{qg}\right)} \tag{61}$$

$$K_p^P = \left(\frac{2.15\omega_n^2 L_g}{K_q^P K_i^{qg}}\right) - \frac{1}{K_q^P} + \left(2.15\omega_n^2 \frac{K_p^{qg}}{K_i^{qg}}\right).K_d^P \tag{62}$$

$$K_i^P = \left( \frac{\omega_n^3 L_g}{K_q^P K_i^{qg}} \right) + \left( \frac{K_p^{qg}}{K_i^{qg}} \right) . K_d^P \tag{63}$$

### 7.3. PID Reactive Power Controller Design for Grid-Side CRPWM Voltage Source Inverter

Similarly, the PID reactive power controller is designed and analyzed. The d-axis current of the control winding is selected as the variable to be used to regulate the reactive power, Q. The block diagram of the reactive power control loop is shown in Figure 9. The closed loop transfer function of the reactive power control loop is given by:

$$\left. \frac{Q_d^{eg}(s)}{Q_{\max}^{T*}(s)} \right|_{VOC} = \frac{c_3^Q s^3 + c_2^Q s^2 + c_1^Q s + c_0^Q}{s^3 + d_2^Q s^2 + d_1^Q s + d_0^Q} \cong \frac{\omega_n^3}{s^3 + 1.75\omega_n s^2 + 2.15\omega_n^2 s + \omega_n^3} \tag{64}$$

The PID controller parameters are given by (64-66).

$$K_d^Q = \frac{\left(1.75\omega_n L_g K_i^{dg} - R_g K_i^{dg} - 2.15\omega_n^2 L_g K_p^{qg}\right)}{\left(K_q^Q K_i^{2dg} + 2.15\omega_n^2 K_q^Q K_p^{2dg} - 1.75\omega_n K_q^Q K_p^{dg}\right)} \tag{65}$$

$$K_p^Q = \left( \frac{2.15\omega_n^2 L_g}{K_q^Q K_i^{dg}} \right) - \frac{1}{K_q^Q} + \left( 2.15\omega_n^2 \frac{K_p^{dg}}{K_i^{dg}} \right) . K_d^Q \tag{66}$$

$$K_i^Q = \left( \frac{\omega_n^3 L_g}{K_q^Q K_i^{dg}} \right) + \left( \frac{K_p^{dg}}{K_i^{dg}} \right) . K_d^Q \tag{67}$$

## 8. Intelligent Maximization Control for Double-Sided CRPWM AC/DC/AC Voltage Source Converters

### 8.1. Configuration of the Proposed Intelligent Maximization Control System

In order to control the DC-link voltage of the IG-side CRPWM voltage source converter, active power and reactive power of the grid-side CRPWM voltage source inverter effectively, an intelligent maximization hybrid control system is proposed. The configuration of the proposed hybrid control system, which combines an on-line trained wavelet-neural-network controller (WNNC) with IPSO and a PID compensator, for wind turbine generation system is illustrated in Figures (8 and 9). It basically consists of an PI current controllers in the *d-q* axis, a three PID controllers and three on-line trained WNNCs with IPSO in parallel with the three PID controllers for voltage control of the DC-link side of the CRPWM converter, active power and reactive power of the grid connected CRPWM inverter. Although the desired tracking and regulation characteristics for DC-link voltage, active power and reactive power can be obtained using the PID controllers with nominal parameters, the performance of the system is still sensitive to parameter variations. To solve this problem, a hybrid controller combining the PID controller and the WNNC with IPSO is proposed for the DC-link voltage, active power and reactive power for the double-sided CRPWM AC/DC/AC converters. The control law and error signals are designed as:

$$U_{qs}^{*}=U_{qs}^{*WNNC}+U_{qs}^{*PID} \tag{68}$$

$$i_{qs}^{e*}=\delta i_{qs}^{e*WNNC}+i_{qs}^{e*PID} \tag{69}$$

$$i_{ds}^{e*}=\delta i_{ds}^{e*WNNC}+i_{ds}^{e*PID} \tag{70}$$

$$\begin{aligned} e_v &= (V_{dc}^{*}-V_{dc}) \\ \dot{V}_{dc} &= k_v dV_{dc}/dt \end{aligned} \tag{71}$$

$$\begin{aligned} e_P &= (P^{*}-P) \\ \dot{P} &= k_P dP/dt \end{aligned} \tag{72}$$

$$\begin{aligned} e_Q &= (Q^{*}-Q) \\ \dot{Q} &= k_Q dQ/dt \end{aligned} \tag{73}$$

where $i_{qs}^{e*PID}$ is the $q$-axis current command generated from the PID controller and $\delta i_{qs}^{e*WNNC}$ is produced by the proposed WNNC with IPSO to automatically compensate for performance degradation.

$i_{qs}^{e*PID}=i_{qs}^{eg*PID}$ for CRPWM inverter, $i_{qs}^{e*PID}=i_{qs}^{e*PID}$ for CRPWM converter, $i_{ds}^{e*PID}=i_{ds}^{eg*PID}$ for CRPWM inverter, $\delta i_{qs}^{e*WNNC}=\delta i_{qs}^{eg*WNNC}$ for CRPWM inverter, $\delta i_{qs}^{e*WNNC}=\delta i_{qs}^{e*WNNC}$ for CRPWM converter, $i_{ds}^{e*WNNC}=i_{ds}^{eg*WNNC}$ for CRPWM inverter, $P^{*}=P_{\max}^{T*}$ for CRPWM inverter, $Q^{*}=Q_{\max}^{T*}$ for CRPWM inverter.

### 8.2. Wavelet–Neural–Network Controller with IPSO

Since the squirrel-cage IGs have robust construction and lower initial, run time and maintenance cost squirrel-cage IGs are suitable for grid-connected in wind-energy applications. Therefore, a WNNC with IPSO is proposed to control a SEIG system for grid-connected wind-energy power application. The on-line trained WNNC with IPSO combines the capability of artificial neural-network for learning ability and the capability of wavelet decomposition for identification ability. Three on-line trained WNNCs with IPSO are introduced as the regulating controllers for both the DC-link voltage of the CRPWM AC/DC converter, active and reactive power of the CRPWM DC/AC grid-connected inverter. In addition, the on-line training algorithm based on the backpropagation is derived to train the connective weights, translations and dilations in the WNNs on-line. Furthermore, an IPSO is adopted to optimize the learning rates to further improve the on-line learning capability of the WNN and hence the improvement of the control performance can be obtained.

### 8.3. Wavelet–Neural–Network Structure

The architecture of the proposed four-layers WNN in [15-23] is shown in Figure 10, which comprises an input layer (the *i* layer), a mother wavelet layer (the *j* layer), a wavelet layer (the *k* layer) and an output layer (the *o* layer), is adopted to implement the WNNC. The signal propagation and the basic function in each layer are introduced as follows.

1. *Layer 1: Input Layer*

The nodes in layer 1 transmit the input signals to the next layer. The input variables are the error signal, $e(t)$ , and the rate of change of the DC-link voltage, active power and reactive power. For every node *i* in the input layer, the input and the output of the WNN can be represented as:

$$net_i^1 = x_i^1, \quad y_i^1 = f_i^1(net_i^1) = net_i^1 \quad i = 1, 2 \tag{74}$$

$$x_1^1 = e(t) and\, x_2^1 = \psi(t) \tag{75}$$

where $e(t) = e_v(t) = (V_{dc}^* - V_{dc})$ for the CRPWM converter, $e(t) = e_P(t) = (P^* - P)$ , $e(t) = e_Q(t) = (Q^* - Q)$ , $\psi(t) = \dot{V}_{dc}$ , $\psi(t) = \dot{P}$ , for the CRPWM inverter.

2. *Layer 2: Mother Wavelet Layer*

A family of wavelets is constructed by translations and dilations performed on the mother wavelet. In the mother wavelet layer each node performs a wavelet $\phi_j$ that is derived from its mother wavelet. There are many kind of wavelets that can be used in WNN. In this Chapter, the first derivative of the Gaussian wavelet function $\varphi(x) = -x\exp(-x^2/2)$ , is adopted as a mother wavelet. For the *j*th node

$$net_j^2 = -(x_i^2 - \mu_{ij}) / \sigma_{ij}, \; y_j^2 = f_j^2(net_j^2) = \varphi_j(net_j^2) \, j = 1, \ldots, n \tag{76}$$

where $\mu_{ij}$ and $\sigma_{ij}$ are the translation and dilations in the *j*th term of the *i*th input $x_i^2$ to the node of mother wavelet layer and *n* is the total number of the wavelets with respect to the input nodes.

3. *Layer 3: Wavelet Layer*

Each node *k* in layer 3 (wavelet layer) is denoted by $\prod$ , which multiplies the incoming signal and outputs the result of the product. For the *k*th nodes:

$$net_k^3 = \prod_j \varpi_{jk}^3 x_j^3,\ y_k^3 = f_k^3(net_k^3) = net_k^3 \quad k = 1, \ \ldots\ldots, \ m \tag{77}$$

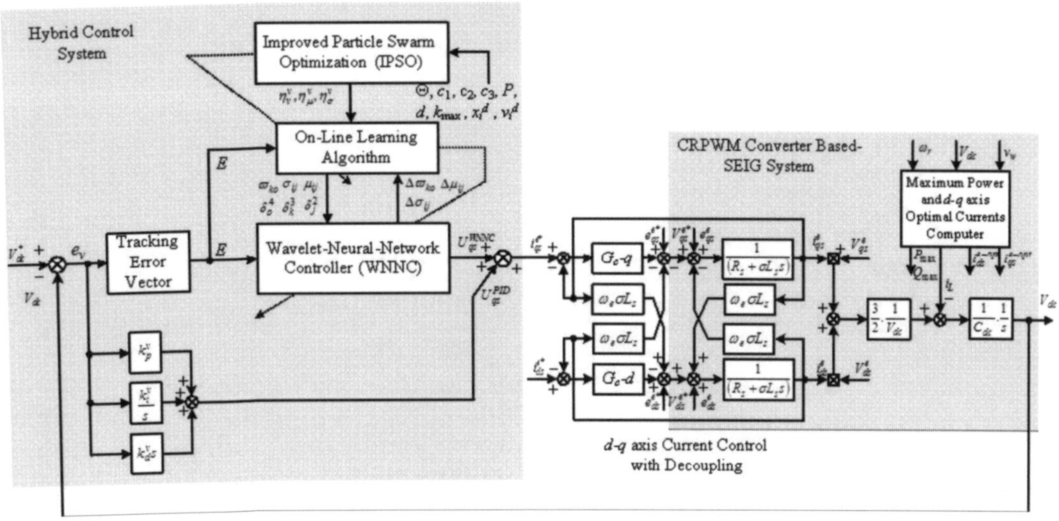

**Figure 8.** Integrated block diagram of the generator-side IFOC CRPWM voltage source converter using WNNC with IPSO control system.

where $x_j^3$ represents the $j$th input to the node of the wavelet layer (layer 3), $\varpi_{jk}^3$ is the weights between the mother wavelet layer and the wavelet layer. These weights are also assumed to be unity; and $m = (n / i)$ is the number of wavelets if each input node has the same mother wavelet nodes.

4. *Layer 4: Output Layer*

The single node $o$ in the output layer is denoted by $\sum$ , which computes the overall output as the summation of all incoming signals to obtain the final results.

$$net_o^4 = \sum_k^m \varpi_{ko}^4 x_k^4,\ y_o^4 = f_o^4(net_o^4) = net_o^4 \ o = 1 \tag{78}$$

$$y_o^4 = U_{qs}^{*WNNC}(t) = \delta i_{qs}^{e*WNNC}(t) \tag{79}$$

where the connecting weight $\varpi_{ko}^4$ is the output action strength of the $o$th output associated with the $k$th wavelet and $x_k^4$ represents the $k$th input to the node of output layer. The control problem is to design the WNNC to improve the convergence of the tracking error for the wind system.

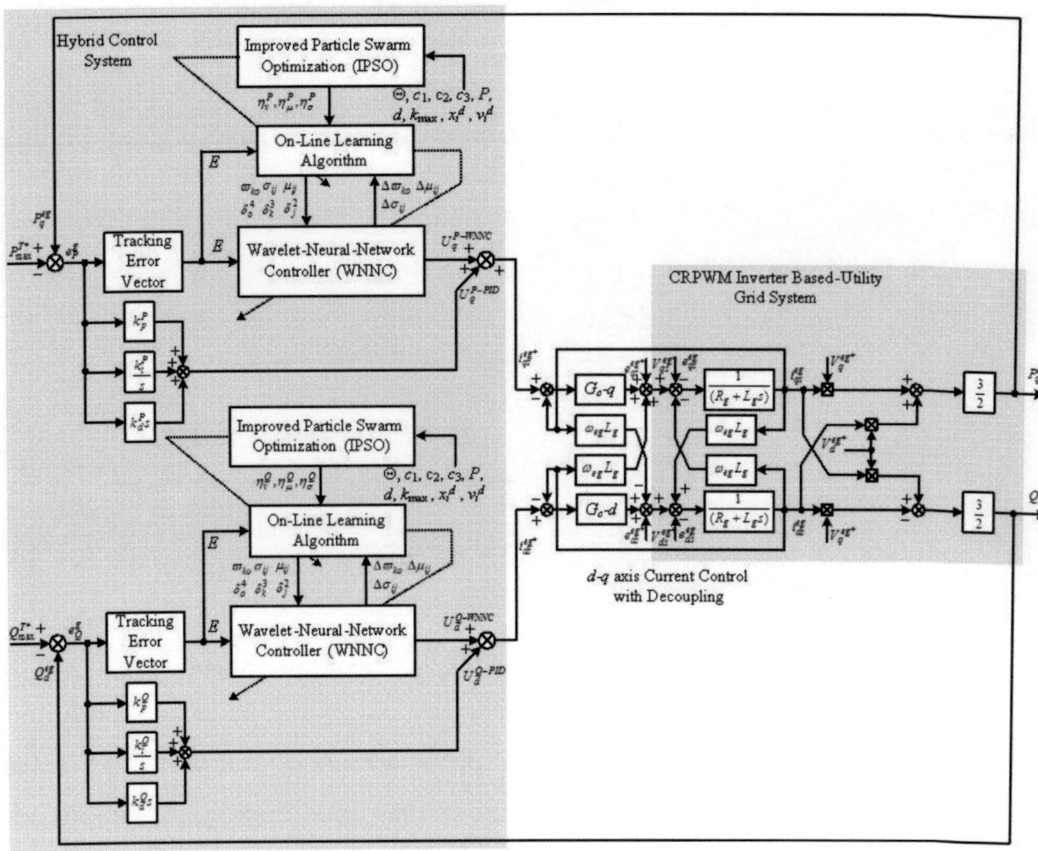


**Figure 9.** Integrated block diagram of the grid-side VFOC CRPWM voltage source inverter intelligent control system.

## 8.4. On-Line Training Algorithm Signal Analysis for WNNC

The essential part of the learning algorithm for an WNN concerns how to obtain a gradient vector in which each element in the learning algorithm is defined as the derivative of the energy function with respect to a parameter of the network using the chain rule. Since the gradient vector is calculated in the direction opposite to the flow of the output of each node, the method is generally referred to back-propagation learning rule in [15-23]. To describe the on-line learning algorithm of the WNNC using the supervised gradient descent method, the energy function is chosen as:

$$E = (1/2)(e)^2 \tag{80}$$

In the output layer (layer 4), the error term to be propagated is calculated as:

$$\delta_o^4 = -\frac{\partial E}{\partial net_o^4} = -\frac{\partial E}{\partial y_o^4}\cdot\frac{\partial y_o^4}{\partial net_o^4} = -\frac{\partial E}{\partial e}\cdot\frac{\partial e}{\partial net_o^4} = -\frac{\partial E}{\partial e}\cdot\frac{\partial e}{\partial \psi}\cdot\frac{\partial \psi}{\partial net_o^4} \tag{81}$$

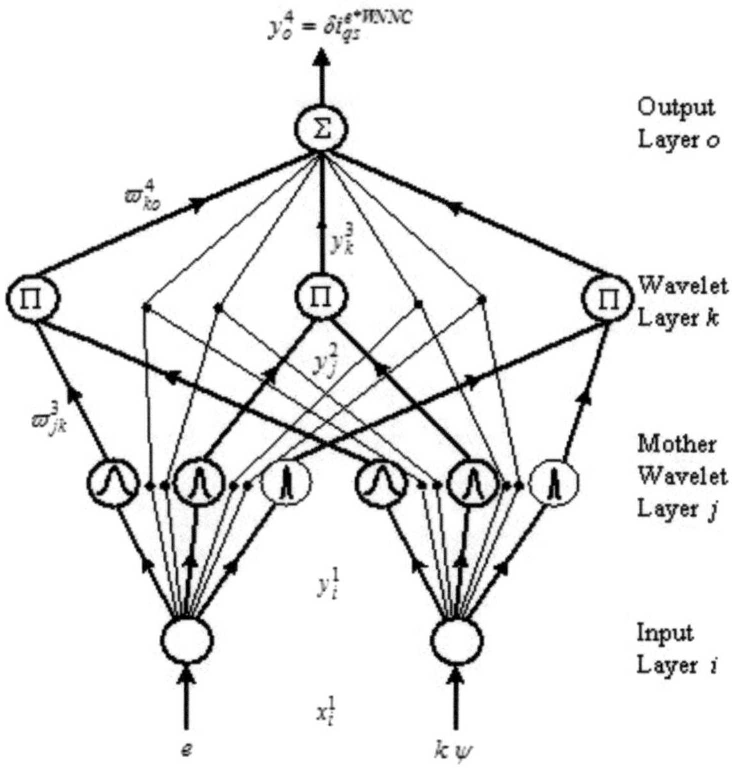


**Figure 10.** Four-layer wavelet–neural–network (WNN) structure.

The weight is updated by the amount:

$$\Delta\varpi_{ko}^4 = -\eta_v\frac{\partial E}{\partial \varpi_{ko}^4} = \left[-\eta_v\frac{\partial E}{\partial y_o^4}\cdot\frac{\partial y_o^4}{\partial net_o^4}\right]\cdot\frac{\partial net_o^4}{\partial \varpi_{ko}^4} = \eta_v\delta_o^4 x_k^4 \tag{82}$$

where $\eta_v$ is the learning rate parameter of the connecting weights of the output layer of the WNNC and will be optimized by the IPSO.

The weights of the output layer (layer 4) are updated according to the following equation.

$$\varpi_{ko}^4(N+1) = \varpi_{ko}^4(N) + \Delta\varpi_{ko}^4 = \varpi_{ko}^4(N) + \eta_v\delta_o^4 x_k^4 \tag{83}$$

where N denotes the number of iterations.

In wavelet layer (layer 3), only the error term needs to be computed and propagated because the weights in this layer are unity.

$$\delta_k^3 = -\frac{\partial E}{\partial net_k^3} = \left(-\frac{\partial E}{\partial y_o^4}\cdot\frac{\partial y_o^4}{\partial net_o^4}\right)\cdot\left(\frac{\partial net_o^4}{\partial y_k^3}\cdot\frac{\partial y_k^3}{\partial net_k^3}\right) = \delta_o^4 \omega_{ko}^4 \tag{84}$$

In the mother wavelet layer (layer 2), the multiplication operation is done. The error term is calculated as follows:

$$\delta_j^2 = -\frac{\partial E}{\partial net_j^2} = \left(-\frac{\partial E}{\partial y_o^4}\cdot\frac{\partial y_o^4}{\partial net_o^4}\cdot\frac{\partial net_o^4}{\partial y_k^3}\cdot\frac{\partial y_k^3}{\partial net_k^3}\right)\cdot\left(\frac{\partial net_k^3}{\partial y_j^2}\cdot\frac{\partial y_j^2}{\partial net_j^2}\right) = \sum_k \delta_k^3 y_k^3 \tag{85}$$

The update law of $\mu_{ij}$ is given by:

$$\Delta\mu_{ij} = -\eta_\mu \frac{\partial E_v}{\partial \mu_{ij}} = \left[-\eta_\mu \frac{\partial E}{\partial y_j^2}\cdot\frac{\partial y_j^2}{\partial net_j^2}\cdot\frac{\partial net_j^2}{\partial \mu_{ij}}\right] = \eta_\mu \delta_j^2 \frac{2(x_i^2-\mu_{ij})^2}{(\sigma_{ij})^2} \tag{86}$$

The update law of $\sigma_{ij}$ is given by:

$$\Delta\sigma_{ij} = -\eta_\sigma \frac{\partial E_v}{\partial \mu_{ij}} = \left[-\eta_\sigma \frac{\partial E}{\partial y_j^2}\cdot\frac{\partial y_j^2}{\partial net_j^2}\cdot\frac{\partial net_j^2}{\partial \sigma_{ij}}\right] = \eta_\sigma \delta_j^2 \frac{2(x_i^2-\mu_{ij})^2}{(\sigma_{ij})^2} \tag{87}$$

where $\eta_\mu$ and $\eta_\sigma$ are the learning rate parameters of the translation and dilation of the mother wavelet which will be optimized by the IPSO. The translation and dilation of the mother wavelet are updated as follows:

$$\mu_{ij}(N+1) = \mu_{ij}(N) + \Delta\mu_{ij} \tag{88}$$

$$\sigma_{ij}(N+1) = \sigma_{ij}(N) + \Delta\sigma_{ij} \tag{89}$$

To overcome the problem of uncertainties of the wind generation system due to parameter variations and to increase the on-line learning rate of the network parameters, a control law is proposed as follows.

$$\delta_o^4 = e + k\psi \tag{90}$$

Moreover, the selection of the values for the learning rates $\eta_v$, $\eta_\mu$ and $\eta_\sigma$ has a significant effect on the network performance. In order to train the WNN effectively, three varied learning rates, which guarantee convergence of the tracking error based on the analyses of a discrete-type Lyapunov function, are adopted. The convergence analyses of the learning rates for assuring convergence of the tracking error is similar to [14] and is omitted here.

### 8.5. Improved Particle Swarm Optimization (IPSO)

In the PSO system, each particle adjusts its position according to its own experience and the experiences of neighbors, including the current velocity, position, and the best previous position experienced by itself and its neighbors. However, the efficiency of the PSO algorithm is affected by the randomly generated initial state. Therefore, the inertia weight Θ is adopted in the IPSO to balance between the local search ability and global search ability. Moreover, the inclusion of the worst experience component in the behavior of the particle in the IPSO gives additional exploration capacity to the swarm. Since the particle is made to remember its worst experience, it can explore the search space effectively to identify the promising solution region in [24]. Thus, the algorithm of the IPSO is derived as follows:

$$\begin{aligned} v_i^d(k+1) &= \Theta v_i^d(k) + c_1 \times r_1 \times (Pbest_i^d - x_i^d(k)) \\ &+ c_2 \times r_2 \times (Gbest_i^d - x_i^d(k)) + c_3 \times r_3 \times (Pworst_i^d - x_i^d(k)) \end{aligned} \tag{91}$$

$$x_i^d(k+1) = x_i^d(k) + v_i^d(k+1) \tag{92}$$

where $v_i^d(k)$ is the current velocity of $i$th particle, $i = 1,..., P$, in which $P$ is the population size; the superscript $d$ is the dimension of the particle; $Pbest_i^d$ is the best previous position of the $i$th particle; $Pworst_i^d$ is the worst previous position of the $i$th particle; $Gbest_i^d$ is the best previous position among all the particles in the swarm; $x_i^d(k)$ is the current position of the $i$th particle; $c_1$, $c_2$, and $c_3$ are the acceleration factors; and $r_1$, $r_2$ and $r_3$ represent the uniform random numbers between zero and one. In addition, the inertia weight Θ is set according to the following equation in [27]:

$$\Theta = \Theta_{max} - \frac{\Theta_{max} - \Theta_{min}}{k_{max}} \times k_n \tag{93}$$

where $k_{max}$ is the maximum number of iterations and $k_n$ is the current number of iteration. Equation (92) restricts the value Θ to the range $[\Theta_{max}, \Theta_{min}]$. In this Chapter, the maximum and minimum values of the inertia weights are $\Theta_{max} = 0.7$ and $\Theta_{min} = 0.4$, respectively.

### 8.6. WNN Learning Rates Tuning Using IPSO

To further improve the online learning capability of the proposed WNN, the IPSO algorithm is adopted in this Chapter to adapt the learning rates $\eta_v^v$, $\eta_\mu^v$, $\eta_\sigma^v$, $\eta_v^P$, $\eta_\mu^P$, $\eta_\sigma^P$, $\eta_v^Q$, $\eta_\mu^Q$ and $\eta_\sigma^Q$ in the backpropagation learning methodology of the WNN. Moreover, the procedure of the IPSO algorithm is shown in Figure 11 and is described as follows.

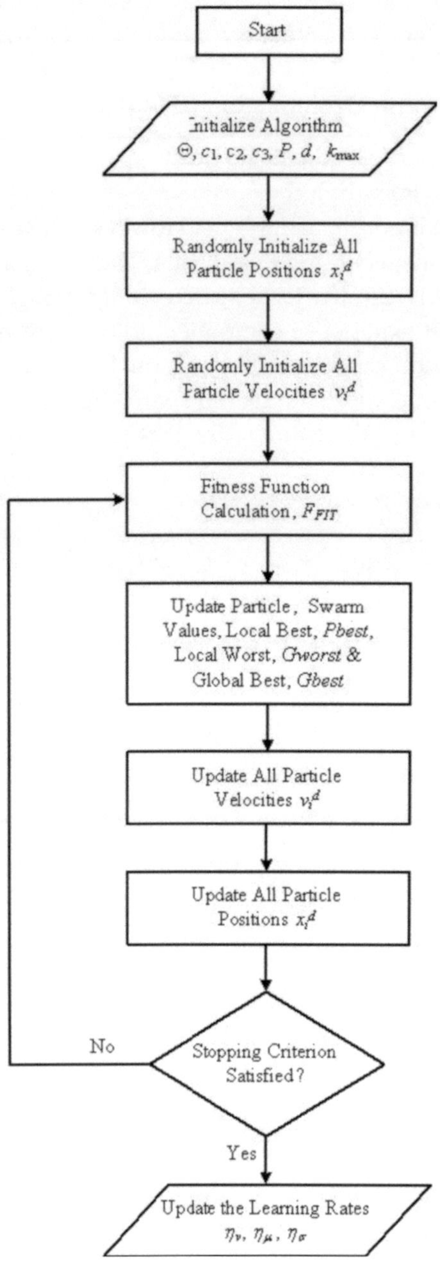


**Figure 11.** Flowchart implementation of the IPSO algorithm.

*1) Initialization:* Randomly generate the initial trial vectors $x_i^d(k)$, which indicate the possible solutions for the learning rates. Moreover, the population size is set to $P = 15$, and the dimension of the particle is set to $d = 9$ in this Chapter. This step is accomplished by setting $x_i^d = [x_i^0, x_i^1, x_i^2, x_i^3, x_i^4, x_i^5, x_i^6, x_i^7, x_i^8]$ represent the desired values of the learning rates $\eta_v^v$,

$\eta_\mu^v$ , $\eta_\sigma^v$ , $\eta_v^P$ , $\eta_\mu^P$ , $\eta_\sigma^P$ , $\eta_v^Q$ , $\eta_\mu^Q$ and $\eta_\sigma^Q$ , respectively. Furthermore, the elements in vector $x_i^d$ are randomly generated as follows:

$$x_i^d \sim U[\eta_{\min}^d, \eta_{\max}^d] \tag{94}$$

where $U[\eta_{\min}^d, \eta_{\max}^d]$ designates the outcome of a uniformly distributed random variable ranging over the given lower- and upper-bounded values $\eta_{\min}$ and $\eta_{\max}$ of the learning rate.

*2) Determination of fitness function:* For each trial vector $x_i^d$ , a fitness value should be assigned and evaluated. In this project, a suitable fitness function is selected to calculate the fitness value and defined as

$$F_{FIT} = \frac{1}{0.1 + abs(V_{dc}^* - V_{dc}) + abs(P^* - P) + abs(Q^* - Q)} \tag{95}$$

where $F_{FIT}$ is the fitness value and *abs*() is the absolute function; 0.1 is added in the dominant part to avoid the fitness value approaching infinite when the error of the DC-link voltage approaches zero.

*3) Selection and memorization:* Each particle $x_i^d$ memorizes its own fitness value and chooses the maximum one that is the best so far as $Pbest_i^d$ , and the maximum vector in the population $Pbest = [Pbset_1^d, Pbest_2^d, \ldots, Pbest_p^d]$ is obtained. Moreover, each particle $x_i^d$ is set directly to $Pbest_i^d$ in the first iteration, and the particle with the best fitness value among *Pbest* is set to be the global best $Gbest^d$ .

*4) Modification of velocity and position:* The modification of each particle is based on (90, 91).

*5) Stopping rule*: Repeat steps (1)–(4) until the best fitness value for *Gbest* is obviously improved or a set count of the generation is reached. The solution with the highest fitness value is chosen as the best learning rates of the WNN. By using the online tuning learning rates based on IPSO, the WNNC can regulate the DC-link voltage of the CRPWM AC/DC converter, active and reactive power of the CRPWM DC/AC inverter effectively.

In the IPSO, since the global best $Gbest^d$ has higher priority than the local best $Pbest_i^d$ and local worst in the optimal algorithm, the acceleration factors are chosen to be $c_1 = c_2 = 0.6$ and $c_3 = 3.10$. Moreover, to achieve better global search ability for the IPSO, larger movement is required for the particle with the chosen larger inertia weight $w$ in the beginning of the optimization process. Then, a smaller inertia weight $\Theta$ is required to improve the searching accuracy after several times of optimization. Furthermore, the inertia weight $\Theta$ must be less than one to avoid the divergence of the particle. Therefore, the maximum and minimum values of the inertia weights are chosen to be $\Theta_{\max} = 0.7$ and $\Theta_{\min} = 0.4$, respectively.

## 9. Numerical Simulation Results

In this section, a computer simulation results for the proposed wind generation system are provided to demonstrate the effectiveness of the proposed control schemes. The wind turbine SEIG system simulation is carried out using MATLAB/SIMULINK package. Since this Chapter is dealing with an isolated wind energy conversion system with maximum power control, the more realistic approach for an isolated wind power control system is to choose the DC-link voltage, active power and reactive power as the controlled variables.

| Wind Speed | Tip Speed Ratio λ | Power Coefficient $C_P$ | Reference Rotor Speed of WTE | Wind Turbine Output Power $P_m$ (W) | IG Output Power $P_{IG}$ (W) | DC-Link Power $P_{DC}$ (W) |
|---|---|---|---|---|---|---|
| $V_w$=16 m/sec | 6.7 | 0.37 | ≈ 296 rad/sec | ≈ 1580 | ≈ 1500 | ≈ 1400 |
| $V_w$=14 m/sec | 6.7 | 0.37 | ≈ 259 rad/sec | ≈ 1086 | ≈ 1030 | ≈ 965 |
| $V_w$=12 m/sec | 6.7 | 0.37 | ≈ 222 rad/sec | ≈ 705 | ≈ 670 | ≈ 637 |
| $V_w$=10 m/sec | 6.7 | 0.37 | ≈ 185 rad/sec | ≈ 422 | ≈ 400 | ≈ 392 |
| $V_w$=8 m/sec | 6.7 | 0.37 | ≈ 148 rad/sec | ≈235 | ≈ 223 | ≈ 212 |
| $V_w$=6 m/sec | 6.7 | 0.37 | ≈ 111 rad/sec | ≈ 110 | ≈ 104 | ≈ 95 |

**Table 1.** Parameters of the wind turbine emulator (WTE) at various wind speeds.

Therefore, the DC-link voltage control, active power control and reactive power control using the PID controllers and WNNCs with IPSO are carried out for comparison. The dynamic performance of the wind generation system using double-sided CRPWM AC/DC/AC power converter system connected to utility grid subjected to three different wind speed variation profiles are shown in Figures (12-16). The first wind speed variation profile is the stepwise, the second is the sinusoidal variation profile and the last is the trapezoidal variation profile as given in the following section. The performance of the whole system at six operating conditions of wind speeds 6, 8, 10, 12, 14 and 16 m/sec is studied as shown in Table 1. The corresponding reference rotor speeds of the IG are 111, 148, 185, 222, 259 and 296 rad/sec, respectively. The respective wind turbine output power, DC-link power commands and IG output power are also shown in Table 1.

### 9.1. Wind Generation System Performance with CRPWM AC/DC/AC Converters Using Stepwise Wind Speed Profile

The dynamic response of the wind generation system feeding the double-sided CRPWM AC/DC/AC power converter connected to utility grid based on the maximum power point tracking (MPPT) control scheme using stepwise profile for wind speed variations of 10 m/s, 12 m/s, 14 m/s and 16 m/s are shown in Figures 12 and 13 utilizing both PID controller and WNNC with IPSO. These responses are the wind speed, rotor speed of the IG, the q-axis torque control current of the IG, the DC-link voltage $V_{dc}$, the DC-link power $P_{dc}$ and the DC-link current $i_{dc}$, respectively, for the CRPWM converter fed from the SEIG. Furthermore, the maximum active and reactive power injected to the grid at unity power factor, d-q axis currents, the phase voltage and currents, respectively, at the AC side of the CRPWM inverter connected to the utility grid. The dynamic responses of the wind speed, rotor speed of the IG, the q-axis torque control current of the IG, the DC-link voltage $V_{dc}$, the DC-link power $P_{dc}$ and the DC-link current $i_{dc}$, respectively, are shown in Figure (12-X) for both PID and WNNC with IPSO controllers for the CRPWM converter fed from the IG. In this simulation, the wind speed is changed from 10 m/s to 12 m/s, then changed back from 12 m/s to 10 m/s and the reference voltage for the DC-link is changed from 0 to 539 V. From the simulation results shown in Figure 12-Xa, sluggish DC-link voltage tracking response is obtained for the PID controller owing to the weak robustness of the linear controller. Moreover, approximately 2 sec is required for the PID-controlled SEIG system to generate the maximum output power. In addition, from the simulation results, fast dynamic response for the DC-link voltage can be obtained for the hybrid control of the SEIG wind generation system owing to the on-line training of the WNNC with IPSO. Moreover, the robust control performance of the proposed hybrid control system using the WNNC with IPSO at different operating conditions is obvious. Furthermore, approximately 1 sec is required for the SEIG to generate the maximum output power. In addition, the dynamic response of the wind generation system using the hybrid control scheme with the WNNC using IPSO is much better as shown in Figure 12-Xb. As a result, comparing the results of PID controller with the WNNC, the proposed hybrid voltage controller is more suitable to control the DC-link voltage of the CRPWM converter-based SEIG wind generation system under the possible occurrence of load disturbance and parameter variations.

The output voltage of the DC-link is fed to the CRPWM inverter connected to the utility grid. The dynamic response of the CRPWM inverter system feeding the utility grid using PID controllers and WNNC with IPSO for active and reactive power control at the same condition of wind speed variations and the DC-link voltage command is shown in Figure 12-Y with MPPT control scheme. These responses are the maximum active and reactive power, d-q axis currents of the CRPWM inverter, the grid voltages and currents at the AC side of the CRPWM inverter, respectively. It is obvious that zero reactive power and zero d-axis current which confirms unity power factor operation at different wind speeds. At the same time the q-axis current and the active power follow their references to give the MPPT. From the simulation results shown in Figure 12-Ya, sluggish active power tracking response is obtained for the PID controller owing to the weak robustness of the linear controller. Moreover, approximately 1.6 sec is required for the PID-controlled CRPWM inverter system to track the maximum power. In addition, from the simulation results, fast dynamic response for the active power can be obtained for the hybrid control of the CRPWM inverter system owing to the on-line training of the WNNC with IPSO. Moreover, the robust control performance of the proposed hybrid control system using the WNNC with IPSO at different operating conditions is obvious. Furthermore, approximately 0.8 sec is required for the CRPWM inverter system to track the maximum power. In addition, the dynamic response of the CRPWM inverter system connected to the utility grid using the hybrid control scheme with the WNNC with IPSO is much better as shown in Figure 12-Yb. As a result, comparing the results of PID with the WNNC-based IPSO, the proposed hybrid active and reactive power controllers are more suitable to control the power of the CRPWM converter/inverter system connected to the utility grid under the possible occurrence of parameter variations. Additionally, from these figures, it is evident that a unity power factor operation is achieved at different wind speeds. Furthermore, it is obvious that the proposed control scheme illustrates satisfactory performance and good tracking characteristics.

To confirm the effectiveness of the proposed control schemes, the wind speed is changed from 14 m/s to 16 m/s, then changed back from 16 m/s to 14 m/s. The dynamic response of the wind generation system using double-sided CRPWM AC/DC/AC power converters is shown in Figure 13. As result, comparing the results of PID controllers and the WNNCs with IPSO, the proposed hybrid controller gives robust performance for both the DC-link voltage, active and reactive power of the AC/DC/AC CRPWM converter considering the existence of parameter variations and load disturbances for the wind generation system.

### 9.2. Wind Generation System Performance with CRPWM AC/DC/AC Converters Using Sinusoidal Wind Speed Profile

In order to investigate the effectiveness of the proposed control schemes, the sinusoidal profile for wind speed variations. The dynamic response of the wind generation system using double-sided CRPWM AC/DC/AC power converters using both PID controllers and WNNCs with IPSO technique for the DC-link voltage, active and reactive power is shown in Figure 14. It is obvious from Figure 14 that good dynamic performance is achieved and the DC-link actual voltage, actual active and reactive power follow their references. In addition, the dynamic performance of the wind generation system using the hybrid control scheme with the WNNCs utilizing IPSO is much better as shown in Figure 14 and provide robust performance considering the existence of parameter variations and load disturbances for the wind generation system.

### 9.3. Wind Generation System Performance with CRPWM AC/DC/AC Converters Using Trapezoidal Wind Speed Profile

The wind generation system is re-subjected to trapezoidal profile for the wind speed variations to study the effectiveness of the proposed control schemes. The dynamic response of the wind generation system using double-sided CRPWM AC/DC/AC power converters using both PID controllers and WNNCs with IPSO technique for the DC-link voltage, active and reactive power is shown in Figure 15.

It is obvious that good dynamic performance is achieved and the DC-link actual voltage, actual active and reactive power follow their references. The line current and voltage at the AC side of the CRPWM inverter at different wind speeds showing unity power factor operation are shown in Figure 16. As a result, comparing the results of PID controller with the hybrid control scheme with the WNNC-based IPSO, the proposed hybrid controllers are more suitable to control the voltage and power of the CRPWM converter/inverter system connected to the utility grid under the possible occurrence of parameters variations. Additionally, it is evident that unity power factor operation is achieved at dif-

http://dx.doi.org/10.5772/51253

ferent wind speed profiles. It is clear that the proposed control scheme illustrates satisfactory performance and good tracking characteristics.

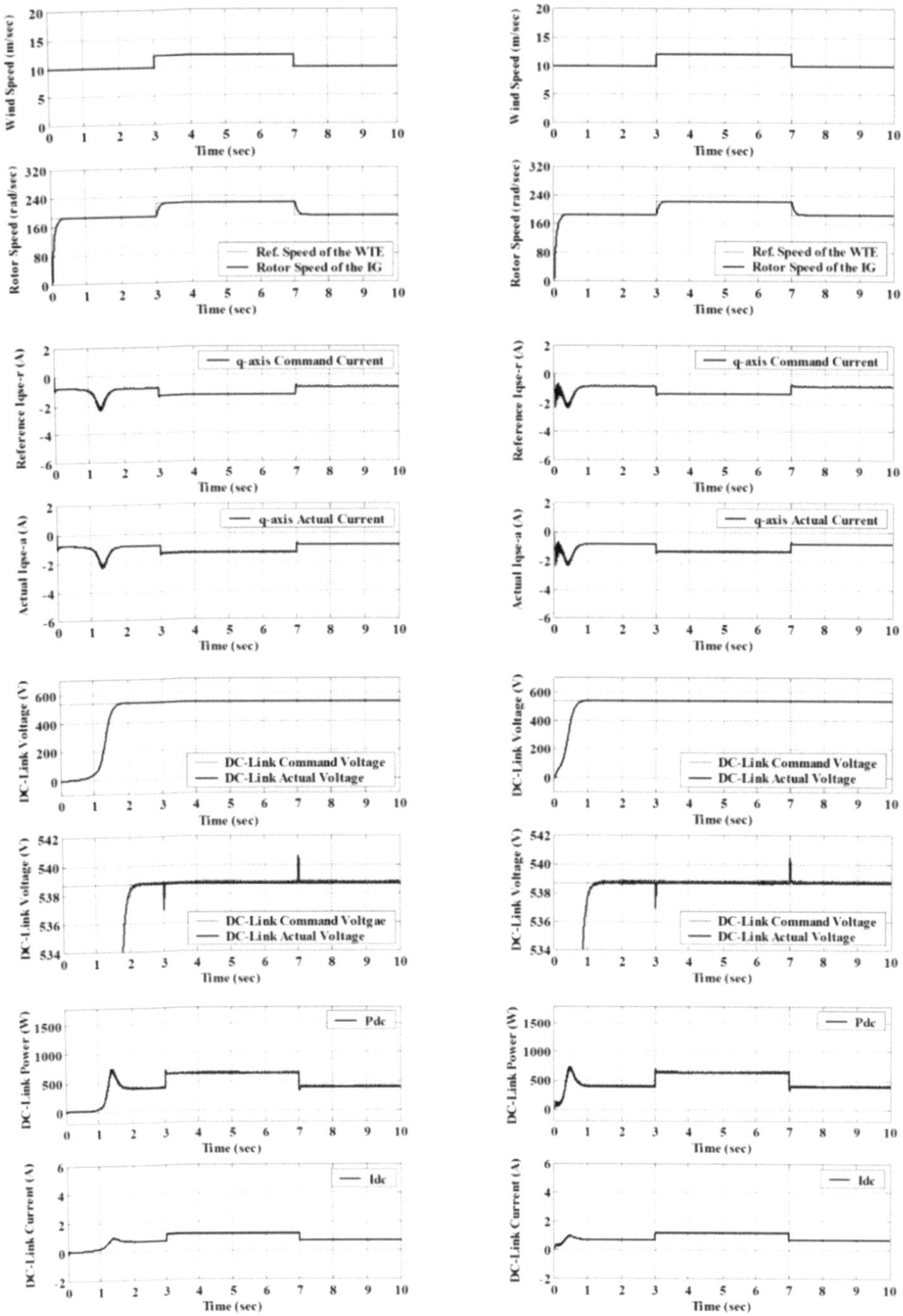


(a) (b)

(X) Dynamic response of the DC-link voltage controlled SEIG system

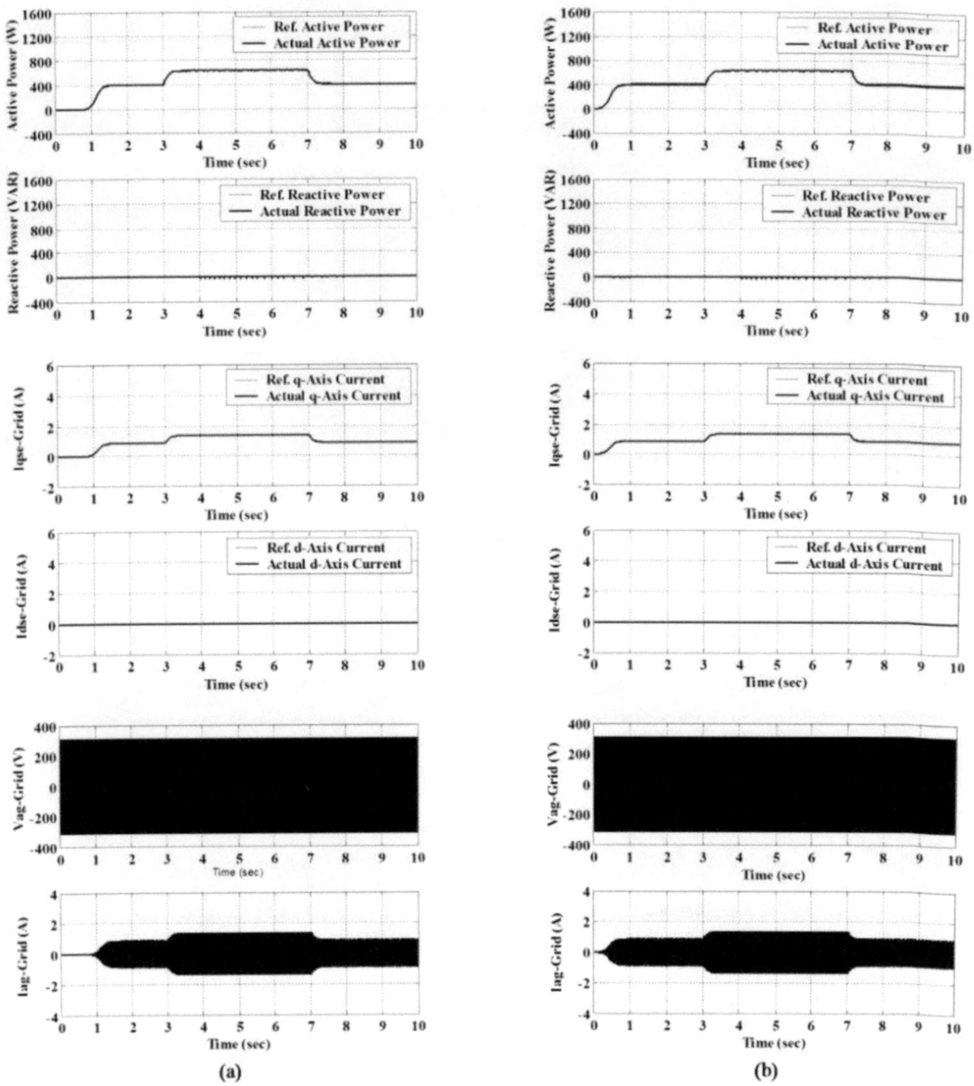


(Y) Dynamic response of the CRPWM inverter connected to the utility grid

**Figure 12.** Dynamic performance of the wind generation system using stepwise profile wind speed changed from $V_w$ =10 m/sec to $V_w$=12 m/sec to $V_w$=10 m/sec. (a) Using PID controller (b) Using WNNC with IPSO.

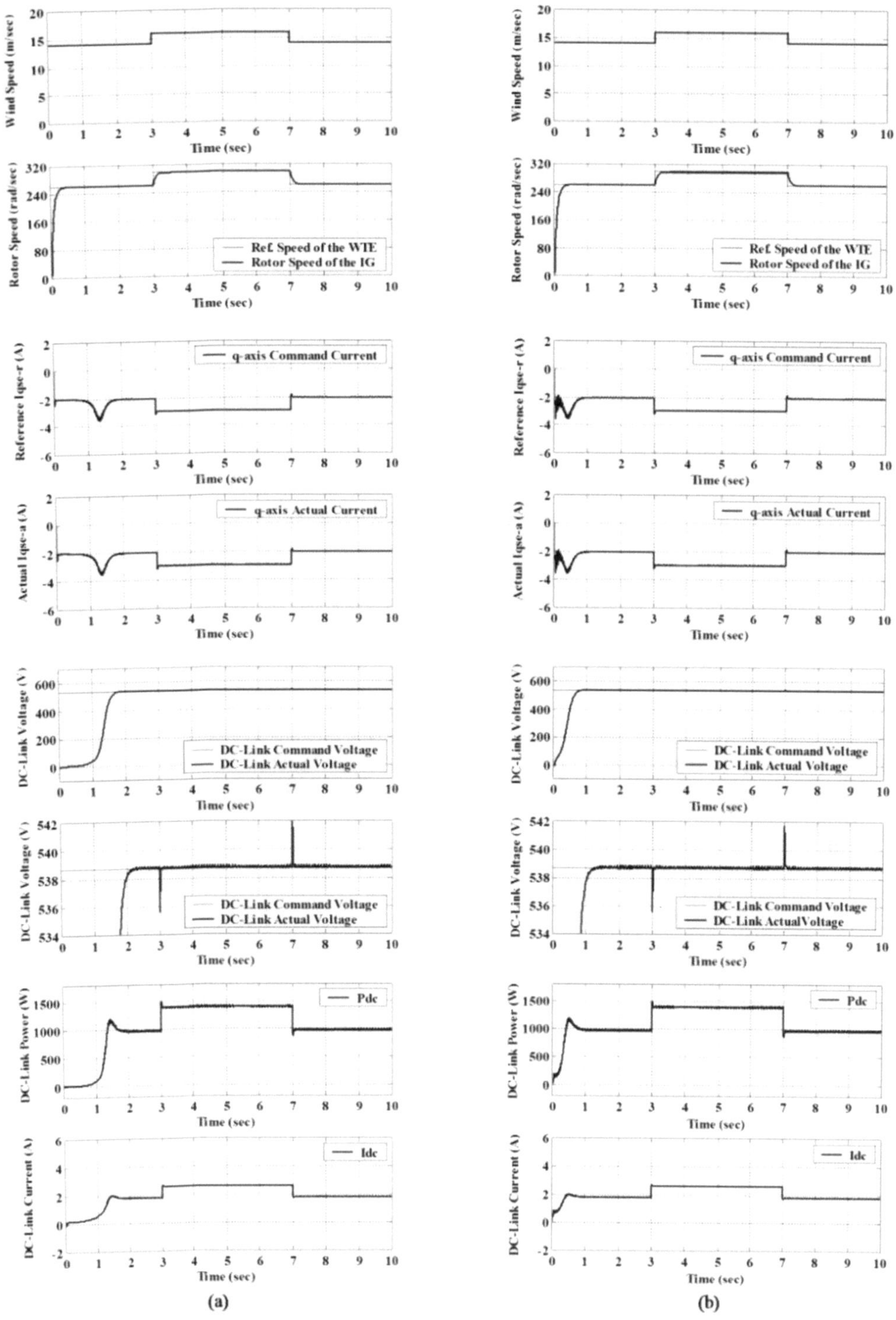


(X) Dynamic response of the DC-link voltage controlled SEIG system

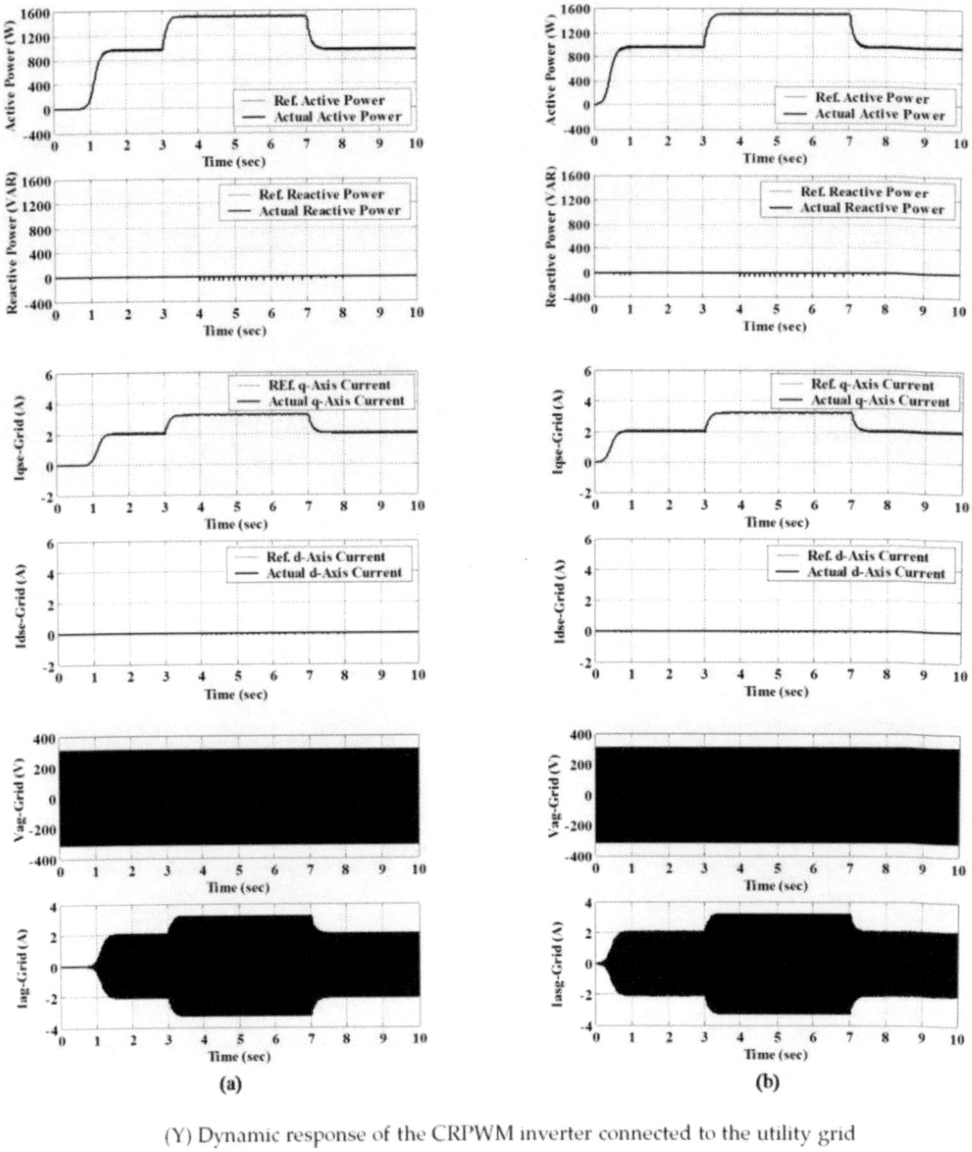


**Figure 13.** Dynamic performance of the wind generation system using stepwise profile wind speed changed from $V_w$ =14 m/sec to $V_w$=16 m/sec to $V_w$=14 m/sec. (a) Using PID controller (b) Using WNNC with IPSO.

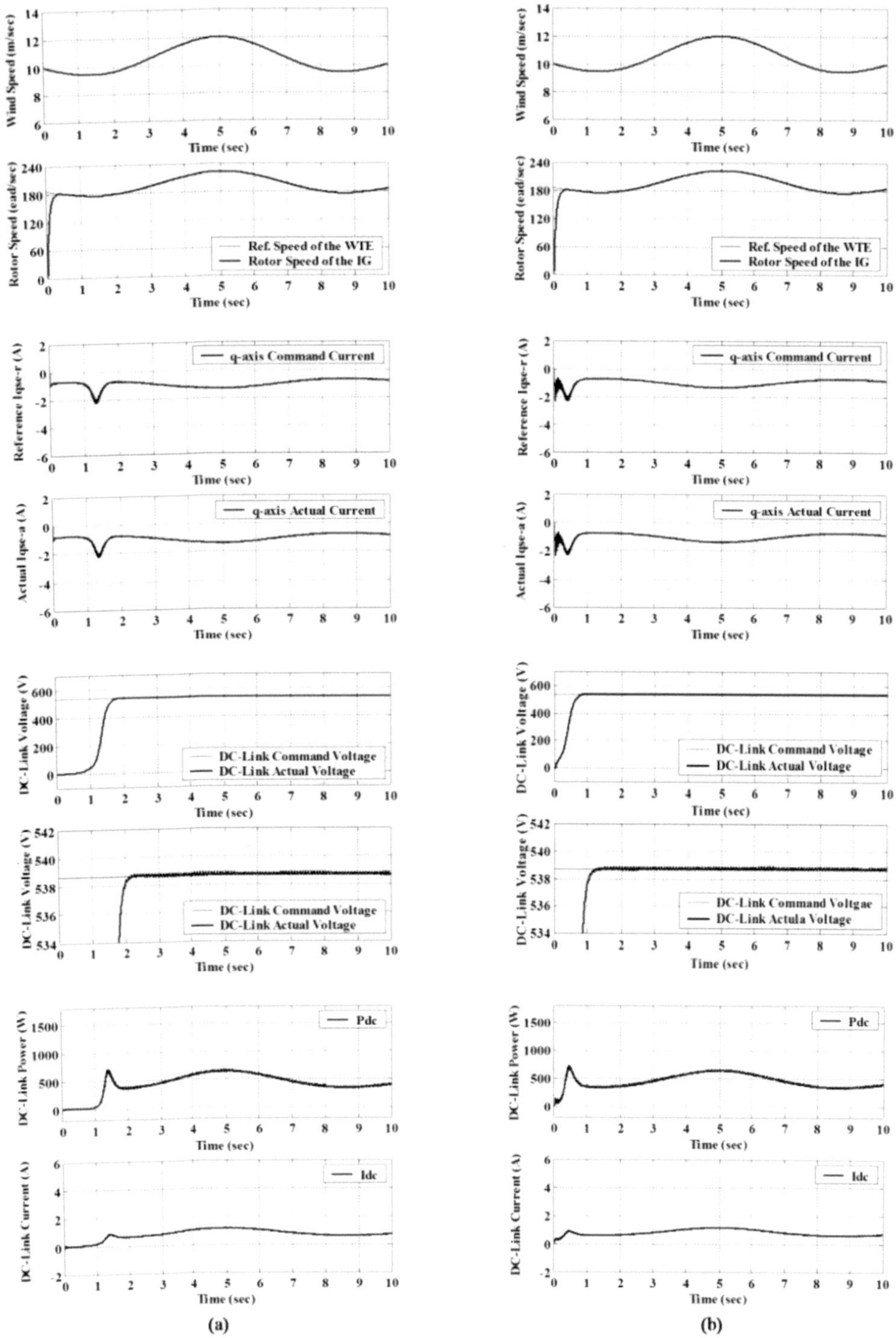


(X) Dynamic response of the DC-link voltage controlled SEIG system

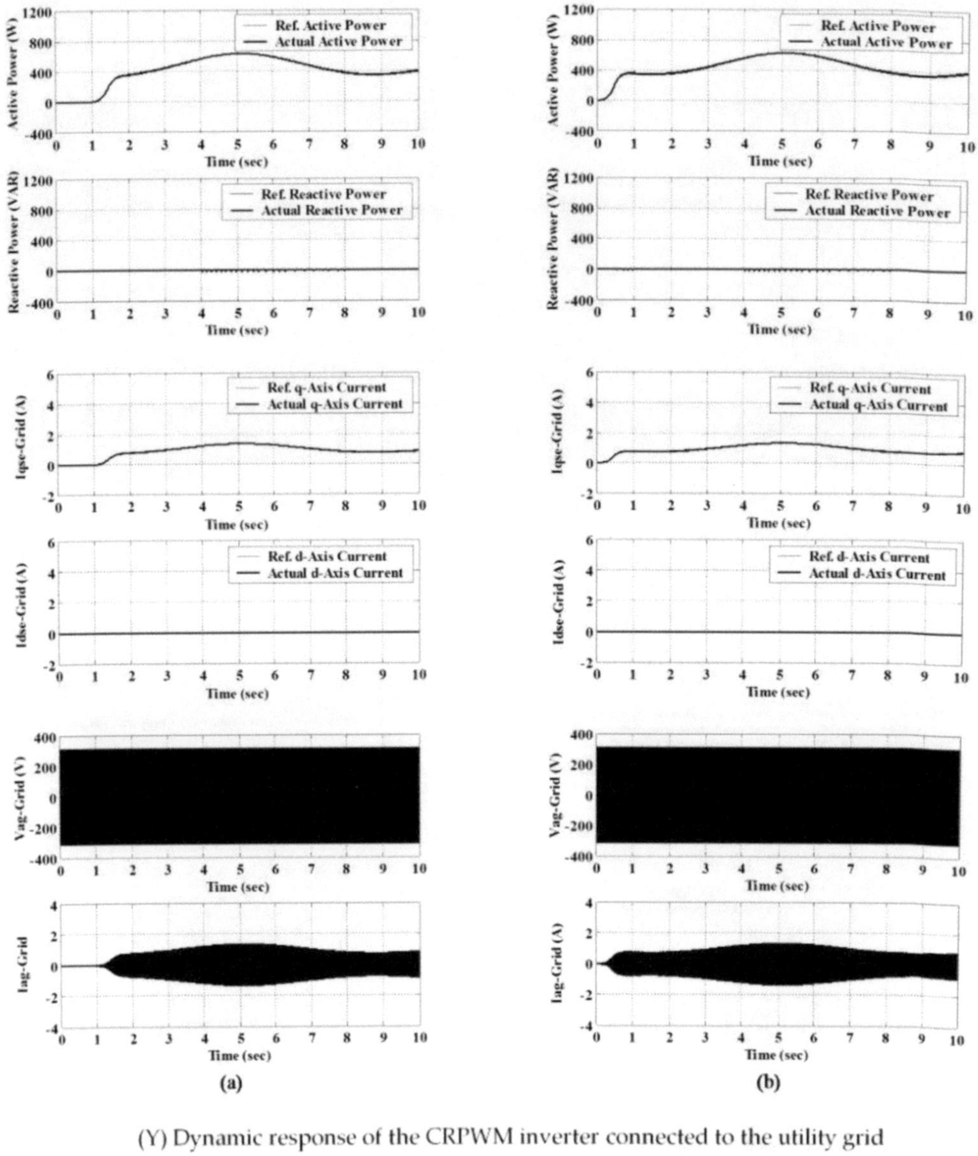


**Figure 14.** Dynamic performance of the wind generation system using sinusoidal profile wind speed variations. (a) Using PID controller (b) Using WNNC with IPSO.

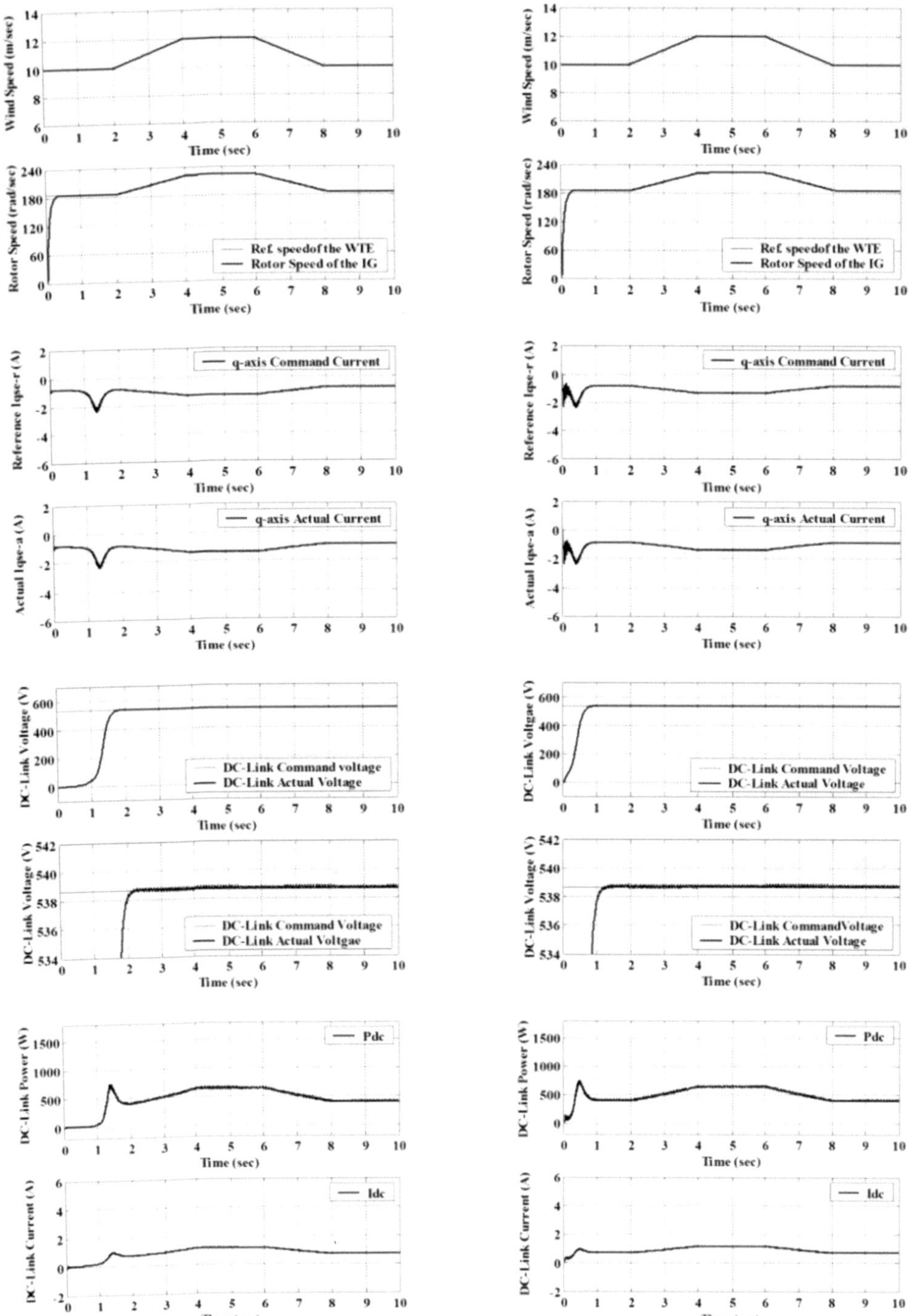


(X) Dynamic response of the DC-link voltage controlled SEIG system

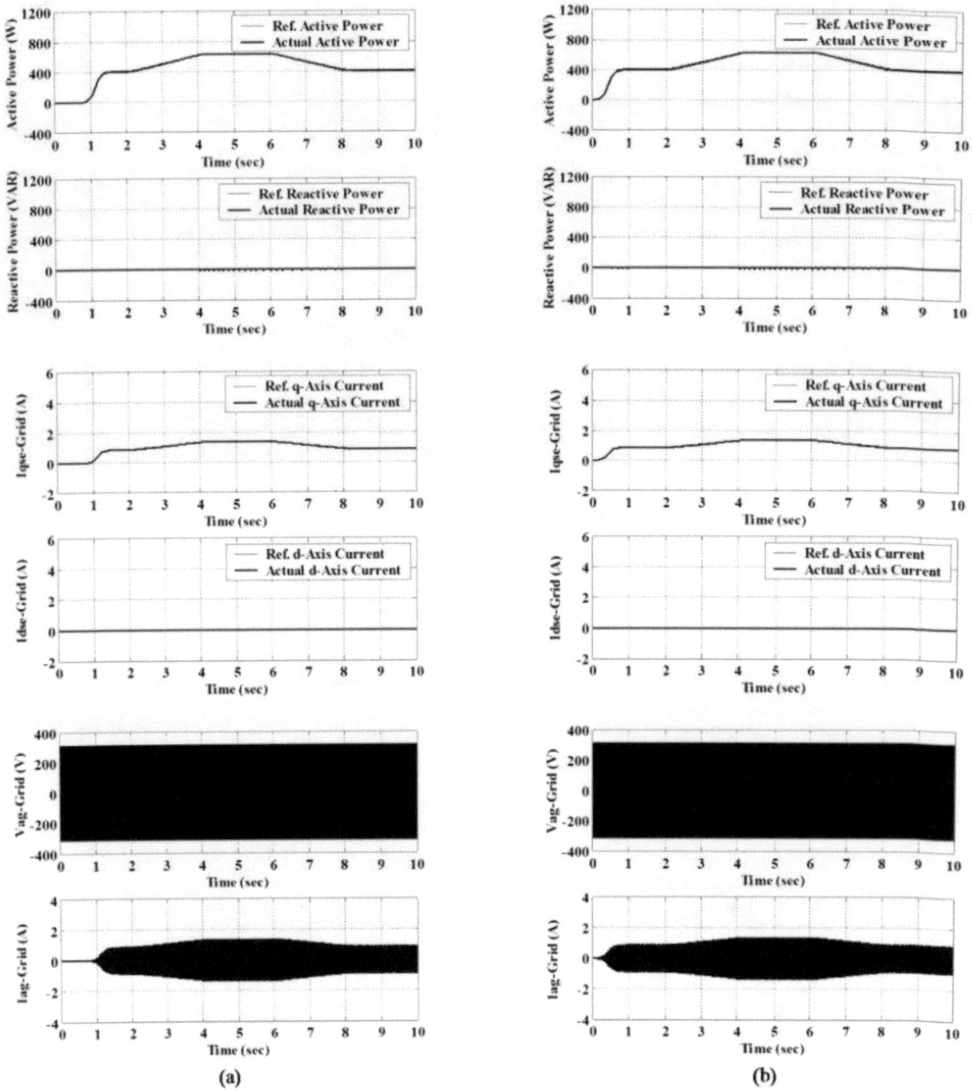


(Y) Dynamic response of the CRPWM inverter connected to the utility grid

**Figure 15.** Dynamic performance of the wind generation system using trapezoidal profile wind speed variations. (a) Using PID controller (b) Using WNNC with IPSO.

http://dx.doi.org/10.5772/51253

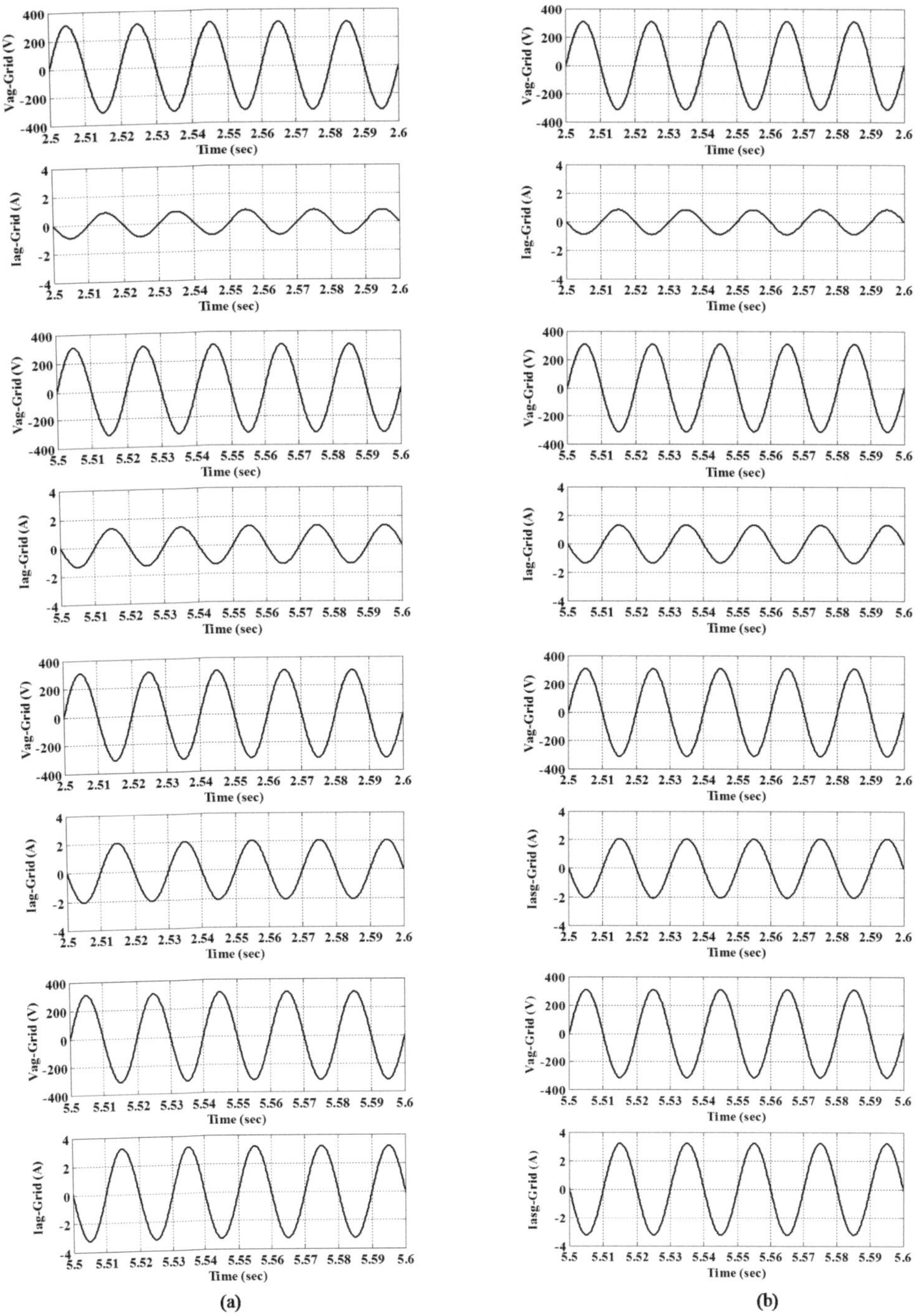


**Figure 16.** Line side voltage and current showing unity power factor operation at different wind speeds $V_w$ =10 m/sec, $V_w$ =12 m/sec, $V_w$ =14 m/sec and $V_w$ =16 m/sec from top to bottom (a) Using PID controller (b) Using WNNC with IPSO

## 10. Conclusion

This Chapter proposed a hybrid control scheme utilizing WNNCs with IPSO for the voltage control of DC-link voltage, active power and reactive power of the CRPWM AC/DC/AC power converter feeding from a wind turbine SEIG system. The double-sided AC/DC/AC CRPWM converter is connected to the utility grid and operated under IFOC and VFOC which guarantees the robustness in the presence of parameter uncertainties and load disturbances. The IG is controlled by the maximum power point tracking (MPPT) control technique below the base speed and the maximum energy can be captured from the wind turbine. The proposed hybrid controller consists of a three feed-back PID controller in addition to a three on-line trained WNNC with IPSO. Also, this Chapter successfully demonstrated the application of the PID control and WNN control systems to control the voltage of the DC-link, active power and reactive power of the CRPWM AC/DC/AC power converter. Therefore, the DC-link voltage tracking response, active power and reactive power can be controlled to follow the response of the reference commands under a wide range of operating conditions. Simulation results have shown that the proposed hybrid control scheme using the WNNC with IPSO grants robust tracking response and good regulation characteristics in the presence of parameter uncertainties and external load disturbances. Moreover, simulations were carried out at different wind speeds to testify the effectiveness of the proposed hybrid controller. Finally, the main contributions of this Chapter are the successful development of the hybrid control system, in which a WNNC with IPSO is utilized to compensate the uncertainty bound in the wind generation system on-line and the successful application of the proposed hybrid control scheme methodology to control the DC-link voltage, active and reactive power of the AC/DC/AC CRPWM converter considering the existence of parameters uncertainties and external load disturbances.

## Author details

Fayez F. M. El-Sousy[1] and Awad Kh. Al-Asmari[2*]

*Address all correspondence to: alasmari@ksu.edu.sa

1 College of Engineering, Department of Electrical Engineering Salman bin Abdulaziz University, Al-Kharj, Saudi Arabia

2 College of Engineering, King Saud University, Riyadh, and Vice Rector for Graduate Studies and Research, Salman bin Abdulaziz University, Saudi Arabia

## References

[1] Zinger, D. S., & Muljadi, E. (1997). Annualized Wind Energy Improvement Using Variable Speeds. *IEEE Trans. on Industry Applications*, 33(6), 1444-1447.

[2] Seyoum, D., Grantham, C., & Rahman, M. F. (2003). The Dynamic Characteristics of an Isolated Self-Excited Induction Generator Driven by a Wind Turbine. *IEEE Trans. on Industry Applications*, 39(4), 936-944.

[3] Malik, N. H., & Al-Bahrani, A. H. (1990). Influence of the Terminal Capacitor on the Performance of a Self-Excited Induction Generator. *IEE Proc.*, 137(2), 168-173.

[4] Wang, L., & Ching-Huei, L. (1997). A Novel Analysis on the Performance of an Isolated Self-Excited Induction Generator. *IEEE Trans. on Energy Conversion*, 12(2), 109-117.

[5] Dixon, J. W., & Ooi, B. T. (1998). Indirect Current Control of a Unity Power Factor Sinusoidal Boost Type 3-Phase Rectifier. *IEEE Trans. on Industrial Electronics*, 35(4), 508-515.

[6] Sugimoto, H., Moritomo, S., & Yano, M. (1988, 11-14 April 1988). A High Performance Control Method of a Voltage-Type PWM Converter. Kyoto, Japan. *Proceedings of the19th Annual IEEE Power Electronics Specialists Conference, PESC*, 360-368.

[7] Datta, R., & Ranganathan, V. T. (2003). A Method of Tracking the Peak Power Points for a Variable Wind Energy Conversion System. *IEEE Trans. on Energy Conv.*, 18(1), 163-168.

[8] Martinez, F., Gonzalez, J. M., Vazquez, J. A., & De Lucas, L. C. (2002, 5-8 Nov.) Sensorless Control of a Squirrel Cage Induction Generator to Track the Peak Power in a Wind Turbine. *Proceedings of the 28th Annual IEEE Conference of the Industrial Electronics Society IEEE-IECON*, 169-174.

[9] Simoes, M. G., & Bose, B. K. (1997). Design and Performance Evaluation of a Fuzzy-Logic-Based Variable-Speed Wind Generation System. *IEEE Trans. Industry Appli.*, 33(4), 956-965.

[10] Cardenas, R., & Pena, R. (2004). Sensor-Less Vector Control of Induction Machine for Variable-Speed Wind Energy Applications. *IEEE-Trans. on Energy Conversion*, 19(1), 196-205.

[11] Seyoum, D., Rahman, M. F., & Grantham, C. (2003, 9-13 Feb.) Terminal Voltage Control of a Wind Turbine Driven Induction Generator Using Stator Oriented Field Control. *Proceedings of the Eighteenth Annual IEEE Applied Power Electronics Conference and Exposition, IEEE-APEC'03*, 846-852.

[12] El -Sousy, F. F. M., Orabi, M., & Godah, H. (2006). Maximum Power Point Tracking Control Scheme for Grid Connected Variable Speed Wind Driven Self-Excited Induction Generator. *Journal of Power Electronics (JPE)*, 6(1), 52-66.

[13] Lin, F. J., Huang, P. K., Wang, C. C., & Teng, L. T. (2007). An Induction Generator System Using Fuzzy Modeling and Recurrent Fuzzy Neural Network. *IEEE Trans. Power Electron.*, 22(1), 260-271.

[14] Lin, F. J., Teng, L. T., Shieh, P. H., & Li, Y. F. (2006). Intelligent Controlled Wind Turbine Emulator and Induction Generator System Using RBFN. *Proc. Inst. Elect. Eng.*, 153(4), 608, 618.

[15] Zhang, Q., & Benveniste, A. (1992). Wavelet Networks. *IEEE Trans. on Neural Networks*, 3(6), 889-898.

[16] Zhang, J., Walter, G. G., Miao, Y., & Lee, W. N. W. (1995). Wavelet Neural Networks for Function Learning. *IEEE Trans. on Signal Processing*, 43(6), 1485-1496.

[17] Zhang, Z., & Zhao, C. (2007, May 30 - June 1). A Fast Learning Algorithm for Wavelet Network and its Application in Control. China. *Proceedings of the IEEE International Conference on Control and Automation, IEEE ICCA*, 1403-1407.

[18] Sureshbabu, N., & Farrell, J. A. (1999). Wavelet-Based System Identification for Nonlinear Control. *IEEE Trans. on Automatic Control*, 44(2), 412-417.

[19] Billings, S. A., & Wei, H. L. (2005). A New Class of Wavelet Networks for Nonlinear System Identification. *IEEE Trans. on Neural Network*, 16(4), 862-874.

[20] Giaouris, D., Finch, J. W., Ferreira, O. C., Kennel, R. M., & El -Murr, G. M. (2008). Wavelet Denoising for Electric Drives. *IEEE Trans. on Industrial Electronics*, 55(2), 543-550.

[21] Hsu, C. F., Lin, C. M., & Lee, T. T. (2006). Wavelet Backstepping Control for a Class of Nonlinear Systems. *IEEE Transactions Neural Networks*, 17(5), 1175-83.

[22] Astrom, K. J., & Wittenmark, B. (1995). *Adaptive Control*, New York, Addison Wesley.

[23] Slotine, J.-J., & Li, W. (1991). *Applied Nonlinear Control*, Englewood Cliffs, NJ, Printice-Hall.

[24] Kennedy, J., & Eberhart, R. (1995, Nov. 27 - Dec. 1). Particle Swarm Optimization. Perth-Australia. *Proceedings of the IEEE International Conference on Neural Networks, IEEE-ICNN*, 1942-1948.

[25] Maurice, C. (2006). *Particle Swarm Optimization*, Paris, France, France Télécom.

[26] Jacob, R., & Yahya, R. S. (2004). Particle Swarm Optimization in Electromagnetics. *IEEE Trans. Antennas Propag.*, 52(2), 397-407.

[27] Gaing, Z. L. (2004). A Particle Swarm Optimization Approach for Optimum Design of PID Controller in AVR System. *IEEE Trans. Energy Conv.*, 19(2), 384-391.

[28] Juang, C. F., & Hsu, C. H. (2005). Temperature Control by Chip-Implemented Adaptive Recurrent Fuzzy Controller Designed by Evolutionary Algorithm. *IEEE Trans. Circuits Syst. I*, 52(11), 2376-2384.

[29] Parrott, D., & Li, X. (2006). Locating and Tracking Multiple Dynamic Optima by a Particle Swarm Model Using Speciation. *IEEE Trans. Evolutionary Computat.*, 10(4), 440-458.

[30] Valle, Y., Venayagamoorthy, G. K., Mohagheghi, S., Hernandez, J.-C., & Harley, R. G. (2008). Particle Swarm Optimization: Basic Concepts, Variants and Applications in Power Systems. *IEEE Trans. on Evolutionary Computation*, 12(2), 171-195.

[31] Eberhart, R. C., & Shi, Y. (1998, 4-9 May). Comparison Between Genetic Algorithm and Particle Swarm Optimization. Anchorage, AK USA. *Proceedings of the IEEE International Conference on Evolutionary. Computation*, 611-616.

[32] Angeline, P. J. (1998, 4-9May). Using Selection to Improve Particle Swarm Optimization. Anchorage, AK USA. *Proceedings of the IEEE International Conference on Evolutionary. Computation*, 84-98.

[33] Yoshida, H., Kawata, K., & Fukuyama, Y. (2000). A Particle Swarm Optimization for Reactive Power and Voltage Control Considering Security Assessment. *IEEE Trans. on Power Systems*, 15(4), 1232-1239.

[34] Teng, L. T., Lin, F. J., Chiang, H. C., & Lin, J. W. (2009). Recurrent Wavelet Neural Network Controller with Improved Particle Swarm Optimisation for Induction Generator System. *IET Electr. Power Appl.*, 3(2), 147-159.

[35] Marra, E. G., & Pomillio, J. A. (2000). Induction-Generator-Based System Providing Regulated Voltage with Constant Frequency. *IEEE Trans. Ind. Electron.*, 47(4), 908-914.

[36] Ojo, O., & Davidson, I. E. (2000). PWM-VSI Inverter-Assisted Stand-Alone Dual Stator Winding Induction Generator. *IEEE Trans. Ind. Appl.*, 36(6), 1604-1611.

[37] Wekhande, S., & Agarwal, V. (2001). Simple Control for a Wind-Driven Induction Generator. *IEEE Ind. Appl. Mag.*, 7(2), 44-53.

[38] Portillo, R. C., Prats, M. M., Leon, J. I., Sanchez, J. A., Carrasco, J. M., Galvan, E., & Franquelo, L. G. (2006). Modeling Strategy for Back-to-Back Three-Level Converters Applied to High-Power Wind Turbines. *IEEE Trans. Ind. Electron.*, 53(5), 1483-1491.

[39] Chatterjee, J. K., Perumal, B. V., & Gopu, N. R. (2007). Analysis of Operation of a Self-Excited Induction Generator with Generalized Impedance Controller. *IEEE Trans. Energy Convers.*, 22(2), 307-315.

[40] Hilloowala, R. M., & Sharaf, A. M. (1996). A Rule-Based Fuzzy Logic Controller for a PWM Inverter in a Stand Alone Wind Energy Conversion Scheme. *IEEE Trans. Ind. Appl.*, 31(1), 57-65.

[41] Battista, H. D., Mantz, R. J., & Christiansen, C. F. (2000). Dynamical Sliding Mode Power Control of Wind Driven Induction Generators. *IEEE Trans. Energy Convers.*, 15(4), 451-457.

[42] Mirecki, A., Roboam, X., & Richardeau, F. (2007). Architecture Complexity and Energy Efficiency of Small Wind Turbines. *IEEE Trans. Ind. Electron.*, 54(1), 660-670.

[43] Kojabadi, H. M., Chang, L., & Boutot, T. (2004). Development of a Novel Wind Turbine Simulator for Wind Energy Conversion Systems Using an Inverter Controlled Induction Motor. *IEEE Trans. Energy Convers.*, 19(3), 547-552.

[44] Teodorescu, R., & Blaabjerg, F. (2004). Flexible Control of Small Wind Turbines with Grid Failure Detection Operating in Stand-Alone and Grid-Connected Mode. *IEEE Trans. Power Electron.*, 19(5), 1323-1332.

[45] Wang, Q., & Chang, L.-C. (2004). An Intelligent Maximum Power Extraction Algorithm for Inverter-Based Variable Speed Wind Turbine Systems. *IEEE Transactions on Power Electronics*, 19(5), 1242-1249.

[46] Song, Y., Dhinakaran, B., & Bao, X. (2000). Variable Speed Control of Wind Turbines Using Nonlinear and Adaptive Algorithms. *Journal of Wind Engineering and Industrial Aerodynamics*, 85(3), 293-308.

[47] Chinchilla, M., Arnaltes, S., & Burgos, J.-C. (2006). Control of Permanent-Magnet Generators Applied to Variable-Speed Wind-Energy Systems Connected to the Grid. *IEEE Transactions on Energy Conversion*, 21(1), 130-135.

[48] Koutroulis, E., & Kalaitzakis, K. (2006). Design of a Maximum Power Tracking System for Wind-Energy-Conversion Applications. *IEEE Transactions on Industrial Electronics*, 53(2), 486-494.

Chapter 8

# Demodulation of FM Data in Free-Space Optical Communication Systems Using Discrete Wavelet Transformation

Nader Namazi, Ray Burris, G. Charmaine Gilbreath, Michele Suite and Kenneth Grant

Additional information is available at the end of the chapter

http://dx.doi.org/10.5772/52433

## 1. Introduction

Free-space optical (FSO) communications links have the potential to deliver very high bandwidth due to the high carrier frequency as compared with RF links. They have the advantages of being rapidly deployable and less expensive to install than optical fiber systems. The low divergence of laser beams means that FSO systems are intrinsically low in probability of intercept in comparison to RF, and being 'line-of-sight' avoids wasteful use of both the frequency domain (bandwidth allocation) and the spatial domain. Another advantage of FSO communication links over RF communications is the large unregulated bandwidth as compared with the heavy traffic and expensive bandwidth allocations for RF links.

However, one of the main factors reducing SNR in FSO communications is scintillation noise due to turbulence. Atmospheric turbulence produces temporary pockets of air with slightly different temperatures and pressures, and therefore with slightly different indices of refraction. These turbulence cells act as small, weak lenses that refract the light slightly and cause distortions in the wave front as a laser beam propagates through the atmosphere. The resulting variation in the arrival time of various components of the beam produces constructive and destructive interference at the receiver, causing fluctuations in laser beam intensity. These rapid fluctuations are known as scintillation and occur on a time scale comparable to the time it takes these cells to move across the beam path due to the wind (typically on the order of a millisecond). These intensity fluctuations become amplitude fluctuations in the case of analog modulation of the laser beam. In addition, atmospheric turbulence can cause beam break-up and beam wander which can cause very large swings in the average received power, on the order of tens of dB, on frequency scales from dc up to several kilohertz. This causes the average received AC signal to not be clamped at zero due to inadequate AC coupling.

There are many applications in which data is collected from an analog sensor or system and transmitted long distances to the end user. Typically the data would subsequently be digitized and transmitted over an RF or fiber optic communication link. Problems occur if the platform containing the sensor system is size, weight, or power (SWaP) constrained, since high speed digitizers can greatly add to the SWaP burden. Also, if the data or required communication is of a sensitive nature and secure communication links are not available, the user runs the risk of having the communication detected and/or intercepted. In these cases, it would be of great benefit to have the capability of transmitting unprocessed analog sensor data over a secure channel. Free-space lasercomm using analog or RF modulation of the transmitted laser beam can provide a method for transmitting un-digitized data over a high speed communication link that has a very low probability of detection and intercept, as well as being highly resistant to jamming efforts due to the relatively narrow field-of-view of the receivers. However, atmospheric turbulence as discussed above makes this process problematic.

Methods to correct the aberrations caused by atmospheric turbulence and to thus enable transmission of analog data over a FSO link are currently being explored. This work deals with scenarios in which a frequency-modulated waveform is transmitted through an FSO channel. Several applications of the DWT are employed in the receiver end to demodulate the transmitted data.

The chapter is organized as follows. Section 2 reviews recent advances in using analog FM to transmit data over the free space channel. Section 3 describes the mathematical modeling of the received FSO signal. Section 4 is dedicated to de-noising of the FSO signal using the DWT and Section 5 is devoted to the simulation experiments. Finally, we present the summary and conclusions in Section 6.

## 2. Applications

The transmission of RF modulated laser beams through optical fibers and the characterization of the information transmitted have been the subject of research for many years [1-3]. More recently, however, the potential advantages of the free space channel have led to research into its use as a medium for transmission of RF analog data. Refai *et al.* [4] undertook a comparative study of fiber optic links and FSO links. They concluded that FSO is suitable for RF transmissions; that it can perform comparably with fiber-based links; and that FSO can be an attractive substitute for fiber optic links when a clear line-of-sight is available. Bucholtz *et al.* [5] performed a statistical study of RF analog FSO links. In fiber-based systems, most of the significant parameters such as RF gain, noise figures, and linearity can, in the absence of component degradation or change, be treated as constants. In FSO systems, on the other hand, these parameters are not constant. In particular, the received power can vary by tens of decibels due to atmospheric turbulence. They reported that the link parameters of gain, noise factor and third-order spurious free dynamic range depend entirely on the statistics of the received optical power.

Since 2005, there have been several reports in the literature on demonstrations of FSO analog links, with increasing range and performance. In a bench top demonstration, Refai *et al.* [6] transmitted cable TV signals using wavelength division multiplexing. This was done with a view to eventual deployment in "last mile" situations. Murphy *et al.* [7] described an optical link using a modulating retro-reflector (MRR) [8]. The laser beam was encoded with a FM signal of carrier frequency ~750 kHz, and successfully transmitted an audio signal over bench top distances.

Analog modulation has been successfully applied to FSO transmission of video signals. Baseband AM provides optimum use of bandwidth, and transmission of composite video has been demonstrated using amplitude modulation [9], although this suffers from signal degradation due to atmospheric scintillation. A technique employing dual wavelengths has been demonstrated to be effective in mitigating scintillation noise by using common mode rejection to remove co-channel noise [10, 11], but the utility of this is limited by the complexity of the system and linearity constraints in the amplitude domain. This constraint was removed by using frequency modulation of a sub-carrier to transmit audio/video signals over a 1.5km terrestrial path [12, 13]. This work has now been extended to include bidirectional audio transmission, and has been demonstrated at ranges up to 3km in the maritime environment using a modulating retro-reflector [14]. Burris *et al.* showed analog FM to be effective in long range links, by transmitting audio/video signals over a folded 32 km maritime path [15].

## 3. Mathematical modeling of received FSO signal

The received FSO signal can be described as

$$r(t) = x_{FM}(t)\sigma(t) + m(t) + w(t) \tag{1}$$

in which $x_{FM}(t)$ characterizes the frequency-modulated signal and $\sigma(t)$ signifies the atmospheric scintillation noise. In addition, the model (1) assumes two types of additive noise. The first noise component, $m(t)$, is the relatively low-frequency fluctuations of the signal mean value caused by insufficient AC-coupling. The second additive term $w(t)$, portrays the additive white Gaussian noise (AWGN) with zero-mean. Furthermore the frequency-modulated waveform is formed as,

$$x_{FM}(t) = A\cos[\omega_c t + k_f \int_{-\infty}^{t} \mathrm{d}(\alpha)d\alpha] \tag{2}$$

in which $d(t)$ represents the information (analogue) data, $A$ is a gain, $k_f$ is the modulation index and $\omega_c$ is the carrier frequency [16].

In the following section we use the Discrete Wavelet Transformation (DWT) to process $r(t)$ for noise reduction.

## 4. De-noising of FSO signal using discrete wavelet transform

This section deals with the application of the Discrete Wavelet Transformation (DWT) to the de-noising of the received FSO waveform $r(t)$ expressed in (1).

The DWT is a powerful iterative technique for decomposition of a signal into *approximation* (low frequency) and *detail* (high frequency) waveforms [17]. The process begins by decomposing the coefficients of the first level of decomposition of the signal into coefficients of *approximation*, $cA_1$, and coefficients of *detail*, $cD_1$. Accordingly, the coefficients $cA_1$ are further decomposed into $cA_2$ and $cD_2$ to generate the second level of decomposition. The process can continue for the $i^{th}$ level of decomposition for which $cA_i$ and $cD_i$ are evaluated from $cA_{i-1}$. At each level, the DWT coefficients can be used to reconstruct the *approximation* and the *detail* of the original signal. Figure 1 illustrates three levels of decomposition of the DWT coefficients.

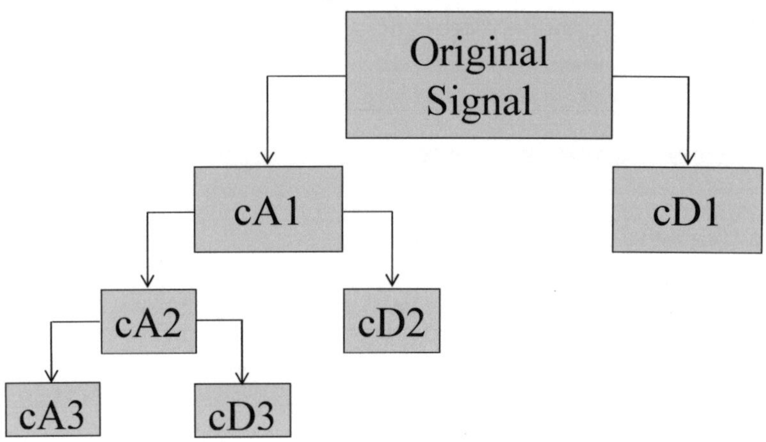


**Figure 1.** A Three Level Decomposition of the DWT Coefficients

A specific strength of the DWT is its ability to decompose a signal into low-frequency and high-frequency waveforms at any desired level. This property can be directly applied into the received FSO waveform of (1) in order to identify and remove the unwanted low-frequency signal $m(t)$ and the undesirable low-frequency scintillation waveform $\sigma(t)$. Moreover, the energy of the high-frequency component of the white noise $w(t)$ can be considerably reduced using the decomposition property of the DWT.

The process of removing the low-frequency noise $m(t)$ is performed in two consecutive steps. We first find the *approximation* of $r(t)$ in an appropriate level to obtain $\hat{m}(t)$. We consequently form a subtraction process as follows:

http://dx.doi.org/10.5772/52433

$$r_1(t) = r(t) - \hat{m}(t) \tag{3}$$

Hence, the received FSO signal (1) after cancellation of $m(t)$ becomes

$$r_1(t) = x_{FM}(t)\sigma(t) + w_1(t) \tag{4}$$

where $w_1(t)$ is the noise term that includes $w(t)$ as well as the error caused due to the determination of $m(t)$. The next step deals with the cancellation of the low frequency scintillation noise $\sigma(t)$. As an intermediate step, it is conceivable to form the square of the new signal shown in (4); that is,

$$r_2(t) = r_1^2(t) = x_{FM}^2(t)\sigma^2(t) + w_1^2(t) + 2w_1(t)x_{FM}(t)\sigma(t) \tag{5}$$

Application of (2) in (5) results in a low-frequency signal $\frac{A^2\sigma^2(t)}{2}$ plus a collection of high-frequency signals shown by *HF*:

$$r_2(t) = \frac{A^2\sigma^2(t)}{2} + HF \tag{6}$$

It is observed from (6) that the square process has enhanced the difference between the low and high frequency components of the received signal; hence, it is more effective to use DWT for signal separation. Subsequently, by finding the DWT *approximations* of $r_2(t)$ in an appropriate level, $\hat{\sigma}(t)$ after a square root device, can be determined. To continue, multiply $r_1(t)$ in (4) by the inverse of $\hat{\sigma}(t)$; hence,

$$r_3(t) = \frac{r_1(t)}{\hat{\sigma}(t)} = x_{FM}(t) + w_3(t) \tag{7}$$

where in (7) it is assumed that $w_3(t) \triangleq w_1(t)/\hat{\sigma}(t) + \varepsilon$, $\varepsilon$ is an error due to the approximation of $\sigma(t)$ and $\hat{\sigma}(t) \neq 0$. The FM signal $\hat{x}_{FM}(t)$ can be finally demodulated using any conventional FM demodulator to provide the analog data $\hat{d}(t)$. The noisy waveform $\hat{d}(t)$ can be further de-noised using an additional application of the DWT. This signal is denoted as $\hat{d}_{DN}(t)$. It is noticed that we have de-noised $\hat{d}(t)$ not $r_3(t)$. This is due to the fact that the demodulated message $\hat{d}(t)$ is characteristically a baseband waveform which can be de-noised more effectively than the relatively high-frequency waveform $r_3(t)$. Figure 2 illustrates the entire process.

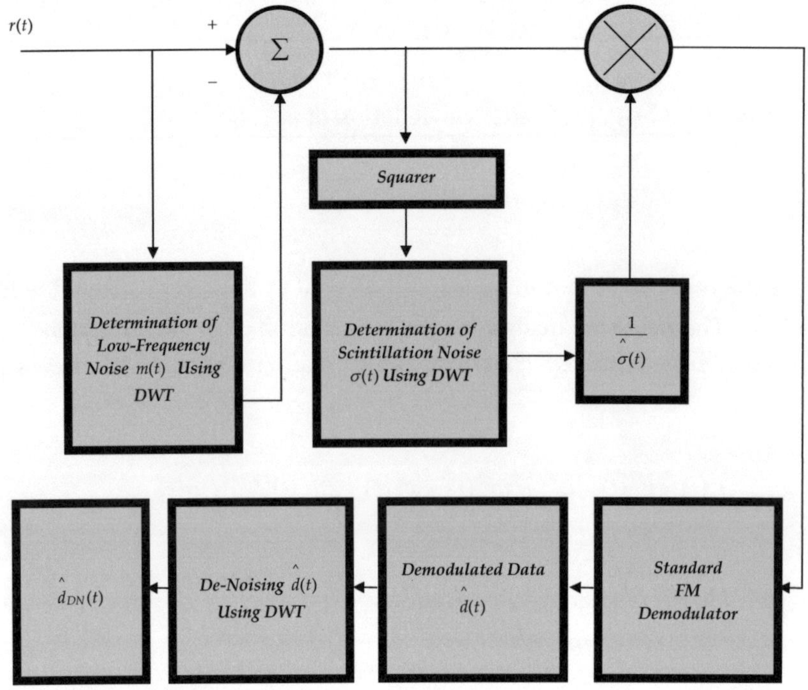


**Figure 2.** Structure of the FM/FSO Receiver

## 5. Simulation experiments

This section presents the results of simulation experiments. We present the results in two sets of experiments. Experiment I uses a 1-D time signal and deals with the sensitivity of the algorithm to the variations of *SNR* and *SV* (defined below). This experiment is primarily presented for quantitative evaluations of the method. Experiment II employs a 2-D single image as the original data and is mainly focused on the qualitative assessment of the algorithm.

### Experiment I

In this experiment the received waveform (1) was synthesized by generating an FM signal with the carrier frequency $\omega_c = 2\pi \times (1.36\text{ MHz})$. The assumed data $d(t)$ was used as follows:

$$d(t) = -0.2\cos(\omega_{d1}t + \pi / 16) + 0.3\sin(\omega_{d2}t - \pi / 8) - 0.1\sin(\omega_{d3}t). \tag{8}$$

with $\omega_{d1}=2\pi \times 60000$; $\omega_{d2}=2\pi \times 30000$; $\omega_{d3}=2\pi \times 10000$. The sampling radian frequency was assumed to be $5\times\ \omega_c$. In addition, the noise signals $\sigma(t)$ and $m(t)$ were duplicated from a real FSO channel and the AWGN noise $w(t)$ was synthetically generated in MATLAB. The data was processed in one frame of 990,000 sample points. The low frequency noise $m(t)$ was extracted as shown in (3) using the DWT with the Daubechies 20 (db20) mother wavelet and 6 decomposition levels. Also the desired signal in (6) was separated using db20 mother wavelet with 10 decomposition levels. In addition, the demodulated message $d(t)$ was de-noised using DWT with db20 mother wavelet and 3 decomposition levels. The Signal-to-Noise Ratio (SNR) was defined as

$$SNR = 10\log_{10}\left(\frac{\sigma_d^2}{\sigma_w^2}\right) \tag{9}$$

where $\sigma_d^2$ is the variance of the data $d(t)$ and $\sigma_w^2$ is the variance of $w(t)$ in (1). To study the sensitivity of the algorithm to the scintillation changes we define the Scintillation Variation (SV) parameter as

$$\mathrm{SV} = 20\log_{10}\left[\frac{\sigma_{\max}(\mathrm{t})}{\sigma_{\min}(\mathrm{t})}\right] \tag{10}$$

This quantity is a measure of the abrupt variation of the scintillation noise $\sigma(t)$.

Figures 3 through 9 represent the results of this experiment. Figure 3 illustrates the FM/FSO signal $r(t)$ represented by Equations (1) and (2). Figure 4 highlights, for SNR = 0 dB, the frequency descriptions of the transmitted FM signal, the received FSO/FM waveform, and the processed FM signal after removal of $m(t)$ and $\sigma(t)$. The middle figure in this set indicates that the spectrum of the FSO/FM waveform carries a relatively large amount of low-frequency components. This is primarily due to the presence of the slowly-varying terms $m(t)$ and $\sigma(t)$. It is shown in Figure 4 that the DWT is quite successful in reshaping the spectrum of the FSO/FM signal from the middle figure to the one shown at the bottom figure. Figure 5 highlights, for SNR = 0 dB, the time history of the transmitted FM signal and the processed FM signal after extracting $m(t)$ and $\sigma(t)$. Figure 6 displays a close-up views of the transmitted message $d(t)$, demodulated message $\hat{d}(t)$, and de-noised demodulated message $d_{DN}(t)$ for SNR = 0 dB. This figure indicates that the original data $d(t)$ is closely extracted from the FSO/FM signal. Further, the de-noising of the demodulated data appears to be quite effective. Figure 7 displays, for SNR = 20 dB, the transmitted FM signal and the processed FM signal after removing $m(t)$ and $\sigma(t)$. Figure 8 displays a close-up views of the transmitted message $d(t)$, demodulated message $\hat{d}(t)$, and de-noised demodulated message $d_{DN}(t)$ for SNR = 20 dB. Figure 9 shows Mean-Square Error for the message $d(t)$ versus SV for various levels of SNR. This figure highlights the important result that the performance of the algorithm is nearly identical under various SV values and for fixed SNR. In other words, the method tends to be insensitive to the variations of the scintillation noise, especially for large levels of SV.

**Experiment II**

As a demonstration of the efficiency of this algorithm, we consider the situation in which the transmitted message $d(t)$ is the row-ordered vector of the still image shown in Figure 10. The scintillation variation, SV, is fixed to 20 dB in this experiment. Similar to Experiment I, the data is frequency modulated using $\omega_c = 2\pi \times (1.36 \text{ MHz})$. Figures 11, 12 and 13, respectively, highlight the demodulated FM/FSO signal for SNR = 10 dB, and SNR = 20 dB and SNR = 50 dB. It is seen from these figures that as the SNR improves, the performance consistently improve.

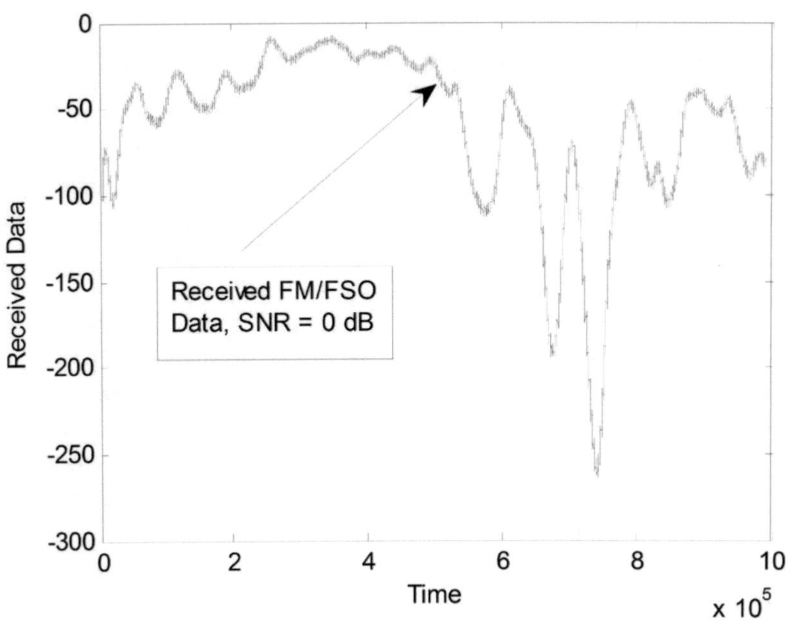


**Figure 3.** A Typical FM/FSO Signal.

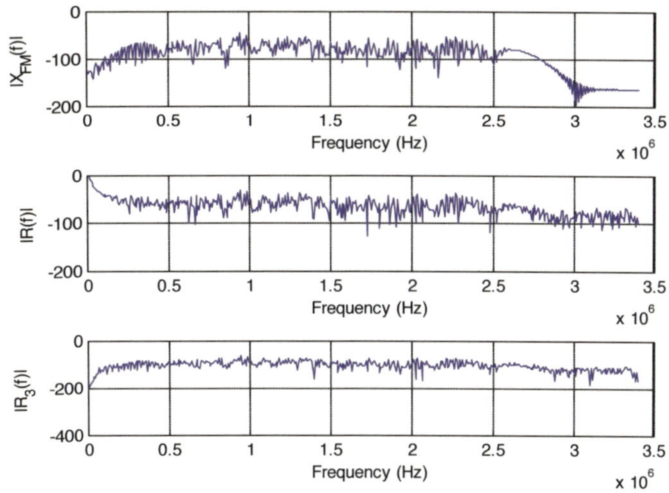


**Figure 4.** From Top to Bottom and for SNR = 0 dB: The Absolute Amplitude Spectrum of Transmitted FM signal, $X_{FM}(f)=\Im\{x_{FM}(t)\}$, The Absolute Amplitude Spectrum of Received Noisy FSO/FM Signal, $R(f)=\Im\{r(t)\}$ shown in Figure 3, The Absolute Amplitude Spectrum of Processed FM Signal after removal of $m(t)$ and $\sigma(t)$, $R_3(f)=\Im\{r_3(t)\}$, where $r_3(t)$ is defined in (7).

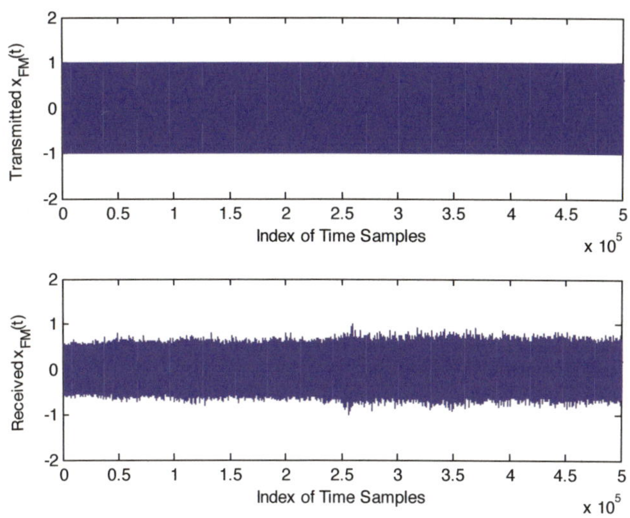


**Figure 5.** Top: The Transmitted FM Signal, $x_{FM}(t)$, Bottom: The Processed FM Signal after Extracting $m(t)$ and $\sigma(t)$ for SNR = 0 dB.

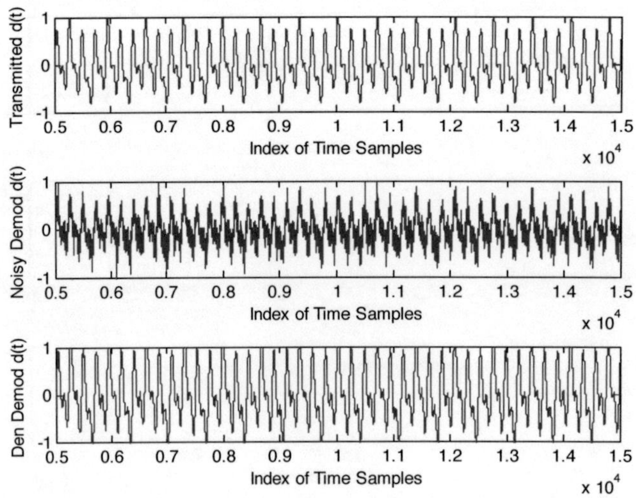


**Figure 6.** From Top to Bottom, SNR = 0, Close-Ups of: Transmitted Message $d(t)$, Demodulated Message $\hat{d}(t)$, De-noised Demodulated Message $\hat{d}_{DN}(t)$.

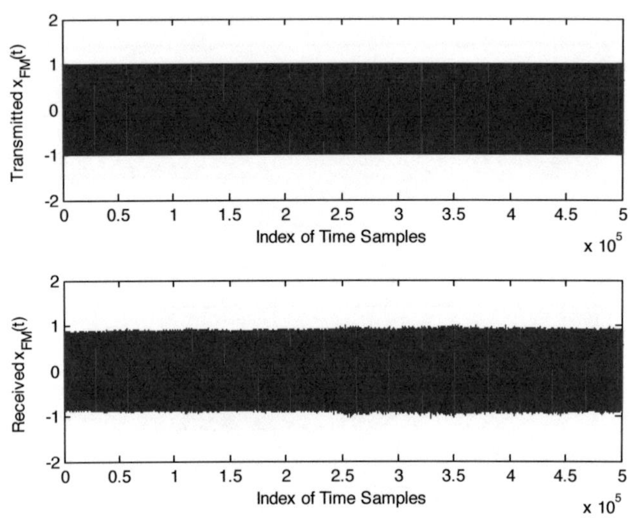


**Figure 7.** Top: The Transmitted FM Signal, $x_{FM}(t)$, Bottom: The Processed FM Signal after Extracting $m(t)$ and $\sigma(t)$ for SNR = 20 dB.

http://dx.doi.org/10.5772/52433

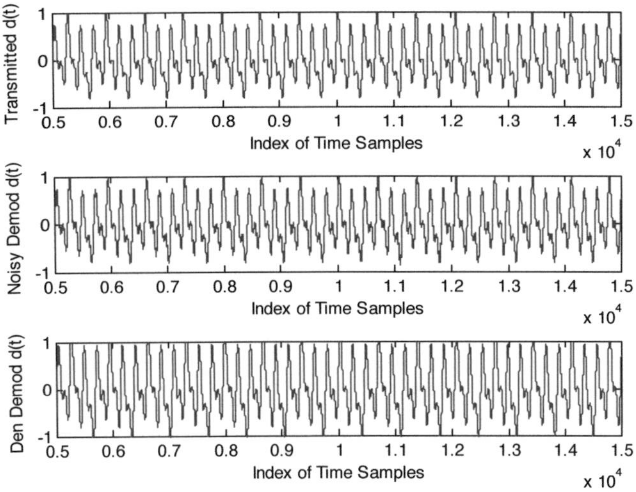


**Figure 8.** From Top to Bottom, SNR = 20, Close-Ups of: Transmitted Message $d(t)$, Demodulated Message $\hat{d}(t)$, De-noised Demodulated Message $\hat{d}_{DN}(t)$.

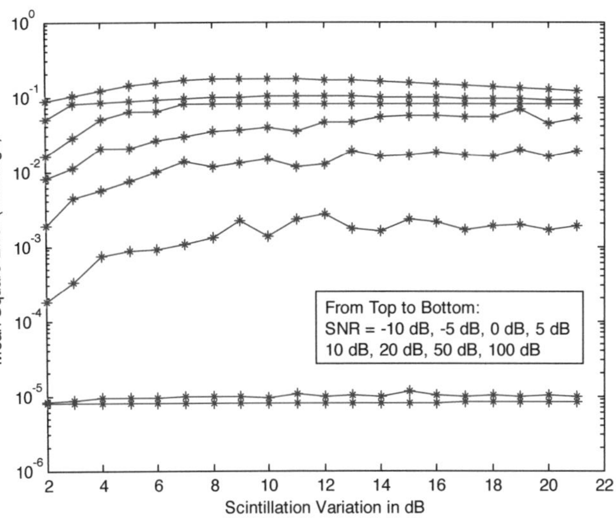


**Figure 9.** Mean-Square Error versus SV for various levels of SNR

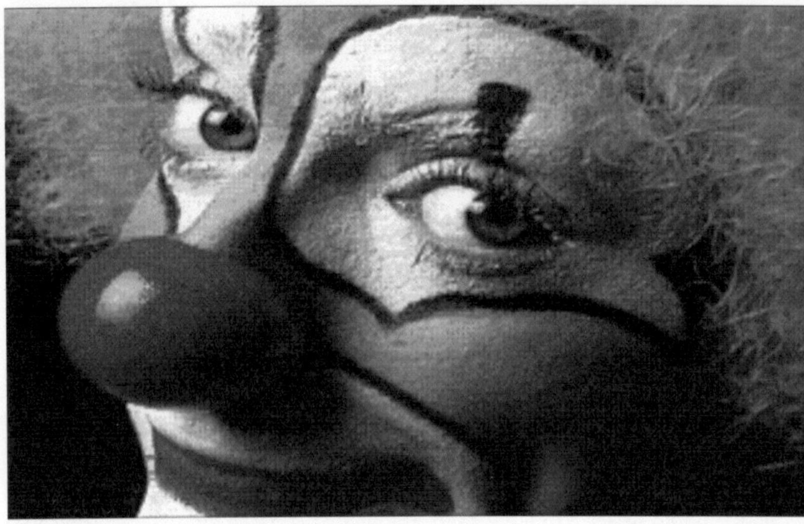

**Figure 10.** Transmitted Image

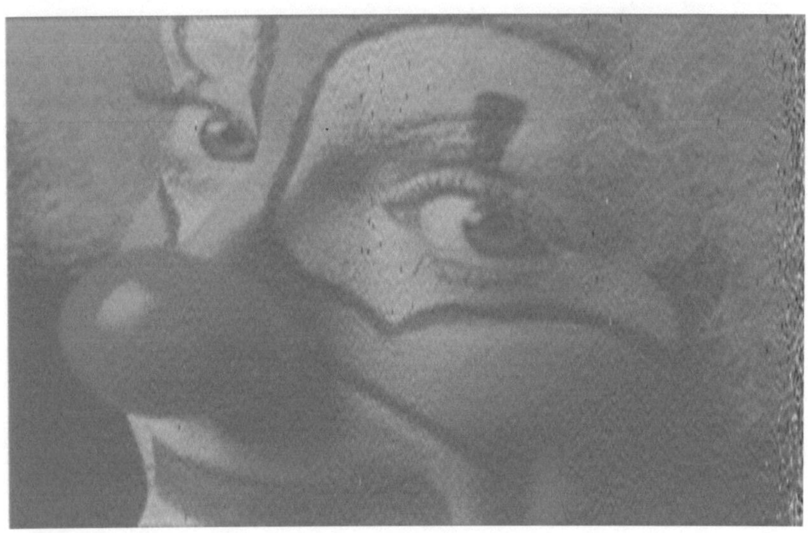

**Figure 11.** De-noised demodulated Image, SNR = 10 dB, SV = 20 dB

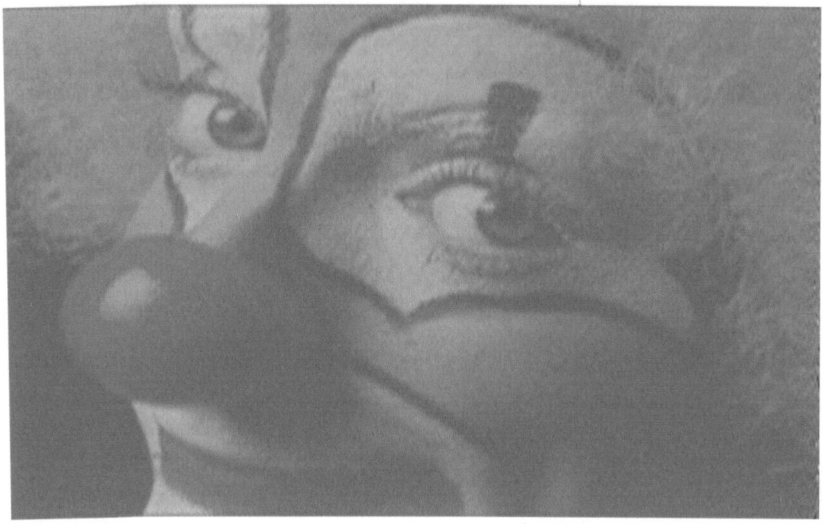

**Figure 12.** De-noised demodulated Image, SNR = 20 dB, SV = 20 dB

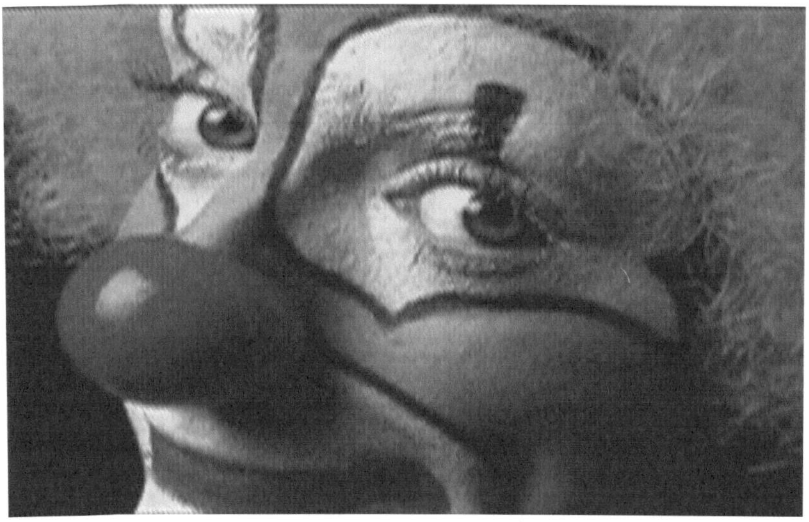

**Figure 13.** De-noised demodulated Image, SNR = 50 dB, SV = 20 dB

## 6. Summary and conclusions

Atmospheric noise signals are a fundamental limitation of free-space optical communications. In this work we presented the limitations that this imposes, and investigated the use of the discrete wavelet transformation (DWT) to overcome them. Simulation experiments were performed to validate the use of the DWT in the demodulation of the FM data in the presence of scintillation noise, noise due to insufficient AC-coupling, and AWGN. It was demonstrated that the use of the DWT, as explained in the paper, is quite effective in reducing the joint effects of the atmospheric as well as the additive white Gaussian noises.

Several concluding remarks are in order. It is noted that despite the fact that FM was the modulation type presented in this paper, our algorithm can be extended to other constant-envelope (digital or analog) modulation scheme. This stems from the fact that in constant-envelope modulations, the message is solely modulating the phase of the carrier. Consequently, any changes in the magnitude of the received FSO signal are exclusively due to the noise terms, $m(t)$, $\sigma(t)$ and $w(t)$, that are removed using the DWT scheme, as described in Section 4.

Finally, the method presented in this paper is a post-processing of the received data to validate the feasibility of the use of DWT in FM/FSO applications. The next phase of this work should be an FPGA implementation of the algorithm for a real time execution of the whole system in the receiver end.

## Author details

Nader Namazi[1], Ray Burris[2], G. Charmaine Gilbreath[2], Michele Suite[2] and Kenneth Grant[3]

1 Department of Electrical Engineering and Computer Science, Catholic University of America, Washington, USA

2 Naval Research Laboratory, Washington, USA

3 Defence Science & Technology Organisation, Edinburgh, Australia

## References

[1] Wilson B., Ghassemlooy Z., Darwazeh I., Analogue Optical Fiber Communications, IEE (1995).

[2] Chang W. S. C., RF Photonic Technology in Optical Fiber Links, (CUP, Cambridge, 2002).

[3] Cox C. H. III, Analog Optical Links: Theory and Practice, (CUP, Cambridge, 2002).

[4] Refai H. H., Sluss J. J. Jnr, Refai H. H., Attiquzzaman M., "Comparative Study of the Performance of Analog Fiber Optic Links versus Free-Space Optical Links," Opt. Eng., (45)2, 025003-1 (2006).

[5] Bucholtz F., Burris H. R., Moore C. I., McDermitt C. S., Mahon R., Suite M. R., Michalowicz J. V., Gilbreath G. C., Rabinovich W. S., "Statistical Properties of a Short, Analog RF Free-Space Optical Link," Proc. SPIE, Vol. 7324, Atmospheric Propagation VI, Edited by L. M. Wasiczko, G. C. Gilbreath, (SPIE, Bellingham, WA, 2009), p. 73240D-1.

[6] Refai H. H., Sluss J. J, Refai H. H., "The Use of Free-Space Optical Links for CATV Applications," Proc. SPIE, Vol. 5825, Opto-Ireland 2005, Edited by J. G. McInerney, G. Farrell, D. M. Denieffe, L. P. Barry, H. S. Gamble, P. J. Hughes, A. Moore, (SPIE, Bellingham, WA, 2005), pp. 408-15.

[7] Murphy J. L., Gilbreath G. C., Rabinovich W. S., Sepantaie M. M., Goetz P. G., "FM-MRR Analog Audio System," Proc. SPIE, Vol. 5892, Free-Space Laser Communications V, Edited by D. G. Voelz, J. C. Ricklin, (SPIE, Bellingham, WA, 2005), p. 58921X-1.

[8] Rabinovich W. S., Mahon R., Burris H. H., Gilbreath G. C., Goetz P. G., Moore C. I., Stell M. F., Vilcheck M. J., Witkowsky J. L., Swingen L., Suite M. R., Oh E., Koplow J., "Free-Space Optical Communications Link at 1550nm Using Multiple-Quantum-Well Modulating Retroreflectors in a Marine Environment," Opt. Eng. (44)5, 056001-1 (2005).

[9] Grant K. J., Murphy J., Mahon R., Burris H. H., Rabinovich W. S., Moore C. I., Wasiczko L. M., Goetz P. G., Suite M. R., Ferraro M. S., Gilbreath G. C., Clare B. A., Mudge K. A., Chaffey J., "Free-Space Optical Transmission of AM Composite Video Signals using InGaAs Modulating Retro-Reflectors," Conference on Optoelectronic and Microelectronic Materials and Devices (COMMAD), University of Western Australia, December 2006.

[10] Grant K. J., Corbett K. A., Clare A. B., Davies J. E. & Nener B. D., "Mitigation of Scintillation Noise by Common Mode Rejection," Proc. SPIE, Vol. 5793, Atmospheric Propagation II, Edited by C. Y. Young, G. C. Gilbreath, (SPIE, Bellingham, WA, 2005), pp. 106-117.

[11] Grant K. J., Clare B. A., Mudge K. A., Sprey B. M., Oermann R. J., "Real-Time Scintillation Noise Mitigation for Free Space Optical Transmission of Analogue and Digital Signals," Proc. SPIE, Vol. 6951 Atmospheric Propagation V, Edited by L. M. Wasiczko, G. C. Gilbreath, (SPIE, Bellingham, WA, 2008), p. 69510H-1.

[12] Grant K. J., Clare B. A., Martinsen W., Mudge K. A., Burris H. R., Moore C. I., Overfield J., Gilbreath G. C. & Rabinovich W. S., "Free Space Optical Transmission of FM Audio/Video Signals using InGaAs Modulating Retro-Reflectors," Conference on

Optoelectronic and Microelectronic Materials and Devices (COMMAD), Aust. National University, Canberra 2010.

[13] Grant K. J., Clare B. A., Martinsen W., Mudge K. A., Burris H. R., Moore C. I., Overfield J., Gilbreath G. C., Rabinovich W. S. & Duperre J., "Laser Communication of FM audio/video Signals using InGaAs Modulating Retro-Reflectors," Proc. SPIE, Vol. 8038, Atmospheric Propagation VIII, edited by L. M. Wasiczko Thomas, E.J. Spillar, (SPIE, Bellingham, WA, 2011), p. 80380K-1.

[14] Grant, K.J., Mudge, K.A., Clare, B.A. & Martinsen, W.M., "Ship-to-shore Free Space Optical Communications", Australian Institute of Physics Congress, Sydney, (2012).

[15] Burris H. R., Bucholtz F., Moore C. I., Grant K. J., Suite M. R., McDermitt C. S., Clare B. A., Mahon R., Martinsen W., Ferraro M., Sawday R., Xu B., Font C., Thomas L. M., Mudge K. A., Rabinovich W. S., Gilbreath G. C., Scharpf W., Saint-Georges E., Uecke S., "Long Range, Analog RF Free Space Optical Communication Link in a Maritime Environment," Proc. SPIE, Vol. 7324 Atmospheric Propagation VI, Edited by L. M. Wasiczko, G. C. Gilbreath, (SPIE, Bellingham, WA, 2009), p. 73240G-1.

[16] Ziemer R. E. and Tranter W. H., Principles of Communications, Systems, Modulation and Noise, (5th Edition, John Wiley & Sons, Inc., 2002).

[17] Rao R. M. and Bopardikar A. S., Wavelet Transforms: Introduction to Theory and Applications, (Addison Wesley Longman, Inc., 1998).